THE CELL BLOCK PRESENTS…

THE MILLIONAIRE PRISONER 5

Published by: The Cell Block™

The Cell Block
P.O. Box 1025
Rancho Cordova, CA 95741

Website: thecellblock.net
Facebook/thecellblock.net
Instagram: @mikeenemigo
Email: info@thecellblock.net

Cover Design: Mike Enemigo

Send comments, reviews, interview and business
inquiries to: info@thecellblock.net

WARNING DISCLAIMER

This book is designed to provide helpful and informative material on prosperity, building a better life, and achieving your dreams. It contains the opinions and ideas of its author on getting free stuff, including money. It is sold with the understanding that the reader requires personal assistance or advice, a competent professional should be consulted.

It is not the purpose of this book to require every tip, tactic, and/or strategy that is available to a prisoner for achieving prosperity, but instead to compliment, amplify, and supplement other books. You are urged to read all the available information and material, including any books listed throughout this work, learn as much as you can, and then develop your own strategies and work your own plan.

Getting free stuff (including free money) is not some pie-in-the-sky get-rich-quick scheme. Anyone who wishes to achieve success must decide to invest a lot of time and effort into it. The advice and strategies contained in this book may not be suitable for every situation. The purpose of this book is to educate and entertain. However, there will probably be errors, both typographical and in content. Because of this, it should be used as a guide, and not the be-all, end-all book on getting free money and success for prisoners. The fact that a website, business, organization, and/or association is listed or referred to in this book as a citation and/or a potential source of further information does not mean the author or publisher endorses the website, business, organization and/or Association, or what those entities may offer. It should also be noted that the Internet websites listed, and other entities referred to, may have, by the time you are reading this warning, changed, disappeared, closed and/or dissolved.

Some terms mentioned in this book are known to be or are suspected of being trademarks of different entities. Use of a term in this book should not be regarded as affecting the validity of any trademark or service mark.

The author and publisher specifically disclaim any responsibility for any liability, loss, or risk, personal or otherwise, which is included as a consequence, directly or indirectly, of the use and application of any of the contents of this book.

CONTENTS

INTRODUCTION

Who doesn't love free stuff, especially free money? I know I do. Most of us prisoners received some, if not all, of the COVID-19 stimulus money passed out. While that was great, you should know there are many other ways a prisoner can get free money. Or other free stuff, like books or pen pals. And in this book, I will give you some tips on how to get it. It will then be up to you to take the steps to get some free money.

> *"A journey of a thousand miles begins with a single step."* –Lao Tzu

At the beginning of the 2016 movie *The Ticket* the main character is telling his wife a story. It's relevant for our purposes. A man prays and prays every day for 50 years asking God to let him hit the lottery. Finally, one of the angels goes to God and asks him, "Sir, why don't we let him hit the lottery? He's been faithful and prayed for 50 years." God replies, "I really want him to hit the lottery and I'd help him win. But first he has to buy a ticket!" Therein lies the moral of the story. You have to buy the ticket you've been given. You have to take action. Everything in this book requires you to take action. So, get up and do something.

> *"Nothing moves until you move."*
> *–Robert Ringer*

Who I Am and My Role in Your Life

I'm a 43-year-old author serving a life sentence for felony murder. I started doing time when I was 14. On this bid I've been down since 1999. I used to be in a gang in a central Illinois town. I sold drugs and did armed robberies. I was dumb as hell. Even though we grew up poor in Section 8 housing and on food stamps so we could eat, I still had every opportunity to go down a different path. I had a job offer to work at UPS. I was in college to become an architect. I also had a good paying job at a major distribution center in the Midwest. But I couldn't stay the course and the streets kept calling me. So, I wound up back in jail fighting the death penalty.

While in the county jail my baby mama gave birth to beautiful twin girls, and it was then that I had to change my life. At the bench trial in the year 2000, I received a directed verdict of acquittal when the State of Illinois refused to participate over an evidence dispute. I was released, but eventually rearrested after the state successfully got the Not Guilty verdict vacated on appeal. See *People v. Kruger*, 327 Ill. App. 3d 839, 764 N.E.2d 138 (4th Dist. Ill. 2002). At the 2003 jury trial, I was acquitted on intentional murder, but convicted of felony murder and sentenced to life in prison without parole.

After reading several of Zig Ziglar's books, I reached out to the late, great motivational speaker and began corresponding with Ziglar. I adopted Zig's philosophy that you can have everything you want in life if you just help enough people get what they want. Tired of depending on friends and family for support, I signed up for, and graduated from Crown Financial Ministries. I decided to leverage my extensive juvenile and adult prison experiences into a freelance writing career. In 2011, I launched my micropublishing empire from my prison cell by self-publishing two booklets, *How To Get Free Pen-Pals* and *How To Win Your Football Pool*. Prison authorities seized my property and threw me in segregation by alleging that I was violating prison rules. Not to be dismayed, I kept going and published my first book, *The Millionaire Prisoner*™. It took me only 30 days to write my second book, *Pen Pal Success*, which is based on my personal experiences from behind the iron veil of prison. After the success of both of those books a lot of prisoners started asking me how I did it. I wrote my third book, *Cellpreneur: The Millionaire Prisoner's Guidebook*, to show prisoners how to legally start a business from their prison cell. *TMP4: Pen Pal Mastery* shows you all the tips I've learned over the last 27 years in the pen pal game. And *Prison Picasso* shows prisoners how to get rich off arts and crafts.

For the past 15 years I've been obsessed with finding strategies that prisoners can use to better their lives. I've written about a lot of them in my books. Becoming an author has helped me in all areas of my life. It has certainly helped me financially. But the thing I love most is when I get letters from other prisoners thanking me for writing the books that I have. That's worth more to me than all the royalty checks I've ever gotten. I hope you'll be one of those prisoners as well. But that is my mission in a nutshell: to deliver quality information to your cell that you can use right away to make things happen.

How This Book Was Written

This book is a collaboration between both me and Mike. Some years ago, IDOC confiscated all of the typewriters from us in maximum security. I haven't let that stop me from writing. I write out my manuscripts in longhand with little, 3-inch, flexible ink pens. Then I send my handwritten pages to Mike Enemigo who edits them and gets them typed up. So even though this book sounds like it was mostly written by me (Josh), it's the work of both of us. And we hope to continue to bring you addition books in *The Millionaire Prisoner* lineup.

How To Get Your Money's Worth From This Book

Read it, peruse it, study it. Master it. But the only way the knowledge in this book can become wisdom is if you implement it into your life. To help you do this I came up with a simple formula for reading and studying how-to information that can help you master it. (I had the help of my mentor, the late, great motivational speaker and author, Zig Ziglar, in coming up with this formula.) Here's how you can read this book to get the most from it:

1. Read through this book quickly to get the gist of the message, underlining or highlighting the things that really "grab" you. Only stop to look up words you don't know or write them down to look up later. This first reading allows you to become familiar with the book.

2. As you read this book the second time, keep a notebook of ideas generated by the book that you can personally use. The objective is not to see how quickly you can get out of the book, but what you can get out of the book.

3. In your third reading, invest time and patience in gleaning additional ideas you may be missing in your second reading. Carefully examine each chapter. Go over what you have highlighted or underlined. Put anything you missed in your notebook.

4. The fourth reading will enable the book to become an integral part of you, enhancing your effectiveness. After this reading, you can place the book in your collection, and it will be a treasure trove, ready and willing to supply you with any knowledge you may need.

5. Find other prisoners who have read this book, or share it with them, and then discuss it together to see what you got out of it. You may gain additional insights from their ideas and thoughts that you didn't see on your own.

A Few Final Words

We invite you to stay in touch with us. The tips, tactics, and strategies that I advocate using in this book will need to be updated as better processes become available. I intend to learn those new processes and use them . . . and share them with you. If you find some success systems that a prisoner can use to get free money, or if you experience success using this book, write and let me know about it. I just might put you in the next edition of this book or other *Millionaire Prisoner*™ products. Also, so that we can congratulate you, not just for what you achieved, but for making the world a better place by beginning to break the cycle of prison. Let's get to it. You can start by turning the page and taking a step forward on your *FREE MONEY* journey.

"Knowledge is of two kinds. We know a subject ourselves, or we know where we can find information on it."
–Samuel Johnson

CHAPTER 1
Lay the Foundation First

When you build a house, you have to lay the foundation first. Or else the weight of the house will over time sink it. This analogy applies to anything you're trying to build. A lot of you want to start a business, so you have to lay that foundation by protecting your entity legally. If you want to learn how to do that from a prison cell you may want to check out my book, *Cellpreneur: The Millionaire Prisoners' Guidebook* (Freebird Publishers). And some of you need money to do this. Then this book can help you get some of this money. But buyer beware.

Money, especially FREE money, is not always the answer. I was glad I didn't start with money. I actually started with a typewriter and $300 saved up from the money pen pals sent me over the years. And slowly but surely, I kept building my foundation. Could I have done it faster with crowdfunding? Probably. Could I have done it faster with a grant? Probably. Would I have learned as much? Probably not. What is more valuable to you—wisdom or money? I hope you said wisdom. Why? Because the person with wisdom can take the money from the ignorant every time.

Now, I'm not telling you this to discourage you from trying to get FREE money. Trust me, I love FREE money. I published my first book from a maximum-security segregation cell without access to a phone or tablet. How did I do that? With a $3,000 gift from a family member (Which I have since repaid even though I didn't have to.). So, I'm all for obtaining FREE money. What you must have is a plan. What do you intend to do with this FREE money? But a TV, tablet, some commissary, and some books (hopefully more of mine)? That's fine. I'm not here to judge why you want FREE money or what you're going to do with it. No matter what you want it for, I want you to stick with your plan. Lay the foundation first.

In 2021 I read an article in *Inc.* magazine by Carey Smith titled, "The Evils of Free Money." For those of you who don't know who he is let me explain. Smith is the founder of Big Ass Fans and took that company from $0 to a $500 million sale. Now he runs Unorthodox Ventures, a firm that focuses on funding small companies so they can grow big. He knows about money. His company has an AFH model, or the "Actual fucking help" model. I loved that because that's what I try to do with my books, actually help convicts! So, before we get into how, and where to get free money, and other free stuff, I need to caution you on a few things. That way I'm actually helping you!

> *"Most real entrepreneurs will be the first to acknowledge that they need advice from people who have been in their shoes and done what they're trying to do."*
> — Carey Smith

Prison's Seizure of FREE Money

To be aware is to be alive. Do you know your prison system's rules regarding money you receive to your trust fund account? Most state prisons have confiscation rules regarding any money we get. They justify it saying they need it to offset cost of incarceration, fines, court fees, and other things. You need to learn your prison's rules on this.

But just because they have rules for this doesn't mean they can seize any, or all the money you get FREE. There are numerous legal cases on Westlaw or Lexis-Nexus dealing with this issue. Search for "Cost of Incarceration" and your state. A great case to read is *Scholl v. Mnuchin*, 494 F.Supp. 3d 661 (N.D. Cal. 2020). In that case, the federal district court ruled we were all entitled to receive the stimulus payments. Some states have tried (or did) to seize prisoners' stimulus money. Arkansas did. But as I write this, there's an ongoing class action regarding that law in the Arkansas system. See *Hayes v. Rutledge*, USDC-ED AR, Case No. 4:21-cv-347-LPR. No matter where you're currently doing your time, be sure to learn your system's rules regarding your money. I hate for you to get FREE money and start a successful business only to see you lose it all, because the state sued you for cots of incarceration.

Ownership vs. In Your Own Name?

A young brother was talking to me the other day and told me he wanted to get everything "in his own name." I asked him what he meant. He said, "I want my own OkCupid page, my own TikTok page, and . . ." He kept going. This brother told me he was all about "the science" in everything. So, I had to break it down to him.

Just because you have your own OkCupid profile or TikTok page doesn't mean you "own" that page. They do. The same for Penacon or WriteAprisoner pages. Here's a simple formula to remember: if someone in that company can press a few computer keys and erase your profile, you don't own it. True ownership comes from owning something. You can do whatever you want with it. You may own the actual content you post online on TikTok. But anytime they want, they could shut you down. Instead, if you own your own website, that's totally different. You can do whatever you want with it. I hope you take some of the FREE money that you get from the avenues in this book and purchase something that you own. Preferably, items that grow in value and don't decrease in value. Like dividend paying stocks in great companies. Or starting your own business. Or buying some legal books to help win your case. Invest in knowledge and wisdom. Become a producer, not a consumer. Just remember to check your prison system's rules about cost of incarceration first. I don't write this to scare you or try to dismay you. Only to caution you. Proper preparation prevents poor performance.

Getting Help in Reaching Out

Some of you will not be able to contact any of the resources in this book. You may need some outside help. You can enlist your family and friends. What you need them to do is simple. You need the applications that most of the grantees in this book use. Until you get those applications you should not hire anyone to help you. And before you hire anyone, you should always check with the special government offices around the country. They are called Small Business Development Centers (SBDC). There are thousands of them in America. To find the nearest office to you and your family, you should contact:

US Small Business Administration (SBA)
409 3rd Street SW
Washington, DC 20416
1-800-8-ASK-SBA
https://ww.sba.gov/sbdc/sbdcnear.html

When you have your family member or friend contact the agencies in this book have them ask a general question at first. For instance:

> "Hi, my name is _____, and I'm trying to get a description of all the _____ programs that are available for _____."

You can fill in the blanks. I'll show you how. Let's say I wanted my personal assistant to contact an office about getting free money to publish a book. I would have them ask:

> "Hi, my name is Jane Doe, and I'm trying to get a description of all the free money programs that are available for writers."

If the person on the other end does not know the answer to your question, ask them to point you in the direction of the person (or website) that does. You can contact them by mail, e-mail, telephone, or in person after you get out. Here's what I'd do:

1. Go to their website (or have my assistant do it) and review what programs and guidelines they have. I also would be looking for the contact name of the person in charge.

2. Once I got the above information, I would contact them by telephone and ask the above question. If I found something that fit me, I'd ask for an application. (They may make these applications readily available on their website.)

3. After I send in my application, I'd follow-up with an e-mail or letter inquiring about the status of my request. And I'd keep following up until I got an answer.

On the last point here's something to think about. Do you remember the movie *The Shawshank Redemption*? Well, in that movie, Andy writes a letter every week, trying to get money for the prison library. He finally gets a $200 check and some donated books. So, he then writes two letters a week and gets more money. That's how you have to be. Don't take no for an answer, and when you find something that works, keep working it.

Another Stupid Disclaimer

My lawyers are always telling me to say this, but it's the truth. In this day and age, with the COVID pandemic raging on, we cannot guarantee that any of the businesses listed are still operable. Some may still be good but have changed addresses or contact info. No matter what, please don't give up. If you see a program or grant that you like, do a web search for it on the following search engines:

https://www.google.com
https://www.dogpile.com
https://duckduckgo.com
https://search.yahoo.com
https://www.bing.com/
https://www.ask.com/

If it's a federal government agency or program you can find it by contacting the Federal Information Center, 1-800-FED-INFO; https://www.pueblo.gas.gov/.

Lastly, if you still can't find the help you need, just contact your federal, state or local elected official. You can find them at www.govengine.com or www.firstgov.gov. You can find your state senator at www.senate.gov. You can find your state representative at www.house.gov. I will list more state agencies in each respective chapter if they apply.

You can also search for help in the databases of some of the biggest non-profit charities in America. They are listed below:

Catholic Charities USA
1731 King St., #200
Alexandria, VA 22314
(703) 549-1390
www.catholiccharitiesinfo.org

Salvation Army National Headquarters
615 Slaters Lane
P.O. Box 269
Alexandria, VA 22313
(703) 684-5500
https://www.redshield.org/

United Way of America
701 North Fairfax Street
Alexandria, VA 22314
(703) 836-7112
www.unitedway.org

> *"People would do better, if they knew better."*
> — Jim Rohn

Grow A Money Tree

When I was a kid, my mother used to tell us "Money doesn't grow on trees." She'd tell us that when we'd ask for stuff, and she didn't have the money. We were poor. I wish someone would have showed me that money does grow on trees. Maybe

I wouldn't be in prison right now. Thankfully, someone did show me and now I'm growing my own money trees. Let me explain.

Some years ago, I got to read *The Millionaire Fastlane* by MJ DeMarco. And in that great book he says that our moms were wrong. Money does grow on trees if you own a money tree. DeMarco said that "Money trees are business systems that survive on their own. They required periodic support and nurturing, but survive on their own, creating a surrogate for your time-for-money trade." He would go on to point out the following five business seedlings to money trees:

1. Rental systems
2. Computer/software systems
3. Content systems
4. Distribution systems
5. Human resource systems

Because of this book I invested into myself and created how-to information and books. That fits a content system.

And every day I make money off my books. That's what I hope you do. Take whatever FREE money you get out of the ideas in this book and invest in your own money tree.

> *"The best money tree in existence sits right in your pocketbook: The good old-fashioned buck. Yes, money. Money is the king of money trees."*
> — MJ DeMarco

If you would like a great read on ideas to building your own money tree, be sure to get a copy of *The Millionaire Fastlane*. Now that I did my duty in pointing you in the right direction, let's talk about getting FREE stuff and money.

Recommended Reading

For more information on how to really tap into the power of Google and other online resources, like *refdesk.com* and Project Gutenberg, get a copy of *How To Find Out Anything* by Don Macleod.

Just remember to never take no for an answer. Be persistent in your search. Be nice to the people you talk to and write. But be persistent and always follow-up on all your requests, letters, e-mails, phone calls, and applications. Be like Andy from *The Shawshank Redemption* and go get your FREE money.

CHAPTER 2

FREE Books and Other Stuff

When I first started doing time, I didn't have much money. Only what my mom could send here and there. So, I did what we all did and do. I hustled. I learned how to play the pen pal game. I learned how to do lawsuits. And I learned a few other tricks of the trade that I can't talk about in this book. But I can honestly say that the thing that helped me the most was the FREE book companies. When I was in seg I would write these companies and get FREE books to help pass the time. While doing that I learned a whole lot that led me down this path. I no longer ask for free books because I believe in "book karma." But you may want to or need to. So here are some of the best places to write and request FREE books.

Free Book Programs

There are lots of FREE book programs. Some serve all 50 states. Most serve only a few of them in a designated area. When you write to them make sure you let them know any restrictions your prison has for incoming books. Don't try to request specific books, like "send me *48 Laws of Power*." Ask for books by subject or genre. Make sure your complete address, name, and ID number are in your letter and on your envelope.

*Disclaimer: Some of the companies and organizations in this book may have gone out of business due to the COVID pandemic.

Asheville Prison Books Programs
67 N. Lexington Ave.
Asheville, NC 28801
Email:
prisonbooks31@hotmial.com
(North Carolina, South Carolina, Georgia and Tennessee prisoners only!)

Athens Books to Prisoners
30 1st Street
Athens, OH 45701
Email:
athensbooks2prisoners@gmail.com

Beehive Books Behind Bars
c/o Weller Book Works
607 Trolley Square
Salt Lake City, UT 84102
(Prisoners in western states only!)

Book 'em
P.O. Box 71357
Pittsburgh, PA 15213
(Pennsylvania prisoners only!)

Books Between Bars
1117 Peach Street
Abilene, TX 79602
(1 book every 60 days to Texas prisoners.)

Books to Prisoners
c/o Left Bank Books
92 Pike St., Box A
Seattle, WA 98101
(206) 442-2013
Email:
bookstopprisoners@live.com
(Can't pay postage in CA or send "New Books.")

Books To Prisoners
c/o Groundwork Books
0323 Student Center
La Jolla, CA 92037

Books Through Bars
4722 Baltimore Ave.
Philadelphia, PA 19143
(Books to prisoners in PA, NY, NJ, DE, MD, WV and VA.)

Books Through Bars-NYC
c/o Bluestockings Bookstore
172 Allen St.
New York, NY 10002

(Specializes in political and history books.)

Books Through Bars-
Providence
c/o Paper Nautilus Books
5 Angell St.
Providence, RI 02906

Chicago Books to Women in
Prison
4511 N. Hermitage Ave.
Chicago, IL 60640
(Women prisoners in AZ, CA,
CT, FL, IL, IN, KY, MO and
OH.)

DC Prison Book Project
P.O. Box 34190
Washington, DC 20043-4190

Human Kindness Foundation
P.O. Box 61619
Durham, NC 27715
(Free spiritual books to
prisoners.)

Inside Books Project
c/o 12th St. Books
827 W 12th St.
Austin, TX 78701
(Free books to prisoners in
Texas.)

International Prison Books
Collective
405 West Franklin Street
Chapel Hill, NC 27514
(919) 942-1740
(Books to prisoners in MS, AL
and NC.)

Louisiana Books 2 Prisoners
3157 Gentilly Blvd., #141
New Orleans, LA 70122
(Books to prisoners in LA, AL,
AR and MS only.)

Maine Books to Prisoners
c/p Norris
P.O. Box 12
Fairmington, NE 04938

Midwest Books to Prisoners
1321 North Milwaukee Ave.,
PMB 460
Chicago, IL 60622
(Books to Midwest prisoners.)

Portland Books to Prisoners
P.O. Box 11222
Portland, OR 97211

Prison Book Program
c/o Lucy Parsons Bookstore
1306 Hancock St., Ste. 100
Quincy, MA 02169

(Doesn't ship to CA, MA, MD, MI, PA, KY, LA, NV or TX!)

Prison Literature Project
c/o Bound Together Books
1369 Haight St.
San Francisco, CA 94117

Prison Book Project
Open Books Bookstore
1040 N. Guillemard St.
Pensacola, FL 32501
(850) 453-6774
openbookspcola.org
(Books to Florida prisoners.)

Prison Books Collective
P.O. Box 625
Carrboro, NC 27510
(Books to southern states, primarily MS, AL and NC.)

Prison Library Project
c/o The Claremont Forum
915-C West Foothill Blvd.,
PMB 128
Claremont, CA 91711
(909) 626-3066
www.claremontforum.org

Read Between The Bars
c/o Daily Planet Publishing
P.O. Box 1589
Tucson, AZ 85702

readbetweenthebars.com
(Books to AZ prisoners only.)

Redbird Books to Prisoners
P.O. Box 10599
Columbus, OH 43201
(Books to OHIO prisoners only.)

Spring Grass Book 'Em
P.O. Box 71357
Pittsburgh, PA 15213
(412) 251-7302
springgrassbookem.org

Transmission Prison Books
P.O. Box 1874
Asheville, NC 28801
(Free Queer/Trans related books.)

Unchained Books
P.O. Box 784
Fort Collins, CO 80522
(Books to prisoners in Colorado.)

UC Books to Prisoners Project
P.O. Box 515
Urbana, IL 61803
(217) 344-8820
books2prisoners.org
(Books to Illinois prisoners.)

Wisconsin Books to Prisoners
Project
c/o Rainbow Bookstore
426 W. Gilman St.
Madison, WI 53703
(LGBTQ books for all states.)

LGBTQ Books to Prisoners
c/o Social Justice Center
Incubator
1202 Williamson Street #1
Madison, WI 53703
(608) 227-0206
(LGBTQ books to all states,
except TX.)

Women's Prison Book Project
c/o Boneshaker Books
2002 23rd Avenue S.
Minneapolis, MN 55404
(612) 671-7110
www.wpbp.org
(All states, except CT, FL, IL,
IN, MA, MI, MS, OH, or PA.)

Other Free Stuff for Prisoners

4 Strugglemag
P.O. Box 97048
RPO Roncesvalles Ave.
Toronto, Ontario
MGR3B3
Canada

(Free mag/newsletter to
prisoners.)

ACCESS SECUREPAK
P.O. Box 50028
Sparks, NV 89435
(Free catalog of food, CDs,
shoes, clothes, etc.)

AFSC Prison Watch Project
89 Market Street, 6th Floor
Newark, NJ 07102
(Free book for primers in
solitary called "Survivors
Manual.")

Amazing Facts
P.O. Box 909
Roseville, CA 95678
(Free sample magazine and
bible studies.)

American Bible Academy
P.O. Box 1627
Joplin, MO 64802
(Free English and Spanish
bible correspondence courses.)

American Rehabilitation
Ministries
P.O. Box 1490
Joplin, MO 64802
(Free bible correspondence
courses.)

B.B.P.D.
P.O. Box 248
Compton, MD 20627
(Sase for free book catalog.)

Berean Prison Ministry
P.O. Box 761
Peoria, IL 61652
(Free bible and bible study
material.)

Buddhist Association of the
United States
Chuang Yen Monastery
2020, Route 301
Carmel, NY 10512
(845) 228-4287
Email: *book@baus.org*
(Free Buddhist books.)

Campaign to End the Death
Penalty
P.O. Box 25730
Chicago, IL 60625
(773) 955-4841
(Free The New Abolitionist
newsletter.)

Chandra Yoga Resources
1400 Cherry St.
Denver, CO 80220
(Free books on devotional yoga
and mantra meditation.)

Crescent Imports &
Publications
P.O. Box 7827
Ann Arbor, MI 48107
(800) 521-9744
www.halalcatalog.com
(Free Islamic products catalog.)

Crossroads Bible Institute
P.O. Box 900
Grand Rapids, MI 49509-0900
(Free bible correspondence
courses.)

Dallas Cowboys Football Club
1 Cowboys Pkwy
Irving, TX 75963
(Free fan information on the
team.)

Dharma Seeds Foundation
P.O. Box 61175
Oklahoma City, OK 73146-
1175
(Free subscription to
meditation newsletter.)

East Bay Prisoner Support
P.O. Box 22449
Oakland, CA 94609
(Sends free zines to CA, AZ,
NM, TX, UT and NV prisoners.
Write for FREE catalog.)

Exotic Fragrances
1645 Lexington Ave.
New York, NY 10029
(Free catalog.)

The Fire Inside
1540 Market St. #490
San Francisco, CA 94102
(Free quarterly newsletter for
female prisoners.)

In-Touch Ministries
P.O. Box 7900
Atlanta, GA 30357
(Free "In-Touch" religious
magazine.)

Islamic Center
2551 Massachusetts Ave., NW
Washington, DC 20008
(Free Koran and study guides.)

Jewish Prisoners Assistance
Foundation
770 Eastern Parkway
Brooklyn, NY 11213
(718) 735-2000
www.prisonactivist.org/resources
(Free weekly newsletter, The
Scroll.)

Liberation Prison Project
P.O. Box 31527

San Francisco, CA 94131
www.liberationprisonproject.org
(Free Buddhist books and
booklets.)

The Lionheart Foundation
P.O. Box 170115
Boston, MA 02117
(Free resource guide with
books and orgs.)

Maoist International Ministry
of Prisons
P.O. Box 40799
San Francisco, CA 94140
(Free subscriptions to "Under
Lock and Key" newsletter.)

Mt. Hope Prison Ministry
25 Summit Ave.
P.O. Box 1511
Hagerstown, MD 21741
(Free bible study
correspondence program.)

National Health Prison Project
32 Greenwood Ave. #4
Quincy, MA 02170-2620
(Free subscription to
prisoners.)

Off Our Backs Magazine
2337B 18th St. NW
Washington, DC 20009

(Free radical feminist news journal to women in prison.)

PEN American Center
588 Broadway, Suite 303
New York, NY 10012
(Free *Handbook For Writers in Prison*.)

Prisoner Diabetes Handbook
c/o Prison Legal News
P.O. Box 1151
Lake Worth Beach, FL 33460
(Free book for prisoners with diabetes.)

Prisoner Express
Cornell University
127 Anabel Taylor Hall
Ithaca, NY 14853
(607) 255-6486
www.prisonerexpress.org
(Free semi-annual newsletter for prisoners.)

Rock of Ages Prison Ministry
c/o Prisoners Bible Institute
P.O. Box 2308
Cleveland, TN 37320
(Free bible and correspondence course.)

San Francisco 49ers Limited
4949 Centennial Blvd.

Santa Clara, CA 95054
(Free fan information on the team.)

Socialist Worker
P.O. Box 16085
Chicago, IL 60616
(Free subscription for prisoners to this newsletter.)

St. Dismas Guild
P.O. Box 2129
Escondido, CA 92033
(Free bible study, bibles, rosaries, pamphlets, etc.)

The Sun Magazine
Attn: Molly Herboth
Circulation Manager
107 North Roberson St.
Chapel Hill, NC 27516

SYDA Foundation Prison Project
P.O. Box 99140
Emeryville, CA 94662
(510) 898-2700, Ext. 4113
Email:
Prisonproject@siddhayoga.org
(Free correspondence course titled "In Search of Self.")

Walkenhorst's
445 Ingenuity Ave.

Sparks, NV 89441   (Free catalog of commissary
(800) 660-9255   products/music.)
www.walkenhorsts.com

How To Get Free Money From Family and Friends

If you have been building your network, you should have some people you can ask for help. But if you don't have anyone to ask, you should get my books *Pen Pal Success* and *Tmp4: Pen Pal Mastery*. They will give you plenty of tips and tactics on building your network. For those of you who want to ask your family and friends for money, let me offer a few suggestions.

Some of you know that I originally self-published my first book, *The Millionaire Prisoner*. I used $3,000 from a family member to start my publishing company and put out *TMP*. I actually asked them for a loan, but they said I didn't have to pay it back. I haven't looked back since. (FYI: Last year I gave them a gift of $3,000. Yes, they took it. And it felt damn good to be able to do it!) Here are a few secrets to remember when requesting money from family and friends:

- Ask them to pay for supplies or books that will help you learn and perfect your craft.
- Have them send the money to the supplier or book company (or Amazon.com) and not to you.
- Don't ask them for money they don't have and force them to say no.

Look at those above. A lot of people won't give prisoners money because they don't know what it will be used for. But instead, if they can put the order in for you, they may say yes. What I used to do before I got on was to fill out the order form and mail it to my family or friends so they could write a check and mail it in. Or have them just order it online for me. It always worked because they'd rather do that than send me money I might blow on candy and cakes from commissary. Here's what I'd say:

"I'm sending you this order for several reasons. One, it just takes too long for my prison's trust fund office to process orders. By the time they do it my ADD mind will have moved on. Two, and the main reason, is because I'm tired of being dependent on you for money. It's not your fault I'm in here. So, I want to better myself and learn how to make my own money. Plus, this way I won't blow the money on coffee and cakes from commissary."

Remember to never ask for money they don't have. There's a big difference between money they *won't* give you and money they *can't* give you. A lot of us come from poor families. We can't ask for $10,000 to start our own business. But we may ask for $50 to order some books. Know beforehand if they can afford your request.

Another tip is to time your requests. I've been more successful on my birthday, Christmas, and tax check time. The key is to show them their money is being used for the greater good. Don't burn your bridges. Instead, build them. After you have asked your family and friends, it's time to branch out. There are other sources of money. The two main ones are grants and crowdfunding. I'll deal with both of those later. For now, we'll discuss a big issue prisoners have: legal help.

"Skills and expertise are waiting just for you. No one drops a book on your lap and gifts knowledge. You have to seek it, process it, and then use it. The acquisition and

application of knowledge will make you rich."
— MJ DeMarco

CHAPTER 3

Free Legal Help

Prisoners only have a Sixth Amendment right to counsel if they are facing criminal prosecution. *See U.S. v. Gouveia*, 467 U.S. 180, 104 S.ct. 2292 (1984). There's also no constitutional right to appointment of an attorney in federal lawsuits. *See Fakner v. Haas*, 990 F.2d 319 (7th Cir. 1993).

Most states have some form of legal assistance office. I will list some of them at the end of this chapter. But you can get a lawyer appointed to represent you in court. I've done it twice. The first time I got members of the University of Illinois Legal Clinic appointed to my case. We settled that minor lawsuit for $1,500. Free money. The second time I got counsel from a multimillion-dollar law firm in Chicago appointed. That case is still pending as I write this chapter. I'll give you a copy of the Motion I used to make that happen at the end of this chapter. But first, let me share with you the law behind getting a lawyer appointed to your case. (Always remember to Keycite® or Shepardize® all case law listed to make sure it's still good law in your circuit.)

Appointment of Counsel Law

A federal court *may* appoint counsel to represent you under the *in forma pauperis'* statute. *See 28 U.S.C.* § (1915 (e)(1). Yet just because an attorney is appointed doesn't mean they have to represent you, and the court can't force them to. *Mallard v. U.S. District Court of Iowa*, 490 U.S. 296, 109 S.ct. 1814 (1989).

You should first go to your prison's law library and ask if your federal (or state) court has any special rules regarding how to go about getting a lawyer appointed. For instance, in my district, you must show the court that you made a reasonable attempt to obtain counsel on your own. Or to show you've been precluded from doing so. *Pruitt v. Mote*, 503 F.3d 647, 654 (7th Cir. 2007). Here's how you do that.

First, you should write to numerous attorneys requesting their help. You do this for several reasons. One, if you get lucky, you may get a lawyer to take your case. Two, you need to show the court that you tried to get counsel on your own. *See Flakes v. Frank*, 322 F.Supp. 2d 981, 983 (W.D. Wis. 2004) (noting usual practice of requiring plaintiff first to contact three lawyers who do civil rights work). Keep all the letters of denial that lawyers write to you so you can use them in your Motion as Proof that you tried to get an attorney.

Second, if you can't write attorneys you need to prove to the court the obstacles stopping you from wiring on your own. I believe it's not reasonable to tell a poor prisoner to write attorney, unless the prison gives out free legal postage. Some courts agree with my sentiments. *See Rose v. Racine, Correctional Institution*, 141 F.R.D. 105, 106-07 (E.D. Wis. 1992); *Cooper v. A. Sargenti Co., Inc.*, 877 F.2d 170, 173-74 (2d Cir. 1989) (". . . [T]he most important disability of the poor claimant may be not so much his lack of funds, but his lack of practical access to attorneys. If the indigent plaintiff is a prison inmate or a homeless vagrant, he may have no effective means of bringing his claim to the attention of the lawyer marketplace to have its merit appraised.")

Once you have tried to obtain counsel on your own (or have been precluded from doing so), you should highlight the following factors:

Merits of Your Case

If your case has no merit a court will not appoint a lawyer to represent you. *See Carmona v. U.S. Bureau of Prisons*, 243 F.3d 629, 632 (2d Cir. 2001); *Risley v. Hawk*, 108 F.3d 1396 (D.C. Cir. 1997). This is easily shown if your case gets past initial merit review.

Ability to Investigate and Conduct Discovery

If you've been transferred from the prison where the facts took place, that will hinder *your* investigation. *See Tucker v. Randall*, 948 F.2d 388, 391-92 (7th Cor. 1991). And when prison officials hinder your ability to conduct discovery or take depositions, you have a better chance of getting a lawyer appointed. *See Montgomery v. Pintchak*, 294 F.3d 492, 502 (3d Cir. 2002); *Parham v. Johnson*, 126 F.3d 454, 459 (3d Cir. 1999).

Whether the Evidence is Conflicting

If it will require cross-examination to resolve conflicting evidence, counsel should be appointed in most prisoner cases. *See Bright v. Hickman*, 96 F.Supp. 2d 572, 577-78 (E.D. TEX. 2000); *Steele v. Shah*, 87 F.3d 1266, 1271 (11th Cir. 1996). And prisoners with little formal education and no legal training are ill-suited to conduct jury trials by themselves. *See Solis v. County of Los Angeles*, 514, F.3d 946, 958 (9th Cir. 2008).

Prisoner's Ability to Present the Case

If you have a lack of education, mental or physical disabilities, or any other hindrance, it should be pointed out to the court. *See Hamilton v. Leavy*, 117 F.3d 742, 749 (3d Cir. 1997); *Hetzel v. Swartz*, 917 F.Supp. 344, 345-46 (M.O. Pa. 1996).

Complexity and Difficulty of Your Case

Sexual abuse and medical care cases are complex and in need of counsel for prisoners. *See Wood v. Idaho Dep't of Corrections*, 391 F.Supp. 2d 852, 867 (D. Idaho 2005); *Moore v. Mabus*, 976 F.2d 268, 272 (5th Cir. 1992). So are cased involving corporations and prison defendants together. *See Agyeman v. Corrections Corp. of America*, 390 F.3d 1101, 1103-04 (9th Cir. 2004).

And just because a judge denies your request for counsel once, you can renew it at a later time. Especially, if the status of your case had changed. In my cases, I always ask the judge to appoint me counsel. Then, if need be, I can renew it at a later time once I get to the discovery or trial phase. You can also get counsel appointed for specific areas of a case. *See Donald v. Cook County Sheriff's Dep't*, 95 F.3d 548, 556 (7th Cir. 1996) (counsel appointed to amend the complaint); *Smith v. Kansas Dep't of Corrections*, 2008 WL 4534242 (D. Kan. Oct. 7, 2008) (appointing counsel to assist at settlement conference); *Dooley v. Quick*, 598 F.Supp. 607, 624 (D.R.I. 1984)(counsel appointed to help frame rules).

For more about litigating lawsuits against prison officials while inside prison, I highly suggest you get a copy of the following books:

- *Prisoners' Self-Help Litigation Manual* (soft-cover, 900+ pages) by John Boston and Daniel E. Manville.
- *Meister Manual for Prisoner Lawsuits* (soft-cover, 700+ pages) by David J. Meister.

Those are my two favorite prison lawsuit books. Dan Manville is a former prisoner turned lawyer and law school professor. David Meister is a prisoner and his book used to be called, *Battling the Administration: An Inmate's Guide to a Successful Lawsuit.* This newer version is even bigger with lots of up-to-date 2019/2020 case law.

One last note about the *Motion for Appointment of Counsel* included at the end of this chapter. You may want to tell the court that you had my help in drafting it. Why? Here's what David Meister says in *Meister Manual for Prisoners' Lawsuits* (Chapter 12, p. 193):

> "The fact of a well-crafted motion for appointment of counsel may be viewed as evidence of an inmate's ability to adequately represent his or her cause in court. If using the services of a jailhouse lawyer in drafting an appointment motion, it may, therefore, be prudent to point out in the motion (or during the subsequent hearing on the motion) that you've had help drafting your papers but remain unable to prosecute your claims without professional assistance."

Pretty good advice. It's up to you how you do it. You have all of the information in this chapter to get you started. Here are some places you can contact to try and get an attorney to take your case:

American Civil Liberties
Union Offices
ACLU-National Prison Project
(NPP)
915 15th St. NW, 7th Fl.
Washington, DC 20005

ACLU of Idaho
P.O. Box 1897
Boise, ID 83701
(208) 344-9750

ACLU-LGBT Rights/Aids
Project
125 Broad St., 18th Fl.
New York, NY 10004

ACLU of Montana
P.O. Box 1317
Helena, MT 59624
(406) 443-8590

ACLU of Northern California
39 Drumm Street
San Francisco, CA 94111
(415) 621-2493

ACLU of San Diego
P.O. Box 87131
San Diego, CA 92138-7131
(619) 232-2121

ACLU of Texas
P.O. Box 8306
Houston, TX 77288
(713) 942-8146

ACLU-Texas Prison and Jail
Accountability Project
P.O. Box 12905
Austin, TX 78711-2905
(512) 478-7300

ACLU of Washington
901 Fifth Avenue, Suite 630
Seattle, WA 98164

ACLU-Reproductive Freedom
Project
125 Broad Street, 18th Fl.
New York, NY 10004-2400

ACLU-Capital Punishment
Project
201 West Main Street, Suite
402
Durham, NC 27701
(919) 682-5659

ACLU
125 Broad Street, 18th Fl.
New York, NY 10004
www.aclu.com

Pro Bono/Contingency Fee Attorneys

Pro Bono means "for the public good." It means a lawyer is working for free. Some lawyers also work on contingency fee basis. That means they don't get paid unless you win your lawsuit. Typically, if you win, they'll get a third, or 33% of your damages award. Here are some of these types of attorneys:

PFAU Cochran Vertetis Amala
(PCVA)
Attorneys at Law
909 A Street, Suite 700
Tacoma, WA 98402
(888) 303-9045
www.pcva.law
(Catastrophic injury/Medical malpractice/Sexual abuse)

John F. Mizner, Esq.
Mizner Law Firm
311 West Sixth Street
Erie, PA 16507
(814) 454-3889
jfm@miznerfirm.com
(Pennsylvania prisoners only.)

Magna Law Firm
2915 South Wayzata Blvd.
Minneapolis, MN 55405
(763) 438-3032
www.magnalaw.net
(Medical neglect/Police brutality)

Matthew Pinix
Pinix Law, LLC
1200 East Capitol Drive,
Suite 360

Milwaukee, WI 53211
(414) 963-6164
info@pinixlaw.com
(Wisconsin prisoners.)

William L. Schmidt
Attorney at Law, P.C.
P.O. Box 25001
Fresno, CA 93729
(559) 261-2222
www.schmidtcivillaw.com
(Civil rights violations nationwide.)

Art Gage
AG Law
2573 N. First Avenue
Tucson, AZ 85719
(520) 881-8300
www.artgagelaw.com
(Veterans benefits lawyer.)

Alaska Disability Law Center
3330 Artic Blvd., Suite 103
Anchorage, AK 99501
(907) 565-1002

Alaska Immigration Justice
Project

431 West 7th Avenue, Suite
208
Anchorage, AK 99501
(907) 279-2457

Alaska Pro Bono Program
P.O. Box 140191
Anchorage, AK 99514-0191

Alabama State Bar Volunteer
Lawyers Program
415 Dexter Avenue
Montgomery, AL 36104
(334) 269-1515

Alabama Equal Justice
Initiative
122 Commerce Street
Montgomery, AL 36104
(334) 269-1803

Arkansas Volunteer Lawyers
for the Elderly
2020 W. 3rd Street, Suite 620
Little Rock, AR 72205
(501) 376-9263

Ozark Legal Services Pro Bono
Project
4083 N. Shiloh Drive, Suite 3
Fayetteville, AR 72703
(501) 442-0600

Legal Services of Arkansas
615 West Markham Street,
Suite 200

Little Rock, AR 72201
(501) 376-8015

Arizona Justice for Children
P.O. Box 45500
Phoenix, AZ 85064
(602) 235-9300

AIDS Project Arizona
1427 N. 3rd Street
Phoenix, AZ 85004
(602) 253-2437

HIV/AIDS Law Project
303 E. Palm Lane
Phoenix, AZ 85004
(602) 258-3434

AZ Federal Public Defender's
Office
222 N. Central Avenue, Suite
810
Phoenix, AZ 85004
(602) 379-3670

California Pro Bono Project
480 N. First Street
San Jose, CA 95112
(408) 998-5298

Bay Area Legal Aid
1735 Telegraph Avenue
Oakland, CA 94612
(510) 663-4755

Asian Pacific Islander Legal
Outreach
1121 Mission Street
San Francisco, CA 94103
(415) 567-6255

Southern Colorado AIDS
Project
1301 S. 8th Street
Colorado Springs, CO 80903
(719) 578-9092

Northwest Colorado Legal
Services
P.O. Box 1904
Leadville, CO 80461
(719) 486-3238

Heart of the Rockies Bar
Association-Pro Bono
Program
1604 H Street
Salida, CO 81201
(719) 539-4251

Colorado Office of the Public
Defender
110 16th Street, Suite 800
Denver, CO 80202
(303) 620-4888

Connecticut Statewide Legal
Services
425 Main Street, #2
Middletown, CT 06457-3371
(800) 453-3320

Connecticut Trial Services
Unit
1 Hartford Square West
Hartford, CT 06106
(203) 566-5328

Delaware State Bar
Association-
Lawyer Referral Service
(800) 773-0606

Delaware Legal Aid Society
913 Washington Street
Wilmington, DE 19801
(302) 575-0660

Georgia Volunteer Lawyer for
the Arts
675 Ponce DeLeon Ave. NE
Atlanta, GA 30308
(404) 873-3911

Georgia Indigent Defense
Council
985 Ponce De Leon Avenue
NE
Atlanta, GA 30306
(404) 894-2595

State Bar of Georgia Pro Bono
Project
104 Marietta Street NW,
Suite 100
Atlanta, GA 30303
(404) 527-8700

Volunteer Legal Services
Hawaii
545 Queen Street, Suite 100
Honolulu, HI 96813
(808) 528-7046

Legal Aid Society of Hawaii
1108 Nuuanu Avenue
Honolulu, HI 96817
(808) 536-4302

Iowa Legal Aid
1111 9th Street, Suite 230
Des Moines, IA 50314
(800) 532-1275

Idaho Legal Aid Services
310 North 5th Street
Boise, ID 83701-0913
(208) 336-8980

Idaho Volunteer Lawyers
Program
P.O. Box 895
Boise, ID 83701
(800) 221-3295

Center for Disability and Elder
Law
79 W. Monroe Street
Chicago, IL 60603
(312) 376-60603

Chicago Volunteer Legal
Services

100 N. LaSalle Street, Suite 900
Chicago, IL 60602
(312) 332-1624

Chicago Legal Clinic
2938 E. 91st Street
Chicago, IL 60617
(773) 731-1762

Heartland Pro Bono Council
151 N. Delaware Street,
Suite 1800
Indianapolis, IN 46204
(317) 614-5304

Indianapolis Legal Aid
Society, Inc.
615 North Alabama Street
Indianapolis, IN 46204
(317) 635-9538

Community Development
Law Center
1802 N. Illinois Street
Indianapolis, IN 46204
(317) 921-8806

Indiana Legal Services
Support
151 North Delaware Street,
18th Floor
Indianapolis, IN 46204
(317) 631-9410

Kansas Legal Services, Inc.

712 South Kansas Avenue,
Suite 200
Topeka, KD 66603
(913)223-2068

The Pro Bono Project-
Louisiana
615 Baronne Street, Suite 203
New Orleans, LA 70113
(504) 581-4043

Civil Justice, Inc.
520 West Fayette Street
Baltimore, MD 21201
(410) 706-0174

Women's Law Center
305 W. Chesapeake Avenue,
Suite 201
Towson, MD 21204
(410) 321-8761

Maryland Volunteer Lawyers
Service
1 North Charles Street,
Suite 222
Baltimore, MD 21201
(800) 510-0050

Maine Equal Justice Partners
126 Sewall Street
Augusta, ME 04330
(866) 626-7059

Maine Volunteer Lawyers
Project

P.O. Box 547
Portland, ME 04112
(800) 442-4293

Michigan Legal Services
220 Bagley Avenue, Suite 900
Detroit, MI 48226
(313) 964-4130

Legal Services of South-
Central Michigan
420 N. Fourth Avenue
Ann Arbor, MI 48104
(734) 665-6181

Minnesota Volunteer Attorney
Program
314 West Superior Street, Suite
1000
Duluth, MN 55802
(218) 723-4005

St. Cloud Area Legal Services
830 W. St. Germain, Suite 300
St. Cloud, MN 56302
(888) 360-2889

Western Minnesota Legal
Services
415 SW 7th Street
Willmar, MN 56201
(888) 360-3666

Legal Aid Society of
Minneapolis
430 First Avenue North,

Suite 300
Minneapolis, MN 55401-1780
(612) 334-5970

Legal Services of Southern
Missouri
1414 East State Route 72
Rolla, MO 65402
(800) 999-0249

Legal Aid of Western Missouri
1125 Gran Blvd., #1900
Kansas City, MO 64106
(816) 474-6750

Legal Services of Eastern
Missouri
4232 Forest Park Avenue
St. Louis, MO 63108
(800) 444-0514

Mississippi Center for Justice
5 Old River Place, Suite 203
Jackson, MS 39202
(601) 352-2269

Mississippi Volunteer
Lawyers Project
P.O. Box 2168
Jackson, MS 39225-2168
(800) 682-6423

Mississippi Legal Services
Coalition
775 North President Street,
Suite 300

Jackson, MS 39205
(601) 944-0765

Montana Legal Services Help
Line
616 Helena Avenue, Suite 100
Helena, MT 59601
(800) 666-6899

Montana Pro Bono Project
P.O. Box 3093
Billings, MT 59103
(406) 248-7113

North Carolina Legal Services
224 South Dawson Street
Raleigh, NC 27611
(919) 856-2121

North Dakota State Bar
Association
Lawyer Referral Service
515½ E. Broadway
Bismarck, ND 58501-4407
(701) 255-1406

Legal Services of North
Dakota
1025 North 3rd Street
Bismark, ND 58502-1893
(800) 634-5263

New Hampshire Pro Bono
Referral System
112 Pleasant Street
Concord, NH 03301

(800) 639-5290

New Hampshire Legal
Assistance
15 Green Street
Concord, NH 03301
(603) 225-4700

Legal Services of New Jersey
100 Metroplex Drive at
Plainfield Ave.,
Suite 402
Edison, NJ 08818-1357
(888) 576-5529

Volunteer Lawyers for Justice
P.O. Box 32040
Newark, NJ 07102
(973) 645-1955

Washoe Legal Services
299 South Arlington Avenue
Reno, NV 89501
(775) 329-2727

Volunteer Attorneys for Rural
Nevadans
904 N. Nevada Street
Carson City, NV 89703
(866) 448-8276

Legal Aid Center of Southern
Nevada
800 S. Eighth Street
Las Vegas, NV 89101
(702) 386-1070

State Bar of New Mexico
Referral Program
P.O. Box 92860
Albuquerque, NM 87199
(505) 797-6066

New Mexico Legal Aid
P.O. Box 25486
Albuquerque, NM 87104
(505) 243-7871

The Legal Aid Society
175 Remsen Street
Brooklyn, NY 11201
(718) 243-6473

Legal Services NYC
350 Broadway, 6th Floor
New York, NY 10013
(646) 442-3600

Urban Justice Center
123 William Street, 16th Floor
New York, NY 10038
(646) 602-4598

Legal Aid Referral Project
(Greater Columbus)
1108 City Park Avenue
Columbus, OH 43206
(614) 224-8374

Volunteer Lawyers Project
(Greater Cincinnati)
215 E. Ninth Street, Suite 200

Cincinnati, OH 45202-2122
(531) 241-6800

Legal Aid Society of Cleveland
Volunteer Lawyers Program
1223 W. Sixth Street
Cleveland, OH 44113
(216) 687-1900

Greater Dayton Volunteer
Lawyers Project
109 N. Main Street, Suite 610
Dayton, OH 45402
(937) 461-3857

Legal Aid Services of
Oklahoma, Inc.
2915 North Classen
Boulevard, Suite 500
Oklahoma, OK 73106
(405) 557-0020

Marion-Polk Legal Aid
1655 State Street
Salem, OR 97301
(503) 581-5265

Center for Non-Profit Legal
Services
225 W. Main Street
Medford, OR 97501
(541) 779-7291

Legal Aid Services of Oregon
921 SW Washington Street,
Suite 500

Portland, OR 97205
(888) 610-8764

Neighborhood Legal Services
Association
928 Penn Avenue
Pittsburgh, PA 15222-3799
(412) 255-6700

Lackawana Pro Bono
321 Spruce Street
Scranton, PA 18503
(570) 961-2715

Pennsylvania Legal Aid
Network
118 Locust Street
Harrisburg, PA 17101
(800) 322-7572

Rhode Island Bar Association
Volunteer Lawyer Program
115 Cedar Street
Providence, RI 02903-1082
(401) 421-7799

Rhode Island Legal Services
56 Pine Street, 4th Floor
Providence, RI 02903
(401) 274-2652

South Carolina Legal Services-
Charleston
2803 Carner Avenue
Charleston, SC 29405
(843) 720-7041

South Carolina Legal Services-
Beaufort
69 Robert Smalls Parkway,
Suite 3-A
Beaufort, SC 29902
(843) 521-0623

South Carolina Legal Services-
Columbia
2109 Bull Street
Columbia, SC 29201
(803) 799-9668

Second Judicial Circuit Pro
Bono Project
335 N. Main Avenue
Sioux Falls, SD 57104
(605) 336-92330

East River Legal Services
335 North Main Avenue, Suite
300
Sioux Falls, SD 57102
(605) 336-9230

Nashville Pro Bono Program
300 Deaderick Street
Nashville, TN 37201
(615) 244-6610

Tennessee Alliance for Legal
Services
50 Vantage Way, Suite 250
Nashville, TN 37228
(888) 395-9297

Lone Stare Legal Aid
1415 Fannin Street
Houston, TX 77002
(800) 733-8394

Texas Legal Aid-Rio Grande
17 Sunny Glen
Alpine, TX 79830
(432) 837-1199

Legal Aid Society of Utah
450 South State Street
Salt Lake City, UT 84111-3101
(801) 238-7170

Utah Legal Services, Inc.
254 West 4th Street, 2nd Floor
Salt Lake City, UT 84101
(801) 328-8891

Virginia Poverty Law Center
201 West Broad Street,
Suite 302
Richmond, VA 23220
(804) 782-9430

Virginia Legal Aid Society,
Inc.
513 Church Street
Lynchburg, VA 24504
(866) 534-5243

Southwest Virginia Legal Aid
Society
227 W. Cherry Street

Marion, VA 24354
(800) 277-6754

Vermont Volunteer Lawyer's
Project
274 North Winooski Avenue
Burlington, VT 05401
(802) 863-7153

Vermont Legal Aid Inc.
P.O. Box 1367
12 North Street
Burlington, VT 05401
(802) 863-5620

Evergreen Legal Services
101 Yesler Way, Suite 300
Seattle, WA 98104
(206) 464-5933

Legal Action of Wisconsin
230 West Wells Street,
Room 800
Milwaukee, WI 53203
(414) 278-7722

West Virginia Legal Service
Plan
1003 Quarrier Street, Suite 700
Charleston, WV 25301
(304) 342-6814

Legal Aid of Wyoming, Inc.
211 West 19th Street, Suite 300
Cheyenne, WY 82001
(877) 432-9955

Legal Services Corporation
(LSC)
3333 K Street NW, 3rd Floor
Washington, DC 20007
https://www.lsc.gov/
(202) 295-1500

National Legal Aid and
Defender Association
(NLADA)
1901 Pennsylvania Avenue
NW, Suite 500
Washington, DC 20006
https://www.nlada.org/

Southern Poverty Law Center
(SPLC)
400 Washington Avenue
Montgomery, AL 36104
https://www.splcenter.org

American Bar Association
(ABA)
321 North Clark Street
Chicago, IL 60654
*https://www.americanbar.org/gro
ups/lawyer-referral/*

Nolo
7031 Koll Center Parkway
Suite 260
Pleasanton, CA 94566
https://www.nolo.com/lawyers

National Lawyers Guild

132 Nassau Street, Room 922
New York, NY 10038
https://jailhouselaw.org/

Vera Institute of Justice
233 Broadway, 12th Floor
New York, NY 10279
https://www.vera.org

The Marshall Project
156 West 56th Street, Suite 701
New York, NY 10019
https://www.themarshallproject.org

Amnesty International
5 Penn Plaza, 16th Floor
New York, NY 10001
https://www.amnestyusa.org

Free Legal Help for Mexican-
Americans
Mexican American Legal
Defense Fund (MALDF)
634 South Spring St.,
11th Floor
Los Angeles, CA 90014
(213) 629-2512
www.maldef.org

Free Money From Class Action Lawsuits

A lot of my fellow convicts in Illinois got free money from the Cook County class action lawsuits about the strip searches and 48-hour hearing mandate. They got a few thousand dollars. I wish I would have been from Cook County and got some of that free money. I wonder how many convicts didn't get their money because they didn't ask for it.

Don't worry. There are websites that monitor all the major class actions in the United States. You can search these websites and find a possible payday for free money. That would pay for the cost of this book and a whole lot more. Here's two websites you can monitor:

www.topclassactions.com
www.sec.gov/divisions/enforce/claims.htm

Free Legal Help for People with Disabilities

Disability Rights Education and Defense Fund, Inc.
2212 Sixth Street
Berkeley, CA 94710
(510) 644-2555
www.dredf.org
edf@dredf.org

Free Legal Help for Welfare Rights

Welfare Law Center
275 Seventh Ave., Suite 1205
New York, NY 10001
(212) 633-6967
www.lincproject.org/
Email: *dirk@welfarelaw.org*
(Contact for closest organization in your state.)

Free Legal Help with Civil Liberties and Religious Freedom

The Rutherford Institute
Legal Department
P.O. Box 7482
Charlottesville, VA 22906
(434) 978-3888
www.rutherford.org

Prisoner Turned Lawyer

How many of you have seen the television series *For Life* that aired on ABC? Well, that show is based in part on the story of Isaac Wright, Jr. He is now a successful lawyer in New Jersey. But back in 1991 he was wrongfully convicted on drug charges in New Jersey and sentenced to life in prison under New Jersey's drug kingpin laws. While in prison he worked as a paralegal and helped overturn the wrongful convictions of twenty other prisoners. Finally, after seven years inside he got this own conviction overthrown and the charges dismissed after a police officer came forward to tell the truth.

After being released from prison he graduated from *Thomas Edison State University* and eventually *St. Thomas University School of Law*. He passed the bar in 2008. After a nine-year investigation into his character the New Jersey Bar Association's Committee approved his application. He started practicing law in 2017 for the New Jersey law firm of Hunt, Hamlin & Ridley. He specializes in defending the wrongly accused and going after corrupt institutions. Curtis "50 cent" Jackson signed a deal to produce a TV series based on Isaac's life. That show aired on ABC-TV and was must-watch TV for us prisoners. If you've been wrongfully convicted in New Jersey or New York, you may want to contact Mr. Wright. His address is below:

Isaac Wright, Jr.
Hunt, Hamlin & Ridley
60 Park Place, 16th Fl.
Military Park Building
Newark, NJ 07102
(973) 242-4471

Maybe you can follow in Isaac Wright's footsteps and become a lawyer yourself. Even if you are innocent, don't give up. Keep fighting. Here are some more examples to get you inspired.

Wilder "Kendric" Berry was wrongfully convicted and spent more than eight years in the Illinois Department of Corrections. He is now a senior paralegal at the high-powered

Chicago law firm of Winston & Strawn, LLP, where he protects the justice that others deserve.

Shon Hopwood was a prisoner who my twin brother did time with, in the federal system. He was sentenced to 12 years in prison at the age of 23 for five bank robberies in rural Nebraska. Instead of participating in the usual prison folly, Hopwood spent most of his time in the prison law library getting an education and helping other prisoners. One case he worked on made it all the way to the U.S. Supreme Court where the court not only accepted the *pro se* brief he filed for prisoner John Fellers but sided with his argument. You can read more about his story in the book, *Law Man: My Story of Robbing Banks, Winning Supreme Court Cases, and Finding Redemption.* Or more on his website, *www.shonhopwood.com.*

Here are some of the people that are willing to help prisoners who are innocent:

The Exoneration Project
312 N. May St., Suite 100
Chicago, IL 60607
(312) 798-4955
(Send for free info package.)

University of Texas School
of Law
Attn: Actual Innocence Clinic
727 E. Dean Keeton St.
Austin, TX 78705

California Innocence Project
225 Cedar St.
San Diego, CA 92101

(619) 525-1485

Northwestern University
School of Law
Attn: Wrongful Convictions
357 E. Chicago Ave.
Chicago, IL 60611-3069
(312) 503-2391

Centurion Ministries
221 Witherspoon
St. Princeton, NJ 08542-3215
(609) 921-0334
(Only LWOP/Death Penalty cases.)

DNA Testing Program
1660 Cross Center Dr.
Norman, OK 73019
(Oklahoma cases only.)

Innocence Project
55 5th Ave., 11th Floor
New York, NY 10003
www.innocenceproject.org
(DNA cases)

Peoples Law Office
1180 N. Milwaukee Ave.
Chicago, IL 60642
(773) 235-0070

Innocence Project
Attn: Kristin Cronia
125 High St.
Boston, MA 02110
(For CT, MA, ME, NH, and RI
only.)

University of Washington
School of Law
Innocence Project
110 NE Campus Parkway
Seattle, WA 98105
(For WA, OR, AK, ID, or MT)

University of Kansas School
of Law

c/o Wilson Project for
Innocence
409 Green Hall
Lawrence, KS 66045

ASIJ-Justice Project
Mail Code 4420
411 N. Central Ave., Ste. 600
Phoenix, AZ 85004
(602) 496-0286
(For Arizona prisoners.)

Alaska Innocence Project
P.O. Box 201656
Anchorage, AK 99520-1656
(907) 279-0454
www.alaskainnocence.org

Chicago Innocence Project
205 West Monroe Street,
Suite 315
Chicago, IL 60606
(312) 263-6213

Colorado Innocence Project
Wolf Law Building – 401 UCB
2450 Kittredge Loop Drive
Boulder, CO 80309
(303) 492-8047

Connecticut Innocence Project
c/o McCarter & English
Cityplace 1

185 Asylum Street, 36th Floor
Hartford, CT 06103
(860) 275-6140

CPCS Innocence Program
Attn: Lisa Kavanaugh
21 McGrath Highway,
2nd Floor
Somerville, MA 02143
(617) 623-0591
(MA prisoners only.)

The Exoneration Initiative
233 Broadway
Suite 2370
New York, NY 10279
(212) 965-9335

Georgia Innocence Project
2645 North Decatur Road
Decatur, GA 30033
(404) 373-4433

Hawaii Innocence Project
Attn: Professor Hench
University of Hawaii
School of Law
2515 Dole Street
Honolulu, HI 96822
(808) 956-6547

Idaho Innocence Project
Boise State University

1910 University Drive
Boise, ID 83725

Illinois Innocence Project
University of Illinois
Springfield
One University Plaza
Springfield, IL 62703-5407
(217) 206-6600
(For Illinois cases outside
Chicago.)

Innocence and Justice Project
University of New Mexico
School of Law
1117 Standford NE
Albuquerque, NM 87131-0001
(505) 277-2671

Innocence Project For Justice
Rutgers University School of
Law
Constitutional Litigation
Clinic
123 Washington St.
Newark, NJ 07102
(New Jersey cases.)

Innocence Project NW Clinic
University of Washington
School of Law

William H. Gates Hall, Suite 265
P.O. Box 85110
Seattle, WA 98145
(Washington cases only.)

Innocence Project of Florida, Inc.
1100 East Park Avenue
Tallahassee, FL 32301
(850) 561-6767

Innocence Project of Iowa
19 South 7th Street
Estherville, IA 51334

Innocence Project of Minnesota
Hamline University School of Law
1536 Hewitt Avenue
St. Paul, MN 55104
(651) 523-3152

Innocence Project of New Orleans
4051 Ulloa Street
New Orleans, LA 70119
https://www.ip-no.org

The Innocence Project of Texas
1511 Texas Ave.

Lubbock, TX 79401
(806) 744-6525

Kentucky Innocence Project
Department of Public Advocacy
100 Fair Oaks Lane, Ste. 302
Frankfort, KY 40601
(502) 564-3948

Medill Justice Project
Northwestern University
1845 Sheridan Road
Evanston, IL 60108
(847) 491-5840
(Murder cases within 250 miles of Evanston.)

Miami Law Innocence Clinic
3000 Biscayne Blvd., Suite 100
Miami, FL 33137
(305) 284-8115

Michigan Innocence Clinic
1029 Legal Research Building
625 State Street
Ann Arbor, MI 48109
(734) 763-9353

Mid-Atlantic Innocence Project
American University-
Washington College of Law

43

2000 H. Street, NW
Washington, DC 20052
(202) 995-4586
(D.C., MD and VA only.)

Midwest Innocence Project
605 West 47th Street
Kansas City, MO 64113
(816) 221-2166
(AR, KS, MO, IA and NE
cases.)

Mississippi Innocence Project
University of Mississippi
School of Law
P.O. Box 1848
University, MS 38677
(662) 915-5206

Montana Innocence Project
P.O. Box 7607
Missoula, MT 59807
(406) 243-6698

Nebraska Innocence Project
P.O. Box 24183
Omaha, NE 68124-0183

New England Innocence
Project
160 Boylston Street
Boston, MA 02116
(857) 277-7858

North Carolina Center on
Actual Innocence
P.O. Box 52446
Shannon Plaza Station
Durham, NC 27717
(919) 489-3268

Northern Arizona Justice
Project
Department of Criminal
Justice
Northern Arizona University
P.O. Box 15005
Flagstaff, AZ 86011-5005
(928) 523-7028

Northern California
Innocence Project
Santa Clara Law School
500 El Camino Real
Santa Clara, CA 95053
(408) 554-4361

Oklahoma Innocence Project
2501 N. Blackwelder
Oklahoma City, OK 73106
(405) 208-6161

Palmetto Innocence Project
P.O. Box 11623
Columbia, SC 29211

Pennsylvania Innocence
Project
Temple University Beasley
School of Law
1719 North Broad Street
Philadelphia, PA 19122
(215) 204-4255

Rocky Mountain Innocence
Center
358 South 700 East, B235
Salt Lake City, UT 84102
(801) 355-1888

Texas Innocence Network
University of Houston Law
Center
100 Law Center
Houston, TX 77204

The Last Resort Innocence
Project
Seton Hall University School
of Law
One Newark Center
1109 Raymond Boulevard
Newark, NJ 07102
(973) 642-8500

Thomas M. Cooley Innocence
Project
300 S. Capitol Ave.
P.O. Box 13038

Lansing, MI 48901
(517) 371-5140

Thurgood Marshall School
of Law
Innocence Project
3100 Cleburne Street
Houston, TX 77004
(713) 313-1139

University of Baltimore
Innocence Project Clinic
1401 N. Charles St.
Baltimore, MD 21201
(410) 837-4468

Wesleyan Innocence Project
1515 Commerce St.
Fort Worth, TX 76102

West Virginia Innocence
Project
West Virginia University
College of Law
P.O. Box 6130
Morgantown, WV 26506
(304) 293-7249

Wisconsin Innocence Project
University of Wisconsin
Madison
975 Bascom Mall

Madison, WI 53706-1399

Wrongful Conviction Clinic
Indiana University School
of Law
530 W. New York St.,
Room 111
Indianapolis, IN 46202-3225
(317) 274-5551

Wrongful Conviction Project
Office of Ohio Public
Defender
250 East Broad St., Suite 1400
Columbus, OH 43215
(614) 466-5394

Recommended Reading

- *Chasing Justice* by Kerry Max Cook
- *The Innocent Man* by John Grisham
- *Actual Innocence* by Barry Scheck, Peter Neufeld, Jim Dyer

"Justice is indiscriminately due to all, without regard to numbers, wealth, or rank."

— John Jay

Online Resources to Find Attorneys

www.lawinfo.com
www.*lawyers*.com
www.alllaw.com
www.attorneyfind.com
www.attorneylocate.com
www.legalmatch.com
www.attorneypages.com
www.lawyerfinder.com
www.uslaw.com
www.attorneyhunter.com
www.lawfirmdirectory.org
www.martindale.com
www.findlegalhelp.org
www.abanet.org/legalservices/probono/directory.html
www.freeadvice.com

CHAPTER 4
How To Get Free Pen Pals

"The arrow shot by the archer may or may not kill a single person. But stratagems devised by a wise man can kill even babies in the womb."
— Kautilya 3rd Century B.C. Philosopher

I previously wrote about these strategies in my booklet, *How To Get Free Pen Pals* and in Chapter 4 of *Pen Pal Success*. I've used the strategies in this chapter all of my life. I currently have 3 pen pals that I've had over 10+ years that I got using these avenues. Prisoners have been using them for years. Let me show you how you can get FREE pen pals.

First, network with your comrades. Ask your friends who have pen pals. Especially, the ones that go on visits and get big mail. Ask them if their pen pal, girlfriend, wife, or sister could find you someone to write? Most will say no, but every once in a while, you'll find someone to write. Remember my homie hooked me up with his friend from Chicago? I wrote her for a few years. My twin brother got a pen pal/visitor this way when one of his friends' girlfriends didn't want to ride to the prison by herself. And she didn't want her girlfriend to sit alone in the car for a few hours while she visited. So, my brother got put in the car with the friend. He ended up writing, emailing, and going on visits with that girl. Sometimes it's not what you know, but *who* you know!

<u>An Untapped Goldmine</u>

In 2005 I was in the law library at Menard Correctional Center and happened to run into a prisoner named "G." We knew each other from juvie and started telling war stories. Eventually, we got around to pen pals. I told him about the 3 pen pals I had. When it was his turn, he told me about his 7 main pen pals. Then he said he had 29 pen pals altogether. So, naturally, I asked him what website he was on. He laughed and said none. He said that he'd never been on any website and would never go on one because there was no reason to.

The statement caught me off guard because every prisoner I knew said that if you wanted to get pan pals, you had to go on one of the prison pen pal websites. But G told me that a true pick-up artist does what everyone else isn't doing. He told me that he didn't want to fish in the same pond as every other prisoner. Instead, he wanted a pond all to himself. You can probably already guess my next question to him.

"So G, how do you get your pen pals?"

"Man, I get them out of the newspaper or wherever I see an address!"

I laughed a little at that and said, "So, you just write any woman's address that you see?"

"Yep," he replied. "That's how I get my pen pals. It's that easy, try it."

If any other prison would've told me that, I'd let it go in one ear and out the other. But I know G and trust him. So, I went looking for a newspaper. I found a prisoner who had a subscription to *The Southern Illinoisan*. Then I started looking through it with a fine-toothed comb. Sure enough, I found seven addresses in the arrest reports. I immediately went to work and started writing. I wrote all seven women. One week later I got two responses and no return to senders. The first woman wanted to know how I got her info. The second was willing to be my pen pal.

Now I'm not stupid. If you show me something works, I'm going to work the hell out of it. So, I kept writing addresses down, and every time I got extra envelopes, I wrote more women. The results? I came up with two lesbian girls who lived together. I got a lonely security guard at a factory who spent her midnight shift writing me. I had multiple pen pals, got mail every day, but I wanted a woman to come visit me every week.

About that time, I started ending my letters with a line where I gave them an option to pass my letter on to someone else if they were not interested. I didn't know if it would work, but I figured it couldn't hurt. I wrote a woman from Carbondale, Illinois, which is about 30 minutes from Menard. A few weeks later I got a letter from Carla, some woman I didn't write or even know. She told me the woman I wrote was married, but she had read my letter and decided to write. She had just gone through a divorce and was lonely. One month later we had our first visit, and every Tuesday after that, I was in the visiting room, eating good food and playing cards with her. Life can be a whole lot better inside prison when you have free-world friends to help out.

I must be honest with you. I was not running game. I told the truth. I never lied to any of the women who wrote me back and told them I had life in prison. I've always found honesty to be the best policy.

There are numerous places to find addresses in your local newspaper, but you should concentrate on four sections:

- Arrest Reports or Court Roundup Section
- Classified for legal notices and real estate deals
- Obituaries; and
- Religious sections

Let's look at each one of these sections in more detail.

Arrest Reports/Court Roundup

Every local newspaper lists the names of people who have been arrested. But not all newspapers list addressed. It may say: "Jane Doe, of the 1200 block of Walnut, was arrested . . ." In that example, they've put the block number and not the actual house or apartment number. Those kinds of newspapers are no good for the arrest reports. But they still may be good for the classifieds and/or the religious sections.

What you need are actual house numbers. If they say: "Jane Doe, 1218 N Walnut, was arrested . . ." then you can write them, knowing that your letter will be delivered to that address. (But that doesn't mean you'll get a response.) The key to looking for addresses in the arrest reports is twofold:

- What were they arrested for?
- Is the address a house or an apartment?

Here's why. If they were arrested for something major, like murder, they're most likely to still be in jail and won't get your letter, unless you can write them at the county jail. But if they were arrested for something minor; like a traffic violation, retail theft, or disorderly conduct; then they're probably back on the street and may get your letter.

The other thing about what they got arrested for is that you can get a sense of what type of person they are. Someone arrested for drugs probably won't write you back. After they're released, they'll go back to their drug of choice, and that's not you. My best successes have come from people arrested for traffic violations. But I have gotten pen pals from other charges as well.

If you're allowed to write prisoners, consider writing some of the people who are locked up in the county jail. I've had great pen pals who were locked up. Because we developed a great friendship while they were inside, they continued to write once they got out. Remember, you're locked up also. You share a common bond and can use that to build a friendship.

Now to the second point: house number or apartment? In my experience, it's better to write people in a house rather than apartments. Why? Because people tend to move more often when they live in apartments. And in a lot of apartments buildings they have a bunch of mailboxes on the first floor. If the name on the mailbox doesn't match the name on the letter it could be returned to sender! With a house, the mail normally is just put in the mailbox or pushed through the mail slot in the door. I've gotten more return to sender letters writing apartments than any other address.

There are a couple more things you can tell by the addresses themselves. First, if you're from the town of that newspaper, you can tell by the street and block numbers in the addresses what type of neighborhood it is. Even if you aren't from that town or area, someone in your prison is and can tell you about that area or street. Sometimes it's good to find out this info and then tailor your letter accordingly.

Second, a lot of newspapers will list different cities or towns in these addresses because the newspaper covers an area, not just one city. Most of the time they don't publish zip codes in the arrest reports. So, you'll have to find them on your own. If the town is over 5,000 people, you can find the zip code in *The World Almanac and Book of Facts*. If you can't find it in the almanac, most prison libraries have a directory where you can find zip codes for different cities in your state. Or you can have someone in the free-world look them up at: www.usps.com, under "Mail & Ship." You can select "look up a zip code." You can also find some zip codes in the newspaper itself. Look at the advertisements. Some companies list their full contact information. Write the city and zip code down. Put it in your notebook. That will save you a lot of research later on when you start finding addresses.

One last thing about these addresses. When you look up a town in the almanac, you'll get the population. This is important. You should have more success writing people in smaller towns instead of larger cities. Why? Because there's nothing to do in a small town. People are bored and you're something new to them and they have time to write.

Newspaper Classifieds

There are still some newspapers out there where you can find personal ads. In my hometown there's a newspaper called the *Thrifty Nickel*. It's nothing but classifieds where people sell stuff. Yes, it has a personal's section. But most personal ads are online now with *Craigslist* or *Backpage.com* and others. Every once in a while, you'll find a personal ad in the newspaper classifieds.

But the main reason to look in the classifieds is the "legal notices." When someone opens a new business, their name and address of their business is placed in a legal notice in the classified section. A lot of these will be women who work from home. Find them and write them down. Some newspapers will also have a listing of the real estate deals in the legal notices. People who are selling houses are not good addresses, because they are moving or have moved. People who have bought the house are good prospects. If you see an address like that, write it down.

Obituaries

I must admit I've never used this one, but a friend I know well has for success. One day we were watching the movie *Wedding Crashers*, and in that movie, they crash funerals to pick up girls. My friend saw that and told me my FREE pen pal system would work for that. I didn't know what he was talking about, so he explained. He said sometimes in the obituaries they list mailing addresses where people can send in donations. Why not send in a card of condolence and tell them you'll be their prayer partner? I could never do that, but he does. And he has got pen pals that way.

Religious Sections

"The church is among the more desirable sources through which one may meet and cultivate people, because it brings people together under circumstances which inspire the spirt of fellowship among people."
— Andrew Carnegie

It was after reading the above quote from one of the richest men ever, that I started writing churches. Yes, I'd write them requesting pen pals. One church I wrote got me 17 different cards and letters the next week. Jackpot! That's the one where the secretary never delivered my responses because she wanted me all to herself.

You can find church addresses in your newspaper. They are listed in the obituaries when that church will hold the memorial service or funeral. There's a religious section sometimes with a bunch of church addresses. You can also get church addresses off the free religious channels on your prison TV cable network. When they give out their mailing addresses, write them down. You can also have someone search online for you. A good website is www.churchangel.com. On church angel you can search by city, state, and zip code. Your prison chaplain can also supply you with a list of addresses of churches as well.

Here's a sample letter you can use:

"Dear _____ church:

I wonder if you could help me out of a little difficulty.

I'm in search of someone who would correspond with me as a pen pal. I'm trying to change my life for good, but all those around me only want to lie, cheat, gossip, and steal, and practice many other forms of evil in this den of iniquity. My present incarceration causes me a limitation in access to those I can have inspirational, uplifting conversations with. I'm looking for someone who will accept me as their brother and friend.

I've tried numerous websites for prisoners to get pen pals, but it has been discouraging because the replies I have received haven't been from the type of people I'm looking for. If your church has a bulletin or prayer request board, would you please post my letter and photo on it? Anyone wishing to contact me may do so by writing me at the below address.

Thank you for taking the time to consider this letter of request. May God bless you and peace be unto you.

Make sure your mailing address is on the bottom of your letter.

There are also places online where you can post free personal ads and profiles looking for pen pals or a date.

For Christians there is:

Christianmingle.com
Bigchurch.com
Christianpenpals.com

Christianconnectionnetwork.com
Christianlifestyle.com
Realchristiansingles.com

For Muslims there is:

Bestmuslim.com
Meetmuslimsingles.com
Muslima.com
Muslimandsingle.com
Muxlim.com
Salamlove.com
Soulfulmuslimsingles.com

For Jewish people there is:

Gefiltefishing.com
Jewishpassions.com
Jsoulmate.com
Menschfinder.com
JDate.com
Lasurim.org

And there are plenty of more online. You just got to find them, then utilize them.

> *"Don't wait for extraordinary opportunities. Seize common occasions and make them great."*
> — Orison Swett Marden

Pen Pal Hall of Fame

Emmanuel "Top Flight" Grant is one of my old cellmates who was knee-deep in the pen pal game, and one of his accomplishments is legendary in Illinois prison lore. When we were cellmates in segregation, an outside minister came to speak to us prisoners. The guy would go door-to-door talking and praying with guys. Emmanuel talked to him, but at the end of the talk told the minister that he was going to go back to his church and not to forget about him. The minister promised he wouldn't. A short time later he received a letter from the minister and their friendship began. Our prison rules dictate that this minister would lose his "volunteer" status once he came to visit a prisoner. But the minister and his wife began visiting him regularly at the prison. They even set up a donation box in their church just for him and every other week they would empty the box and send him the money. The minister also had other people from the church writing Emmanuel and sending him books and magazines. In 2017 I received a letter and photos from him. He had paroled to Wisconsin to go live with his whole adopted church family. His story is proof that churches can help prisoners. You just have to be open-minded about such things.

Become A Sleuth

You do not have to limit your search to just addresses in a newspaper. I've used magazines where I just wrote the person "in care of" the magazine. And they got the letter and replied. This works if the person has a regular column in each magazine issue. One of those responses is still my pen pal today and is a famous writer and editor. I'm not telling you this to brag, but to illustrate that people are willing to write prisoners and help out. You just have to reach out and don't take no for an answer. But there's still other ways to get FREE pen pals that don't involve newspapers. And in the next chapter I'll show you them.

CHAPTER 5

FREE Pen Pals, Part 2

"A good general cultivates resources."
— Sun Tzu

I happened to run into G once again in the law library and he asked me how it was going. I told him how I got 17 responses off that one letter to the St. Louis church. He loved that. As is true, when two or more people come together to discuss things without any animosity between them, they'll form a third mind, and fresh ideas will flow forth. It happened with me and G.

We came up with the idea to put ads up on college campuses saying we needed pen pals. I was game if he had someone who could post our ads for us. One of his friends strategically placed ads around the UIC campus in Chicago. Then we waited. Within a few weeks we were getting people writing us. I can't remember the exact ad we used, but here's how I would do it now:

HELP WANTED-PART TIME
Pen Pal needed. Position available for an
open-minded woman. No experience
required. Rewarding position with lots of
bonuses. If a quality friendship with a
unique, honest, SWM, published author
and poet is what you'd like, apply soon!
Interested parties submit letter to:

Then put your name and prison number and complete mailing address and email if you got it?

This strategy would work in bigger cities like Chicago, New York, and Los Angeles, where there are multiple colleges in one area. Have your friend or family member post your ads on the student boards, union halls, laundromats, and inside the bathrooms. Guerrilla marketing at its finest. I know one prisoner who said in his ad that he was willing to be a "subject" for their class requirements. That was brilliant because a lot of criminal justice/criminology students have a prison and parole class.

In his book, *How to Get Girls While You Are in Prison*, Freedom Jones advises writing criminal justice departments/psychology department/social science departments of colleges to get pen pals. I've seen it work.

Michael Santos is author of *Inside: Life Behind Bars in America* and *About Prison*, among other books. When he was in the fed joint, he used this strategy and developed mentorships with numerous university professors. One of his books became the book students had to read for that class. That helped him make over $200,000 in royalties while in prison. One of those mentors helped him to teach a class at a major university in California after he got released. He became known as "the prison professor." His book, *Success After Prison*, is a must-read for any prisoner going home in the next few years. When he was inside, Santos made sure there was a letter in the outgoing mail every time they picked up the mail! No wonder he created his own network.

> *"People are bridges you must cross to get where you want to go."*
> — Bob Beaudine

Free Pen Pal Programs

There are organizations and programs you can write to get free pen pals. The very first foreign pen pal I got came from a lifer/death row pen pal program. So, I know firsthand the power these programs hold. Here are some of the more popular FREE pen pal programs:

Lifelines to Solitary
c/o Solitary Watch
P.O. Box 11374
Washington, DC 20008
info@solitarywatch.com
www.solitarywatch.org
(Personalized letters and quarterly newsletters to prisoners in solitary confinement across the country.)

Church of the Larger Fellowship (CLF)
Worthy Now Prison Ministry Network
Pen Pals Letter Writing Ministry
24 Farnsworth Street
Boston, MA 02210
(617) 948-6150
www.clfuu.org
worthynow.org
(Matches prisoners with Unitarian Universalists for friendship.)

Forum for Understanding Prisons (FFUP)
29631 Wild Rose Drive
Blue River, WI 53518
(608) 536-3993
www.prisonforum.org

(Write them with your background, areas of interest, and to request a pen pal volunteer.)

National Coalition to Protect Civil Freedoms
P.O. Box 66301
Washington, DC 20035
(855) 248-3733
info@civilfreedoms.org
www.civilfreedoms.org
(Write and request a pen pal volunteer.)

Forgotten Females
c/o McLoyd Services
P.O. Box 3621
Wichita, KS 67201
forgottenfemales@yahoo.com
(Free pen pal service for female prisoners.)

Pen Pal Connection
P.O. Box 11296
Hickory, NC 28603
cppministry.com
(Christian pen pals.)

St. Michael Outreach Ministry
Attn: Prisoner Outreach Program
7765 Tiger Tail Road, Suite One
St. Paul, MN 28384

Texas Prisoners Network
3005 South Lamar Blvd., Suite D-109-224
Austin, TX 78704
(Only for Texas prisoners.)

Jewish Prisoner Services
P.O. Box 85840
Seattle, WA 99814
(Free pen pal for Jewish prisoners.)

Human Rights Pen Pal Program
1301 Clay Street
P.O. Box 71378
Oakland, CA 94612

Lifeline
63 Forest Road
Garston
Watford WD 25 7QP
United Kingdom
(International pen pal for death row prisoners.)

FREE Ads On The Internet

Most prisoners think that prison pen pal websites are the best place to get pen pals. I disagree and think they are a waste of money. I've got more hits off free websites than prison pen pal sites I had to pay for! Here are some websites you can place free profiles on:

Afrontroductions.com	*Alternative hookups.com*
Blackcupid.com	*BBW singlesfinder.com*
Africanamericanpassions.com	*Gothscene.com*
Blackplanet.com	*Gayfriendfinders.com*
Blackscene.com	*Manlive.com*
Blacksingles.com	*Largefriends.com*
Freeblackdates.com	*Fitnessdatelink.com*
Interracialromance.com	*Freealternativedating.com*
Soulsingles.com	*Gays.com*

Isopersonals.com
Iwantu.com
Lesbotronic.com
Savagehearts.com
Vampirefreaks.com
Youloveme.com
Outeverywhere.com
4ppl.com
Allsinglesmeet.com
Be2gether.com
Connectingsingles.com
Cupidmarket.com
Datanta.com
Date.com
Datepad.com
Ecpersonals.com
Freedatingusa.com
Fdating.com
Gofishdating.com
Jumpdates.com
Letslol.com
Love.org
Lulusloveshack.com
Luvfree.com
Matchmaker.com
Match.com
Meeta.com
Mingles2.com
Okfreedating.com
Plentyoffish.com
Singlesnet.com

Seekingsugarmomma.com
Triguladating.com
Youandme.com
Okcupid.com
Webdate.com
Zoosk.com
Asianeuro.com
Asiapassions.com
Cheekyflirt.com
Datememateme.com
Flovedates.com
Globalladies.com
Ezifriends.com
Internationalcupid.com
Ukdatingnow.com
Amor.com
Latinamericancupid.com
Latinlovesearch.com
Latinpassions.com
Latinromance.com
Mexicancupid.com
Sonico.com
Flixter.com
Weread.com
Librarything.com
Oneclimate.net
Over40andsingle.com
Partnerup.com
Wiseearth.com
Deafpassions.com
Shelfari.com

As you can see from the above list there's something out there for everyone. A lot of the above sites you would need email for. Just remember, the more places you place your ad/bio/and photo on, the more opportunities you give yourself.

FREE Pen Pal Sites

A lot of the above websites were dating sites or social networking sites and forums. Here are some of the better known FREE online pen pal sites:

www.penpalworld.com	*www.brownpride.com*
www.penpalparty.com	*www.penpalsonline.net*
www.signalpenpals.com	*www.interpals.com*
www.penpalsplanet.com	*www.penpalsnow.com*
www.palsforfree.com	*www.penpalgarden.com*
www.apenpals.com	*www.penpalscommunity.com*
www.penpalsanywhere.com	*www.sassociations.net*

The thing to remember about the above websites is that they're not "prison pen pal" websites. They are free-world people looking for other free-world people to write. But that doesn't mean you can't utilize them for your own success. A lot of these sites will make you put on your profile page that you're in prison. Don't try to hide that fact. Play it up. You'll be surprised at the results you get.

I have been on *Interpals* and *Penpalsnow*. The first week I was on InterPals I got 22 responses from people wanting to write. They were from all over the world. The first week on PenPalsNow I got 7 responses. I have never gotten 7 hits in one week to any prison pen pal website profile, let alone 22 responses in the first week! If you have someone who can post ads online for you, I'd use both of those websites. You can see all of the profiles I posted online in my book, *Pen Pal Success* (Freebird Publishers).

How To Win Friends & Influence Pen Pals

Using these FREE pen pal websites can boost your pen pals by the hundreds. But to make real and lasting connections you have to get interested in the other person. Here's how to do it online:

1. When a prospective pen pal emails you or writes you at the prison, have your assistant (or family member/friend) go online and print out their profile. Or they can just read it to you over the phone. Of course, those of you who have your own phone can do your own research.

2. Upon receiving their profile pages, read it to learn their likes, wants, favorites, and other vital information. You want to use that information in your response. The key is to enter the conversation they're already having in their mind.

3. You should also use the search options on each pen pal website. That way you can tailor your search. For instance, say you want to find a female pen pal in the USA who is between 31-40 years old, and wants to use snail-mail. You can put those parameters into the search option on the site and see who comes up. Then have them print out those profiles and send them to you so you can see who you want to write.

4. When writing your first letters to these pen pals, use items from their profiles in your emails or letters. Here are some templates you can use:

"I see that you like _____. I never could do that no matter how many times I tried. How do you do it?"

"You mentioned that you're a _____. My dad was a _____, and had _____ years in before he retired."

"Hi, I see that you _____. My personal assistant said that she couldn't get it to work. Can I get you to tell me your trick?"

"Your profile says that you like to _____. Does that mean you're good at it? I like to _____, but I haven't been able to _____."

"Hi there _____. I see you're deeply involved with _____. Can you tell me more about how you got involved?"

These are just a few templates you can use. All you have to do is fill in the blanks with your prospective pen pal's likes and interests. Anything they reply with to the above is great, because all answers except silence are winners.

A Final Parting Thought

Online pen pal websites do two things you can't do yourself. They introduce you to a large population of people who are visiting the website for one reason: looking for someone to write. They also give you access to thousands of possible pen pals, twenty-four hours a day.

Online pen pal strategies should be one of the focal points of your pen pal success. In this chapter, I've dealt with FREE online pen pal websites. Don't forget this chapter if you want to build a stable of pen pals.

For more about getting pen pals, be sure to check out my book, *TMP4: Pen Pal Mastery*, published by The Cell Block of course. See the catalog at the back of this book for more information.

CHAPTER 6

FREE "Public Domain" Money

In *The Millionaire Prisoner, Part 1*, I wrote about "A Goldmine Ready To Be Seized" in the *Imagination* chapter. That goldmine is the "public domain." The public domain consists of works created by others that are not protected by copyright law and are free for all to use. These works include books, art, songs, movies, photos, plays, and lots more. Some of the more famous works that are in the public domain are as follows:

Moby Dick by Herman Melville
Mona Lisa by Leonardo DaVinci
The Jungle Book by Rudyard Kipling
All of Shakespeare's plays
The Autobiography of Benjamin Franklin

Anyone can use works that are in the public domain any way they wish. In this chapter I'll show you how to get FREE money from public domain material.

"One good idea can enable a man to live like a king the rest of his life."
— Ross Perot

How to Find Public Domain Material

All works published in the U.S. before the year 1923 are in the public domain. This means that any newspaper, book, song, painting, magazine, photo, quotation, and letter that was created or published before 1923 is free to use in any way you wish. But the public domain doesn't stop there. All written works of the U.S. government, whether published or unpublished, are in the public domain. All laws and court decisions are in the public domain. Any database is in the public domain, and a list of addresses is a database. The only thing protected in a list of addresses is the order, arrangement, and selection of the addresses. The addresses themselves are not protected. Any fact, idea, or common property is in the public domain.

Another category of works that are in the public domain are works that were published between 1923 and 1963 that *did not* have their copyright renewed within 28 years. But these are a little more difficult to find. It has been said that 85% of all works in this category are in the public domain. For instance, if a book was published in 1962 and did not have its copyright renewed by 1990, the book is in the public domain. If you found such a book, you could use it any way you choose. So, how do you find one of the above gems?

You can look at the following sources to find public domain products:
Catalog of U.S. Government Publications Government Printing Office (GPO); (202) 512-1800
Email: contactcenter@gpo.gov; Website: www.gpo.gov
Project Gutenberg
Email: help2010@pglaf.org; Website: www.gutenberg.org
Library of Congress (202) 707-5000; Website: www.loc.gov
Internet Archive Website: www.archive.org
Open Library.org

Public Domain Sources and Information
Email: malten@airpost.net;
Website: www.public-domain-sources.com
Authorama.com
Feedbooks.com
Manybooks.net
World Public Library www.worldlibrary.org
Google Books
Booksshouldbefree.com
Librivox.org

If you don't have someone who can search the internet for you then how do you find them? The first place to start is the copyright page of the book. Remember, if it was copyrighted before 1923, then it's in the public domain and you do not have to do anymore research. You could use that book freely.

Now, if the book has a copyright date later than 1923, but before 1963, it had to have been renewed within 28 years, or you can use freely. To check to see if a copyright was renewed you do a search at the U.S. Copyright Office. Since you're a prisoner, you have to have someone do it for you. If you have the copyright office, do it, then you'll have to query them by mail, and there's an hourly fee for the search. $150 per hour is normal, and a typical search last an hour. You have to provide the copyright office with the title of the work, author's name, copyright owner's name, year of publication, type of work, and the name or issue of the work. You should send the letter and money order or check payable to the "Register of Copyrights" at:

Reference & Bibliograph Section
LM-451
Copyright Office
Library of Congress

101 Independence Avenue, SE
Washington, DC 20559-6000

Or you can hire a research firm to do the search for you.

Some of these firms may be cheaper and faster than having the copyright office do it. Searches for works published between 1923-63 can be done on Stanford University's Library website at:

https://collections.stanford.edu/copyrightrenewals/bin/page?forward=home

A word of caution is needed here. A lot of prisoners believe that anything on the internet is in the public domain. This is not true. The same copyright laws that apply to offline materials apply to online works as well. One thing is for sure. If the original work is in the public domain, then any copy of it on the internet is in the public domain. Just be careful that you don't use anything that is added to the original work such as a website URL or Hypertext link.

Another great place to find public domain materials is in non-fiction books. Any fact contained in such a book is in the public domain. You can't copyright a fact. You can only copyright how a fact is expressed. Because if someone were able to copyright a fact or idea, then no one would be able to create new works, and knowledge would not flow to others.

One last place to look for public domain material is on your tablet. Log into the "eBooks" app on your prison tablet. Search for older eBooks that you could possibly update and resell. Which leads me to part two of our subject.

> *"Good artists copy. Great artists steal."*
> — Pablo Picasso

How To Use Public Domain Works

What is the price value of works in the public domain? They are priceless. They are an untapped goldmine of riches waiting your excavation. The only limitation on their application and use is what you put on it. Allow your imagination to use public domain materials to supply you with the ideas you need to achieve success and prosperity.

To assist you, allow me to suggest a few avenues that a prisoner could use the public domain for:

Any tattoo artist could find a wealth of material that is in the public domain. that artwork could be used, adapted, and formatted to fit any tattoo pattern. They could put those patterns into a book and sell it. Or just do the tattoos themselves. Either way, all FREE money.

Any prisoner who writes urban novels could comb the case reporters in the law library for ideas. The case reporters supply true life urban crime histories. These stories are free for the taking. I once read a true story about a guy who had sex with the dead body of his male victim. He said he wasn't gay, but instead, he wanted to send his victim to hell as a homosexual. A real-life story straight out of a horror novel. Use your imagination, change people's names, and spin those stories and case law into a bestselling novel.

You could find a public domain book and adapt it into a screenplay, then sell it to a Hollywood movie studio. Or you could republish it yourself. Either way, more FREE money.

You could rearrange address/website lists according to your own qualifications and resell them. That's all these prisoner companies do when they sell pen pal lists or celebrity addresses.

Let me give you some real-life examples from the above tactics.

I started out selling lists of addresses. I had *"100 Wealthy Women"* and *"100 Chicagoland Women."* Where did I get these addresses? Out of magazines and newspapers. You could find them if you know where to look. Another one of my books, *Celebrity Female Star Power* is just a book of celebrity female addresses. I spent a couple months putting all the addresses together. Then I sent it off to my publisher. I've made thousands of dollars in FREE money off that idea.

Richard Vineski spent 24 years in the New York prison system. He spent time working inside the law library and gathered addresses and resource lists that helped prison litigators. Upon his release he started selling a booklet compiled of those resources and addresses. Vineski profited from addresses that were in the public domain.

One of my publishing mentors is Dr. Joe Vitale. In his book, *The Secret to Attracting Money*, he tells the story of how he took some public domain books on Pelmanism and made thousands of dollars off them. Pelmanism was created in London in the 1920s at the Pelman Institute for the Scientific Development of Mind, Memory, and Personality. It's about self-help and spirituality. Dr. Vitale read those books and loved them. So, he scanned those books into eBooks and turned it into an online information course. He said that course became one of his all-time bestsellers with tens of thousands sold. FREE money because he didn't write those books. He just found them, put them online, and started selling them.

Now that you know these FREE public domain money secrets, keep your eye out for stuff you can use. All it takes is one good idea to cement your name in the halls of the successful. It would be a shame if you had that idea and then forgot it. Always remember the maxim: *A short pencil is better than a long memory.*

Everyone is different. You may come up with your own way of keeping track of ideas, but you must secure them. When you're out of your cell, carry a pen or pencil and some paper with you at all times. When something comes to mind, whether an idea, thought, or quote, write it down so it won't be lost.

Of course, when you're in your cell, it will be much easier to capture ideas. Keep a pen or pencil and some paper next to your bed, or by your desk if you have one. This way it will be handy when you want to write something down. You must get in the habit of capturing your ideas. You never know which one will be profitable for you in the future.

> "A man would do well to carry a pencil in his pocket and write down his thoughts of the moment. Those that come unsought are commonly the most valuable and should be secured because they seldom return."
> — Sir Francis Bacon

What has been suggested in this chapter is only the tip of the iceberg. If you would like to know more about the public domain, I highly recommend the following book:

The Public Domain: How to Find & Use Copyright-FREE Writings, Music, Art and More by Stephen Fishman

If you would like more information on how to profit from writing books and selling how-to information while in jail or prison, be sure to check out Mike Enemigo's book *Jailhouse Publishing,* and my book *TMP6: Publishing From Prison.* In my book I show you how to write and publish my books rom a maximum-security prison cell and make thousands of dollars in FREE money every year!

Freedom of Information Act

For years I have been using Freedom of Information laws in both my state (Illinois) and on the federal level. Just last night I got a copy of the TV cable contract at my prison and an itemized listing of IDOC's Inmate Benefit Fund. You will be surprised at what kind of information you can get under these open government rules. A friend of mine got a bunch of declassified documents about Jimmy Hoffa and the investigation into his disappearance. To each his own. I'm no there to judge why you want certain information. I am here to point you in the right direction. It will be up to you to go the distance.

In 1966, the federal government passed the Freedom of Information Act. It established the public's right to obtain information from federal government agencies. And yes, this law allows prisoners to get information from those agencies as well. But not every bit of information is open to the public. There are exemptions. For instance, the FOIA protects records that are classified under national defense or foreign policy rules. It protects trade secrets. And most importantly, it protects investigatory records compiled for law enforcement purposes. That last bit has been used against me when I tried to get copies of the records the FBI has on my corrupt state's attorney that prosecuted me. In his book, *How To Find out Anything*, Don MacLeod says "Not only can you *not* use FOIA to ask for the nuclear launch codes or the combination to the safe at Fort Knox, but there are nine other categories of information that agencies are under no obligation to disclose."

Here are those nine categories taken straight from the FOIA itself:

1. Classified Documents
2. Internal Personnel Rules and Practices
3. Information Exempt Under Other Laws

4. Confidential Business Information
5. Internal Government Communication
6. Personal Privacy
7. Law Enforcement
8. Financial Institutions
9. Geological Information

The problem with these exemptions is that they are subject to the interpretation of the FOIA officer of the respective agency. Every federal agency has someone in charge of FOIA records requests. Most states have their own FOIA laws as well, and you would make your requests from the respective state agencies. You can find out more about the FOIA from your law library. Or ask your local jailhouse lawyer. Any competent litigator will know how to use the FOIA and the case law on prisoners using the FOIA. A great place to find recent court decisions on FOIA is *Prison Legal News*. *PLN*'s parent organization, the Human Right Defense Center, is always winning FOIA records litigation and routinely reports them in issues of *PLN*.

Another law that helps citizens get records is the Privacy Act of 1974. The Privacy Act applies to personal information maintained by agencies in the executive branch of the federal government. Agencies subject to the FOIA are also subject to the Privacy Act. Sometimes it is best to request records under both the FOIA and the Privacy Act. Under either law, the first 50 pages of records produced are free.

Some agencies provide 100 pages for free. Why is this important? Because you can put a line in your records request for them to "Send you the first 50 (or 100) pages for free and tell me how much more it would be to obtain the rest of the records." If you don't do that, the agency officer may hold all of the documents requested until you pay for the rest of them. At the end of this chapter, I will provide some sample FOIA request letters.

There's a wealth of free information on the FOIA on the internet. The Knight Digital Media Center provides a bunch of public records tutorials at the following: *https://multimedia.journalism.berkeley.edu/tutorials/cat/public-records*. The Free Public Records Search Directory from Online Searches, LLC is good for state agency searches. You can find them at the following: *https://publicrecords.onlinesearches.com*. And Virtual Gumshoe has many links to free resources at the following: *www.virtualgumshoe.com/index.asp*.

One of the best books you can get and study on public records research is *The Sourcebook to Public Record Information, 10th Ed.*, by Peter Weber, Michael Sankey, and Peter J. Weber. It's almost 2,000 pages long and if you are going to request tons of documents under the FOIA from multiple agencies, you need it! It will save you time, money, and hassle. I suggest getting the latest version so it's most up-to-date. But you may still be able to find a used, older edition for a few dollars on Amazon.

You can find a thorough guide to FOIA on the National Security Archive at: *www.gwu.edu/-nsarchiv*. One of the best sources is the Reporters' Committee for Freedom of the Press. They have detailed guides that show you how to do government record research. But probably the best thing on their website is the automated "FOIA Letter Generator." You put in what you are trying to get records rise and the FOIA Letter Generator will produce a letter for you. (I wish I could do that for my books! lol) You can find it at: *www.rcfp.org/foia*.

If you are about to start researching documents in criminal cases or appeals, I suggest you get a copy of the Department of Justice's FOIA Guide, which can be found at: *www.justice.gov/oip/foia_guide09.htm*.

Just remember to start with your law library if you have one. Even if you only have access to a Lexis-Nexus kiosk (or search on your tablet), you can search for FOIA or Privacy Act on it and that should be enough to get you started. There's plenty of information out there if you know how to get it.

"A popular government without popular information or the means of acquiring it, is but a prologue to a farce or a tragedy or perhaps both. Knowledge will forever govern ignorance, and a people who mean to be their governors, must arm themselves with the power knowledge gives."
— James Madison

Sample Request Letter Under FOIA

Freedom of Information Act Officer
Name of Agency
Address of Agency
City, State, Zip Code   Date: _____

Re: FOIA Request

Dear _____:

This is a request under the Freedom of Information Act. I request that a copy of the documents containing the following information be provided to me:

[Identify the documents or information as specifically as possible.]

I request a waiver of all fees of this request. I'm an indigent prisoner seeking information for personal use and not for any commercial interest. If fees are not waived, please send me the first 50 (or 100) pages free as is required by law, with the total amount due for the test of the documents.

Thank you for your consideration of this request.

Respectfully Requested,
Your Name
Your Address
City, State, Zip Code
Telephone number (optional)
Email Address (optional)

Freedom of Information Officer
Director Rob Jeffreys
Illinois Department of Corrections
1301 Concordia Court
Springfield, IL 62794-9277   October 18, 2021

Re: IFOIA Request

Dear Freedom of Information Officer:

Pursuant to the Illinois FOIA, 5 ILCS 140/1 et seq., I'm requesting the following documents:

1. A copy of the contract that the Illinois Department of Corrections and its representative signed with Global Tel Link ("GTL") to provide tablet/mp3/video visitations/email services with and for individuals in the custody of IDOC.

2. A copy of the recent contract that the Illinois Department of Corrections and its representative signed with Jpay to provide tablet/mp3/video visitations/email services with and for individuals in the custody of IDOC.

3. All communications, letters, memorandums, emails between IDOC staff in the office of the Director and GTL about providing individuals in custody with phone services, photographs, and Lexis-Nexis Legal research on the GTL tablets they currently have.

4. All communications, letters, memorandums, and/or e-mails from Director Rob Jeffreys to IDOC staff about Securus/Jpay providing individuals in custody with phone services, entertainment, legal, and education services on next generation

tablets, not including the June 22, 2021, Memorandum from Director Jeffreys to individuals in custody.

I look forward to hearing from you within (5) five business days as is required by law.

Respectfully Requested,

Joshua Kruger
#K50216
Pontiac Corr. Center
P.O. Box 99
Pontiac, IL 61764

cc: file

CHAPTER 7
Free Money for College

When I wrote *The Millionaire Prisoner 1* there was no Pell grants for prisoners to enroll in college courses. That has since changed as Congress has since restored them to prisoners. It's still too early to see how that is going to work out. But there's no longer any legitimate excuse for a prisoner not to secure their money to pay for college. (In any future editions of this book I'll update this chapter with prisoner Pell grant information.)

Troy Evans spent seven years locked up in a federal gulag. He wanted to get a college education so that his time behind bars wouldn't be wasted. Unfortunately for him, around that time, Congress cut Federal Pell grants for prisoners. Did Troy let that stop him? No, he set out to obtain scholarships, grants, and foundation assistance. It took him six months of filling out applications, writing essays, begging, pleading, and selling, before he landed a scholarship for one class. That was his start, and he walked out of prison with not one, but two degrees, and a 4.0 GPA, and designation on both the Dean's and President's list. Troy is now a professional speaker and author and took time to share some ways to obtain free money for school with me, and I present them to you.

1. Your first attempts should be through the school or university you have chosen to attend via correspondence. Most institutions will offer some type of scholarship program and/or

package through an alumni association, a foundation, or a scholarship group.

2. Next, apply for federal and state aid. Most scholarships require that you exhaust those possibilities first before seeking their help.

3. Get a list from your state's Department of Commerce of all the civic and service clubs in the area. For example, Kiwanis, Rotary Club, Lions, Elks, etc. Also, try and get one from the state your school is located in. Contact each group individually. Sometimes they offer money for "hard luck" cases such as prisoners.

4. Write any non-profit, social work, or any other association involved with helping others in your area. Contact churches and religious organizations within your area. Ask them to help you in your quest for an education.

5. Look into private scholarships. Troy says these will be your bread and butter in the future. There are scholarships based on every criterion you can think of. There are several great books on scholarships out there. Three are: *Peterson's Scholarships, Grants, and Prizes*; Daniel Jo Cassidy's *Scholarships, Grants, and Loans*; and *The Ultimate Scholarship Book: Billions of Dollars in Scholarships, Grants and Prizes* by Gene I. Kelly Tanabe.

6. Lastly, you'll need to research public and private foundations and trusts. These places must give away money for all kinds of things in order to keep their tax-exempt status. I'll have more to say about this way to get free money in later chapters. But for more information on these resources, you may want to see if your library has a copy of *Foundation Grants to Individuals*, published by The Foundation Center. It will give you the complete contact information, and the criteria for applying for a foundation grant. (Because I was curious, I reviewed the book to see how many foundations and trust I could possibly apply to if I wanted to go to college. If found over 50 of them. These places are out there if you know where to look!)

You must learn how to write essays correctly. Most scholarships are going to require that you write them showing why you deserve the scholarship. Also, in any classes that you're able to get into, do your best. You must be able to show people that their money is going to a worthy investment.

For more information about Troy Evans and his life story, have someone check out his website, *www.troyevans.com*, or read his book, *From Desperation to Dedication: An Ex-Con's Lessons on Turning Failure Into Success.*

> *"There's absolutely no reason why you cannot secure funding for your education while incarcerated. It is only a matter of beating the bushes. The money is there, but the effort has to be there to make it happen. If you're serious about obtaining an education via correspondence while incarcerated, I'm living proof it can happen, you only need to want it bad enough."*
>
> — Troy Evans

Do you want it bad enough? You should, because it's your key to a better life.

Additional Resources

For the prisoner who is truly trying to get an education while behind bars I highly recommend you get all three of the following books:

College in Prison: Resources for Incarcerated Students by Bruce Michaels.
Prison Education Guide by Christopher Zoukis
Prisoners' Guerrilla Handbook to Correspondence Programs in the US and Canada by Jon Marc Taylor

All three of them offer some fresh ideas on how to fund your college costs while in prison. Chris Zoukis was in the federal system when he wrote his books on college from prison. He's not done. He's currently in the free-world and in law school as I write this. Jon Marc Taylor passed away. But before he did, he earned a Doctorate from behind prison walls. They are the godfathers on getting an education from behind bars.

There is one scholarship directly available for prisoners. It's the *Commitment to Change* college grant from the Law Office of Jeremy Gordon. It's only available for tuition and books for one course for four individuals per year. You must have your GED or high school diploma and have to write a 300-word essay. There are four deadlines every year. For more information and the requirements, write to:

Mr. Jeremy Gordon
Attn: Scholarship Contest
215 W. Franklin St., Suite 200
Waxahachie, TX 75165

Some prisoners who are veterans may be eligible for the *Montgomery GI Bill* if they are in federal prison. Others may be eligible for the *Veterans Educational Assistance Program*. You will need to contact your Regional VA office to see if you're eligible. Veterans who are prisoners in Virginia may apply for *state veteran education benefits*. For more information, contact:

Virginia Military Survivors and
Dependents Education Program
1351 Hershberger Rd. NW, Suite 220
Roanoke, VA 24012
(540) 561-6625

Prisoners in Texas who are honorably discharged veterans can apply to the *Hazelwood Act* to try and get a grant. Chris Zoukis in *Prison Education Guide* says you should contact the financial aid office of your school for applications, and approval will be decided by the school.

Female prisoners in Virginia can apply for the *Elizabeth Kates Foundation, Inc.* scholarship. For more information, write to:

Elizabeth Kates Foundation, Inc.
316 Oak Lane
Richmond, VA 23226
(804) 282-1391

There's grant money available for working parents who want to take online courses. See *www.projectworkingmom.com*. You could help your baby mama while you're inside by helping her fund her college.

Remember what I said earlier about applying for federal student aid first. All scholarships and grants for college require this. Here's where you apply for federal student aid:

Federal Student Aid Programs
P.O. Box 7001
Mount Vernon, IL 62864-0071
www.FAFSA.gov

Now that Congress has restored Pell grants for prisoners, I anticipate that several colleges will go back into the prison system. This will open doors to prisoners that have been closed for the last twenty plus years. This chapter is just the tip of the iceberg. There's plenty of money out there. You just have to go get it.

From Prison Cells To PHD

One prisoner who used the power of education was Stanley Andrisse. In research for this book, I read his book, *From Prison Cells To PHD: It is Never Too Late to Do Good*. He went to prison for running a drug ring in the Missouri area. After he got out of prison, he was accepted to St. Louis University PhD program. Andrisse completed that and went to John Hopkins Medicine for his post-doctoral work. He founded the Prison-to-Professionals (P2P) and From Prison Cells to PhD, Inc. programs. He is now a board member of the Formerly Incarcerated College Graduates Network (FICGN). Most importantly, he is a well-published endocrinologist scientist studying insulin resistance. And his P2P Network helps formerly incarcerated people get a college education. I support his work. Andrisse is an example of what's possible with an education. But you do not have to wait anymore till you gut out. You can start right now from your prison cell.

A Final Warning Is Needed

Professor Rebecca Eisenberg is the Director of the Education Justice Project in Illinois. Her home faculty is the University of Illinois in Champaign-Urbana. She does a lot of great work at the Danville Correctional Center in Illinois. In one of the EJP's newsletters she cautioned that it "will be inevitable that predatory institutions will be drawn to offer prison programming by the promise of federal dollars." That is true. One way to stay away from those types of companies is to get the latest version of *Prison Education Guide* by Christopher Zouki. Those colleges that have existed prior to Congress restoring Pell grants to prisoners should still be good to go. Over the years I'm sure that a lot of states will begin to open college classes back up inside the system. They will do this because they will be able to get money from the federal government for it. That's okay. Let them do the work for you. Enroll in any college classes that your prison offers. Don't let anybody stop you from doing what you dream of. Just do your research first. Then go get it. Education can be the key that set you free.

Here are some foundations that offer grants for educational purposes:

Wexner Foundation
6525 W. Campus Oval, Ste. 110
New Albany, OH 43054
614-939-6060

The Buffett Foundation
P.O. Box 4508
Decatur, IL 62525
(402) 451-6011
www.buffettscholarships.org

Point Foundation
P.O. Box 26111
Lakewood, CO 80226
(866)-33-POINT
www.thepointfoundation.org

J. Paul Getty Trust
1200 Getty Center Drive,
Suite 800
Los Angeles, CA 90049-1685
(310) 440-7320
www.getty.edu/grants

The Harry Frank Guggenheim
Foundation
527 Madison Avenue
New York, NY 10022

(212) 644-4907
www.hfg.org

Jack Kent Cooke Foundation
44115 Woodridge Parkway,
Ste. 200
Lansdowner, VA 20176-5199
(800) 498-6478
www.jackkentcookefoundation.org

The Blakemore Foundation
1201 Third Avenue, Suite 4800
Seattle, WA 98101-3266
(206) 359-8778
www.blakemorefoundation.org

The R.O.S.E. Fund, Inc.
175 Federal Street, Suite 455
Boston, MA 02110
(617) 482-5400
www.rosefund.org

The NATSO Foundation
1737 Kings Street, Suite 200
Alexandria, VA 22314
(888) 275-6287
www.natsofoundation.org

Parapsychology Foundation, Inc.
P.O. Box 1562
New York, NY 10021-0043
(212) 628-1550
www.parapsychology.org

John B. Lynch Scholarship Fund
P.O. Box 4248
Wilmington, DE 19807

The Rosario Foundation
100 Broadway Avenue
Carnegie, PA 15106-2421

Welsh Trust
P.O. Box 244
Walla Walla, WA 99362

Larrabee Fund Association
c/o Connecticut National Bank
777 Main St.
Hartford, CT 06115

The Fasken Foundation
500 West Texas Ave., Suite 1160
Midland, TX 79701

Battistone Foundation
P.O. Box 3858
Santa Barbara, CA 93103

Smock Foundation
c/o Lincoln National Bank &
Trust Co.
P.O. Box 960
Fort Wayne, IN 46801

The Perpetual Benevolent Fund
c/o Bay Bank Middlesex
300 Washington Street
Newton, MA 02158

You can find scholarships
and financial aid sources on the
following websites:

Education Resources Information
Center (ERIC)
1-800-538-3742
www.eric.ed.gov

Peterson's
8740 Lucent Boulevard, Suite 400
Highlands Ranch, CO 80129
https://www.petersons.com

Fannie and John Hertz
Foundation
2456 Research Drive
Livermore, CA 94550
(925) 373-1642
www.hertzfoundation.org

The Roothbert Fund, Inc.
475 Riverside Drive, Room 252
New York, NY 10115
(212) 870-3116
www.roothbertfund.org

The Leakey Foundation
P.O. Box 29346
San Francisco, CA 94129-0346
(415) 561-4646
www.leakeyfoundation.org/grants

The Covenant Foundation
1270 Avenue of the Americas
Suite 304
New York, NY 10020
(212) 245-3500
www.covenantfn.org

ESA Foundation
P.O. Box 270517
Forth Collins, CO 80527
(970) 223-2824
www.esaintl.com/esaf/

Here are some resources you can search for free looking for scholarships:

FinAid
https://www.finaid.org

Princeton Review
www.princetonreview.com

The Financial Aid Resource
Network
https://www.theoldschool.org

College Planning Website
https://collegeplan.org

Fast Aid
www.fastaid.com

The Scholarship Page
www.scholarshio-page.com

Go College
www.gocollege.com

FastWEB
https://fastweb.monster.com

Free Scholarship Information
Service
www.freeschinfo.com

College Net
www.collegenet.com

For more about how to get FREE money for college, see if you can find the following books:

8 Steps to Help Black Families Pay for College by Thomas and Will LaViest
Get FREE Cash for College by Kelly Y. Tanabe
How to Go to College Almost for Free by Benjamin R. Kaplan
Winning Scholarships for College by Marianne Ragins

Now that you know about all of these resources, the only thing standing in your way is you. The FREE money is out there for college. It's up to you to go get it.

CHAPTER 8

Free Money for Veterans by Art Gage

Imprisoned veterans across the country need to know about the service-connected disability compensation and rehabilitation benefits they may be eligible for. Even as prisoners, veterans still have options which are not available to the general population that could greatly impact their lives, especially as they work toward release.

An incarcerated veteran with a felony is not limited from applying for service-connected disability compensation, pension, survivors' dependency and indemnity compensation (DIC), or education assistance. However, many of these benefits are limited or greatly restricted. Despite this, there are steps that can be taken while incarcerated that could have a positive impact on life inside, and upon release.

The funds received from VA benefits are protected under federal law throughout imprisonment. They cannot be seized by the government for restitution or for costs of captivity.

Prisoners with family can get them an apportioned amount of their compensation benefits while they serve the remainder of their sentences. Those without family may be entitled to increased benefits which will become available once you are released.

In addition, there are vocational rehabilitation benefits (VR&E) which prisoners can establish the criteria to be eligible

91

for rehabilitation and in some cases start the process to get retraining.

SERVICE-CONNECTED DISABILITY Compensation

To be eligible for service-connected disability compensation, a person must have left the service under circumstances other than a dishonorable discharge. Those with a dishonorable discharge need to get that fixed first, before becoming entitled to service-connected disability compensation. This can prove very problematic while in prison.

Incarceration affects the amount a veteran can personally receive while in prison. The VA will limit entitlement to compensation at a maximum amount of 10% to be provided to the veteran while they are incarcerated. As of the writing of this chapter (in May of 2021), 10% is equivalent to $144.14. If a disability award of 10% is received, then the individual is entitled to receive half this amount.

For a single veteran, the most that can be received while incarcerated is the amount equivalent to 10% which currently is $144.14. The VA provider cost-of-living increases annually. For those able to obtain higher ratings than the amount upon getting out of prison, this would increase to the amount based on service-connected disability. A single veteran who has a 30% disability rating would be entitled to $441.35. A single veteran who has a 50% disability rating would be entitled to $905.04. A single veteran who has a 70% disability rating would be entitled to $1,444.71 a month. A single veteran who is unemployable as a result of their service-connected disabilities would be entitled to $3,146.42 a month.

The importance of establishing an increased disability rating while in prison will go directly to improving chances of being successful upon release. If you have a 50% service-connected disability, then when you get out of prison, you would be entitled to receive $905.04 a month in benefits. If you have limited skills or job opportunities limited to minimum wage work, then receiving an additional $905.04 a month is probably enough to help make it.

Those who are married veterans an/or have dependents may be able to have increased benefits apportioned to the family during periods of incarceration. A married imprisoned veteran with a 50% disability rating would receive $144.14 a month. The remaining amount of the benefits for a married veteran could be apportioned to a spouse and/or dependents.

After release, a married veteran who is receiving a 50% rating is entitled to $992.04 a month. You can also get additional benefits depending on how many dependents you have.

Vocation Rehabilitation (VR&E)

While incarcerated, veterans should look into ideas for what they can do as a vocation once they get out. To be eligible for vocational rehabilitation through the VA, veterans need to either have a VA service-connected disability of at least 20% with an employment handicap or be rated at 10% with a serious employment handicap. In either scenario, they still must be discharged from military service under other than dishonorable conditions.

Veterans in prisons can prepare to receive assistance from VR&E through five separate paths. They are:

Reemployment with previous employer,
Rapid access to employment,
Employment through long-term service, and
Independent living services.

While going through the VR&E program, formerly-imprisoned veterans can also be given a subsistence allowance based on the rate of your attendance for any additional training or the number of dependents supported by the veteran and the type of training. These are all things that you can line up to qualify for prior to getting out. Sometimes these applications can take many months, so it is important to start thinking now about your future.

With service-connected disabilities and monies that are received from that, coupled with a small subsistence allowance while going through the training and a part-time job, former prisoners could get through the retraining which would allow earning a much greater pay.

How to Get Started

Most incarcerated veterans may need help with their claim. Doing a claim without getting a representative is not advised. Given the limited access to resources and abilities to communicate it can be much too difficult to effectively process a claim alone. Those interested should look into getting a Veteran Service Organization (VSO), accredited claimant's agent, or an attorney.

VA law is a vibrant growing practice of law. There are typically 20 to 30 new published opinions from the Court of Appeals for veterans claims or the Federal Circuit that you should read to stay up on this area of law. The VA is annually proposing modifications to the regulations (CFRs) that can affect your claim. There are lots of laws in Congress that are typically either being passed or attempting to be passed which can also affect how these claims are processed. This is not an easy area to stay up on and understand.

VSOs usually do not charge a fee in these cases. Accredited claimant's agents and attorneys typically charge a fee of 20% or 30% of the back due benefits. They are not allowed to charge for an initial claim, only after a decision is rendered can they appeal the claim and get a fee. There are also costs which are in addition to the fees. These can prove to be expensive if you do not have the cooperation of your treating physician.

When a fee is charged, if the fee is 20%, then the VA will withhold that amount from the back due benefits. Because of the case, Snyder v. Nicholson, 489 F.3d 1213 (2007), an accredited claimant's agent or attorney can charge a fee and get the full 20% of the total amount of back due benefits that would normally be due in a claim. Even though the veteran is limited to the 10% of the benefits, the representative will be paid based on the full increase. This is important because if you want help on your claim, to have an accredited claimant's agent and/or attorney will be instrumental to deal with these issues.

If you are a single veteran, then the attorney's fees will minimally affect you because you would only get back due benefits of at most 10%, because of your incarceration. If you are a married veteran, then it would affect some of the back due money that your family could receive; however, given the difficulty of communications and processing this claim, it is well worth it to have a representative.

What You Need to Do

You are going to need to establish medical information to support your claims. It is difficult in prison, but you need to establish treatment to evaluate your service-related conditions. For physical issues, make sure you have whatever objective diagnostic testing is necessary to evaluate the extent of your problem. For mental issues, establish continuity of treatment and give examples of the severity of the conditions and how these conditions relate back to service. It's best to do this immediately.

For veterans with a felony conviction, credibility may be suspect. Establishing lay letters from either people you served with or who are aware of the severity of your conditions since service can be a big help strengthening credibility. These letters should include address, phone numbers and any other contact information. If you have any questions on this process, you can contact me below.

Art Gage is an accredited attorney in Veterans Law and handles cases across the country and abroad. If you have additional questions, you can email him at arthurv@artgagelaw.com, or you can write him a letter at:

Art Gage
Law Offices of Arthur Gage
2573 N. First Avenue
Tucson, AZ 85719
(520) 244-1386

Additional Possible Help For Veterans

Operation Homefront (OH)
1355 Central Parkway S, Suite 100
San Antonio, TX 78232
https://www.operationhomefront.org/
info@operationhomefront.org
(Emergency funding and other help to families of service members and wounded warriors.)

Volunteers of America
1660 Duke Street
Alexandria, VA 22314

https://www.voa.org
(Helps with housing in 40 states.)

Center for Health and Justice
700 S. Clinton St.
Chicago, IL 60607
https://www2.centerforhealthandjustice.org/
(Has a Jail Division for Veterans program.)

US Department of Veterans Affairs
810 Vermont Avenue NW
Washington, DC 20420
https://www.va.gov
(877) 294-6380

You can find your own states Veterans Affairs office at:
https://www.va.gov/statedva.htm
If one of your parents or grandparents were in the military, you may check for any unclaimed life insurance benefits here:

Office of Service Members Group Life Insurance (OSGLI)
290 West Mt. Pleasant Avenue
Livingston, NJ 07039
(800) 419-1473

Veterans can also get a one-time payment to help pay for a car if you have a service-connected disability. In addition to buying a car, you may be eligible to pay to adapt your current car with special equipment to help you to get in and out of the vehicle. Look for "Veterans Compensation   Automobile Allowance." Or you can call the Veterans Benefits Assistance service at 1-800-827-1000. You can also call your local library and ask for the contact information to your local "County Veterans Service Officer."

For more information on this program, see:
https://www.va.gov/disability/eligibility/special-claims/automobile-allowance-adaptive-equipment

If you're a veteran, you need to contact your local National Association of County Veterans Service Officers. They are a network of researchers that help veterans get FREE money and benefits. You can find your local NACVSO office at: *https://www.nacvso.org/*

National Veterans Legal Services Program
2001 S Street, NW, Suite 610
Washington, DC 20009
(202) 265-8305
www.nvlsp.org

CHAPTER 9

Free Grant Money

You may have seen those infomercials selling books saying you can get "free money" from the government. In research for this book, I had my assistant go to the federal government's official website (*https://www.usa.gov*) and download what it said about "Government Grants and Loans."

Here's what it says:

The federal government does not offer grants or "free money" to individuals to start a business or cover personal expenses, contrary to what you might see online or in the media. Websites or other publications claiming to offer "free money from the government" are often scams. Report them to the Federal Trade Commission.

The government does offer federal benefit programs designed to help individuals and families in need become self-sufficient or lower their expenses.

A grant is one of the ways the government funds ideas and projects to provide public services and stimulate the economy. Grants support critical recovery initiatives, innovative research, and many other programs.

The federal government awards grants to organizations including:

State and local governments
Universities and colleges
Research labs
Law enforcement
Non-profit organizations
Businesses

The intent of most grants is to fund projects that will benefit specific parts of the population or the community as a whole. What you might see about grants online or in the media may not be true. The federal government does not offer grants or "free money" to individuals to start a business or cover personal expenses. For personal financial assistance, the government offers federal benefit programs. These programs help individuals and families become financially self-sufficient or lower their expenses.

To search or apply for grants, use the federal government's free, official website, *grants.gov*. Commercial sites may charge a fee for grant information or application forms. *Grants.gov* centralizes information from more than 1,000 government grant programs.

The federal government also provides loans for a specific purpose such as paying for education, helping with housing or business needs, or responding to an emergency or crisis.

Loans are different than grants because recipients are required to repay loans, often with interest. The federal government offers several types of loans, including:

Student loans
Housing loans, including disaster and home improvement loans
Small business loans

You can search for loans on the federal government's free, official website, *Govloans.gov* rather than commercial sites that may charge a fee for information or application forms.

That's what the federal government says on their website. What does it mean for you? It means unless you are starting a business you probably won't use the federal government's money. That's okay. There are plenty of other sources available to get "free" money from.

Where to Find FREE Money

One easy way is to try *www.fastweb.com*. Fastweb is a database of more than 180,000 private sector grants and loans and will let you match yourself to the grants that fit your project for free.

Another great source is the Foundation Center (*www.fdncenter.org*).

After Troy Evans put me up on game about free money, I had my assistant research The Foundation Center. They have a multitude of resources they publish, including the following directories:

Directory of New and Emerging Foundations
Foundation Grants to Individuals
National Director of Corporate Giving

These directories are expensive. You can access these directories online on the Foundation Center's website for a monthly fee. Check your prison's library first to see if they have any of them. Someone could also look at these directories for free in the Foundation Center's Regional offices. They also have 200+ cooperating libraries where you can look at these directories for free. You can find those addresses at *www.foundationcenter.org*.

You can find local foundations within a specific geographical area through the Council of Foundation (*www.cof.org*). Or the Regional Association of Grantmakers (*www.rag.org*). You may also try the Funding Exchange (*www.fex.org*).

For government money you'll want to search the already mentioned (*www.grantsgov* or *Firstgov.org*. The catalog of Federal Domestic Assistance (*www.cfda.gov*) is a database listing information about federal assistance programs. The National Endowment for the Humanities (*www.neh.gov*) and Institute of Museum and Library Services (*www.imla.gov*) both support arts and humanities. Lastly, the Community of Science Funded Research Database (*www.cos.com*) allows you to search grants awarded by five different agencies.

Matthew Lesko said he found 67 government benefits that he was eligible for in two minutes. He said he filled in about 15 blanks online and the below non-profit showed him all the government programs he was eligible for. You can do the same at *www.benefitscheckup.org*. Or you can have your people watch his video at: *https://vimeo.com/257692258*.

If you're an artist and you have no one to access the internet for you I list most of the addresses, you need to get started in

Prison Picasso. But it's a lot easier to use the web. Here's what funding expert Ellen Liberatori says in *Guide to Getting Arts Grants*:

> "Access to public grants has always been very good, in my opinion, and my interaction with government staff has always been very helpful. Nowadays, access couldn't be easier with the internet and instead of chasing around for public grant opportunities, you can simply put your name on an email list and the grant notice will come directly to you."

Even after you find possible sources for free money, you still have to ask a certain way. As my big homie tells me all the time, "Come correct or don't come at all."

How to Win Grant Money

Notice that I said "win" grant money. There will be other people applying for the same grants. It's a competition. Whoever stands out the best with the most compelling application will win. But you have something going for you. That special something is the fact that you're a prisoner. Hardly any other prisoners in the American gulag will try to win grant money, so you'll already stand out. So, with the right mindset and the proper grant application/proposal you can find the money to advance your career. Here's what you need to know and what you need to put together.

1. The first thing you have to do is research and apply for only the grants that you are eligible for. Some grants have age restrictions, geographical restrictions, specific type of business restrictions, education (alumni) restrictions, gender restrictions, and/or all of the above. Do not waste your time applying for

grants that you are not eligible for. Use a website like *fastweb.com* to find the grants that you are eligible for.

2. After you have found a grant that you're eligible for you have to find out what their application process is. Do they have a form online that you're supposed to use? If so, you have to use that form and fill it out properly or you will automatically disqualify yourself from the grant process.

3. If the funder doesn't have a formal application you need to prepare a proposal package that makes you stand out from the crowd. A typical grant proposal will consist of the following:

Cover letter
Title page
Abstract/summation
Introduction
Statement of need
Objectives
Procedures
Budget
Future funding
Appendix

4. Your proposal should be typewritten or done on a computer. If you have no choice but to do yours in your own handwriting, then make sure it's done on plain white typing paper and the handwriting is absolutely legible. Prepare it like you were doing an appeal brief to the court.

5. Make sure your proposal is submitted in a timely fashion. Most funders have specific deadlines that you have to meet. Try to get your proposal in early. It's also good to include a SASE or postcard that the funder can return to you saying they received your proposal. Some funders require that be included, so pay attention.

6. Remember what I said about asking your family and friends for money: don't ask for money they can't give. This applies to foundations, corporations, and other funders. So, ask for moderate amounts from different sources. Do your research and know how much money they have given in the past.

To really understand the whole "free money" from grants process, I suggest you get and study two books:

- *Free Money In America* by Rhonda Turpin
- *The Complete Guide To Getting A Grant* by Laurie Blum

The editions I have in my cell are older, but they are still relevant, especially for prisoners. In *Free Money In America*, Rhonda Turpin explains how Angel Tree was started by a felon after serving a 15-year prison sentence. She started Angel Tree with one X-mas tree and a few donated toys. Now, almost every prisoner in America knows what Angel Tree is. I have used it in the past to send gifts to my children. Maybe you have also? Angel Tree proves that we prisoners can accomplish anything we want in this world if we just apply ourselves. And that you should never let the fact that you don't have any money stop you from achieving your dreams. All you have to do is ask the right people in the right way.

> *"The difference between the right word and the wrong one, is like the difference between lightning and the lightning bug."*
> — Mark Twain

In *Words That Sell*, Richard Bayan has a special section on "Appealing for Contributions." That's what you're doing when you ask someone to give you FREE money. Here are some of my favorite words or phrases from that great book:
Please give . . .

Please try to give *something*.
Your financial support is needed.
We desperately need your help.
We rely entirely on the generosity of friends like you.
The future of _____ lies in your hands.
This is your chance to help . . .
With your help, we can go on . . .
Your gift can help _____ survive.
You can make a difference.
Without your help, all the gains of the last few years could evaporate (disappear).
This is your change to help us meet the challenges of the coming years.
Help us reach our goal.
Give anything you can.
I know you won't let us down.
You'll help assure the future of . . .
Your help makes a critical difference.
In return, you'll gain the satisfaction of . . .
A benevolent gesture.
Your philanthropy.

You can find *Words That Sell* and *Words That Sell 2*, both by Richard Bayan online in used bookstores for pretty low prices. Both are worth having in your personal library. A more updated version of that type of book is *The Big Book of Words That Sell* by Robert W. Gly. Remember that you are selling yourself and your ideas to try to get funding.

Now that you know all of this, we can look at some more ways and means to get FREE money.

CHAPTER 10
Free Money Genius

Some of you may remember who Matthew Lesko is. He's the guy who had the "free money" infomercials and is famous for wearing the question mark suits. He's been studying free money for over 40 years and has written over 100 books on the subject that have sold over four million copies. Here's a little more about him.

Armed with an MBA in computerized management information systems that was paid for by the government with free money because he served in the Vietnam War as a naval officer. Lesko then became a professor in computer science and started a career as an entrepreneur.

His first two businesses failed, and one was a software company Lesko's first successful company was a consulting business that helped Fortune 500 companies tap government programs to finance mergers and acquisitions and enter new markets. In a few short years, that business grew from just himself with a phone and a desk in a one-room apar to 30 researchers in downtown Washington, D.C.

Lesko then left the corporate world to educate the average consumer on how they can also use the same government programs to help their lives. Two of his Free Money books became *New York Times* bestsellers. He has been a columnist for the *New York Times* syndicate and *Good Housekeeping* magazine.

He has appeared on hundreds of radio and TV shows and made regular appearances on late night talk shows—*CNN, Fox,* the *Today Show, Good Morning America,* and *Oprah.* His crazy TV infomercials were among the most popular in the industry and he's easily recognized on the street because he always wears question mark suits.

He says that free money from the government grows every year, no matter what political part is in power. Throughout this book I will share with you the tips I learned from Lesko's books. For now, I'm going to share with you the ten things you should not do when looking for government grants.

Ten Things You Should Not Do When Looking for Government Grants by Matthew Lesko

1. <u>Don't Believe What the Media Says About Budget Cuts</u>
<u>Reality</u>: The overall amount of money given out to the average family grows every year, no matter who is in office.

Total amount of cash sent each year to individual from the federal government:
2016 = $2,777 Billion
2017 = $2,874 Billion
2018 = $2,894 Billion
2019 = $3,116 Billion
2020 = $3,368 Billion
2021 = $3,384 Billion

2. <u>You Should Not Ask for "Grants"</u>
<u>Reality</u>: Over 80% of the free money the government gives out are not called "grants." It's in the form of "Direct Payments," "Transfer Payments," "Forgiveness," and "Loans You Don't Pay Back." The best way to identify these opportunities is to say you

are looking for "Financial Assistance." This way, you won't miss anything.

3. <u>Don't Look for the Money in Washington</u>

<u>Reality</u>: Sure, the money starts in Washington, D.C., but then it goes to your state capital. After that, it goes to your county, and then down to your city and local non-profit organizations.

4. <u>Don't Believe You Have to be Poor to Get Government Money</u>

<u>Reality</u>: Only 12% of the money the government gives out goes to the poor. For some programs, the government considers you poor if you are making $80,000 a year. More importantly, 80% of all the money opportunities have NO income requirements at all.

5. <u>Don't Believe That Government Money is All Set Aside for "Minorities"</u>

<u>Reality</u>: Sure, there are some programs that are available for minorities, but I believe that is less than 5%. There are funds set aside for anyone who wants to start a business, buy a home, train for a new job, or get out of debt.

6. <u>Don't Hire a Grant Writer</u>

<u>Reality</u>: Over 80% of the free money programs are not called grants, and these applications are usually only 2-4 pages of filling in the blanks on a form. Make sure you see the application first before you ever consider hiring a grant writer. Getting a grant writer before you see an application is like buying a prom dress before you are invited to the prom.

7. <u>Don't Give Money to Anyone Who Promises You a Grant</u>

<u>Reality</u>: No one, except the agency handing out the money, can ever promise you will get grant money. Uncle Sam never, never, never asks for money to apply, unlike scam artists.

8. <u>Don't Believe That One Phone Call Will Get You All the Money You Need</u>

<u>Reality</u>: Sure, on occasion, this does happen. But it is better to realize that your efforts can take a few hours, days, or even weeks. But where else are you going to get $20,000 to solve a financial problem that has been nagging you for months or even years?

9. <u>Don't Rely Only on Free Money From the Government</u>

<u>Reality</u>: There are hundreds of other ways to solve financial problems with government programs, like (1) free help getting rid of credit card debt, (2) get your college or training courses paid for, (3) get free dental and healthcare, and (4) free books, condoms, computers; the list goes on.

10. <u>Don't Stop When Someone Says "NO"</u>

<u>Reality</u>: There are over 17,000 free money programs available and no one person can know everything. Here is what to do when you hear that nasty word:

(a) Ask this person if they can suggest another place that may be able to help.

(b) Contact your local reference librarian for free research help.

(c) Call you local hotline for free services and financial assistance—211, or in some areas, 311.

(d) Contact the local office of your congressperson or senator. Each lawmaker has staff aides that help you to try and solve your problem for free.

For more about Matthew Lesko's book and reports on Free Money you can join his membership group or contact him at the address below:

Matthew Lesko
1851 Columbia Rd. NW 402
Washington, D.C. 20009-5107

LeskoHelp.com
LeskoHelp2.com
Leskoreports.com

Lesko has a series of videos on how to get free money. I will list them when they apply to something I'm writing about so you can watch them when you get out. Or you can have your family watch them now.

According to Lesko some of the best places to get help in researching free money sources are your local public library. You can find your local public library at *https://www.usa.gov/libraries*. Another search engine that Lesko says is better than Google for looking for free money is 211. You can find your local 211 at: *https://www.211.org/*

The best place to find FREE consulting help to start any business, non-profit, freelance job, or invention is the Small Business Development Center (SBDC). When we started Barnett Publishing, we used a mentor at our local SBDC for advice. To find your local SBDC you can search: *https://americassbdc.org/*.

Finally, Lesko has a video that shows you how to legally get FREE money from your congressman. He says that every congressman, senator, and other elected officials have case workers on their staff to solve problems that people have. You can have your free-world assistant watch the video at: *https://vimeo.com/194992232*

If you need to find your elected officials, you can at: *https://www.usa.gov/elected-officials/*

Or write your prison law library. They should have the addresses for your congressman or senator.

CHAPTER 11

Unclaimed Funds and Property

There are billions of dollars of unclaimed money and property in the United States. What types of unclaimed stuff am I writing about? How about forgotten bank and credit accounts, undistributed refunds, abandoned insurance policies, apartment rent security deposits, pension deposits, government reimbursements, and a whole lot more. Maybe you have some unclaimed money or property out there with your name on it. How would you find it?

First, you should start with the state you live in. I list the state officers at the end of this chapter. You should write them and ask them if they have any unclaimed money or property in your name.

Second, you can have someone search online records for you. Here are some good places to start:

www.unclaimedassets.com
www.missingmoney.com
www.unclaimed.org
www.unclaimedmoney.usa.gov
www.treasury.gov
https://www.s.fdic.gov/funds
https://webapps.dol.gov/wow

Even if you don't find some free money this way, I'd still do the search every 2 to 3 years. Why? Because the wheels sometimes turn slowly. Also, relatives pass away, and you may be included in the will. You never know. Here are the agencies you should first contact. Find your state. Then write them a letter asking them if they have any unclaimed money or property in your name. Good luck.

State Agencies for Unclaimed Property

Alabama
State Treasury
Unclaimed Property Division
P.O. Box 302520
Montgomery, AL 36130-2520
(334) 242-7500
www.treasury.state.al.us/

Alaska
Department of Revenue
Treasury Division
Unclaimed Property Section
P.O. Box 110405
Juneau, AK 99811-0405
(907) 465-3726
www.revenue.state.ak.us

Arizona
Department of Revenue
Unclaimed Property Unit
P.O. Box 29026
Site Code 9026
Phoenix, AZ 85038-9026
(602) 364-0380

www.revenue.state.az.us/unclm/ index.htm

Arkansas
Unclaimed Property Division
Auditor of State
1400 W. 3rd St., Suite 100
Little Rock, AR 72201-1811
(501) 682-6080
www.accessarkansas.org/auditor

California
State Comptroller
Division of Collections-
Bureau of Unclaimed
Property
3301 C Street, Suite 712
P.O. Box 942850
Sacramento, CA 94250-5873
(916) 445-2636
www.sco.ca.gov

Colorado
Unclaimed Property Division

1120 Lincoln Street
Suite 1004
Denver, CO 80203
(800) 825-2111
*www.treasurer.state.co.us/paych
eck/index.htm*

Connecticut
Unclaimed Property Division
Office of State Treasury
55 Elm St.
Hartford, CT 06106
(800) 618-3404
www.state.ct.us/ott

Delaware
Bureau of Abandoned
Property
P.O. Box 8931
Wilmington, DE 19899
(302) 577-8200
www.state.de.us/revenue

District of Columbia
Office of Finance of Treasury
Unclaimed Property Unit
810 First Street NE, Room 401
Washington, D.C. 20002
(202) 442-8181
www.cfo.dc.gov

Florida

Department of Financial
Services
Bureau of Unclaimed
Property
P.O. Box 1910
Tallahassee, FL 32302-1910
(850) 410-9253
https://up.dbf.state.fl.us/

Georgia
Department of Revenue
Property Tax Division
4245 International Parkway
Suite A
Hapeville, GA 30354-3918
(404) 968-0490

Hawaii
Department of Budget and
Finance
Unclaimed Property Program
P.O. Box 150
Honolulu, HI 96810-0150
(808) 586-1589
www.ehawaii.gov/bf/ucp

Idaho
Idaho State Tax Commission
Unclaimed Property Section
P.O. Box 36
Boise, ID 83722-0410
(208) 334-7627

*www://tax.idaho.gov/unclaimed.
htm*

Illinois
Office of State Treasurer
Unclaimed Property Division
P.O. Box 19495
Springfield, IL 62794-9495
(217) 785-6992
www.cashdash.net

Indiana
Attorney General's Office
Unclaimed Property Division
302 W. Washington, Suite C-531
Indianapolis, IN 46204
(800) 447-5598
*www.state.in.us/attorneygeneral
/ucp/index.htm*

Iowa
State Treasury
Lucas State Office Building
321 East 12th St.
1st Floor
Des Moines, IA 50319
(515) 281-5367
www.treasurer.state.ia.us

Kansas
Unclaimed Property Division
900 Jackson, Suite 201
Topeka, KS 66612-1235

(785) 296-3171
www.treasurer.state.ks.us

Kentucky
Unclaimed Property Division
Kentucky Dept. of Treasury
Suite 183, Capitol Annex
Frankfort, KY 40601
(800) 465-4722
www.kytreasury.com

Louisiana
State Treasurer
Unclaimed Property Division
P.O. Box 91010
Baton Rouge, LA 70821
(225) 342-0010
www.treasury.state.la.us

Maine
State Treasurer's Office
Unclaimed Property Division
39 State House Station
111 Sewall Street, 3rd Floor
Augusta, ME 04333-0039
(207) 624-7477
*www.state.me.us/treasurer/prope
rty.htm*

Maryland
Unclaimed Property Unit
301 W. Preston St.
Baltimore, MD 21201-2385
(800) 782-7383

https://in1.comp.state.md.us/unc
laim/default.asp

(601) 359-3600
www.treasury.state.ms.us/

Massachusetts
Abandoned Property Division
1 Ashburton Place, 12th Floor
Boston, MA 02108
(617) 367-0400
(800) 647-2300
www.state.ma.us/treasury

Missouri
State Treasury Department
Unclaimed Property Section
P.O. Box 1004
Jefferson City, MO 65102
(573) 751-2411
www.treasurer.missouri.gov/u
cpl

Michigan
Department of Treasury
Unclaimed Property Division
P.O. Box 30756
Lansing, MI 48922
(517) 373-3200
www.michigan.gov/treasury

Montanta
Department of Revenue
Unclaimed Property Division
125 N. Roberts, 3rd Floor
P.O. Box 5805
Helena, MT 59604-5805
(406) 444-6900
www.state.mt.us/revenue/

Minnesota
Department of Commerce
Unclaimed Property Division
85 7th Place East, Suite 600
St. Paul, MN 55101-3165
(800) 925-5668
www.commerce.state.mn.us/pa
ges/unclaimedmain.htm

Nebraska
Unclaimed Property Division
P.O. Box 94788
Lincoln, NE 68509
(402) 471-2455
www.nebraska.treasurer.org

Mississippi
Treasury Department
Unclaimed Property Division
P.O. Box 138
Jackson, MS 39205-0138

Nevada
Office of the State Treasurer
Unclaimed Property Division
555 E. Washington Ave.
Suite 4200

Las Vegas, NV 89101-1070
(702) 486-2025
https://nevadatreasurer.gov

New Hampshire
Treasury Department
Unclaimed Property
Department
25 Capitol St., Room 205
Concord, NH 03301
(800) 791-0920
*www.state.nh.us/treasury/divisio
ns*

New Jersey
Department of the Treasury
Unclaimed Property
Department
P.O. Box 214
Trenton, NJ 08695-0214
(609) 984-8234
*www.state.nj.us/treasury
taxation*

New Mexico
Taxation & Revenue
Department
Unclaimed Property Division
P.O. Box 25123
Santa Fe, NM 87504-5123
(505) 476-1774
www.state.nm.us/tax/

New York

State Comptroller Department
State Office of Unclaimed
Funds
110 State Street, 8th Floor
Albany, NY 12236
(518) 270-2200
www.osc.state.ny.us

North Carolina
Department of State Treasury
Escheat & Unclaimed
Property
325 North Salisbury Street
Raleigh, NC 27603-1385
(919) 508-5176
www.treasurer.state.nc.us

North Dakota
State Land Department
Unclaimed Property Division
P.O. Box 5523
Bismarck, ND 58506-5523
(701) 328-2800
www.land.state.nd.us

Ohio
Department of Commerce
Division of Unclaimed Funds
77 South High Street, 20th
Floor
Columbus, OH 43266-0545
(614) 466-4433
*www.com.state.oh.us/odoc/unfd/
default.htm*

Oklahoma
State Treasury Office
Unclaimed Property Division
4545 North Lincoln Blvd.
Suite 106
Oklahoma City, OK 73105-3413
(405) 521-4273
www.unclaimed.state.ok.us

Oregon
Division of State Lands
Unclaimed Property
Department
775 Summer Street NE
Suite 100
Salem, OR 97301-1279
(503) 378-3805
https://statelands.dsl.state.or.us/upintro.htm

Pennsylvania
State Treasury Department
Unclaimed Property Division
P.O. Box 1837
Harrisburg, PA 17105-1837
(800) 222-2046
www.treasury.state.pa.us/unclaimed.html

Rhode Island
Department of Treasury

Unclaimed Property Division
P.O. Box 1435
Providence, RI 02901-1435
(401) 222-6505
www.treasury.ri.gov/money/st.htm

South Carolina
Office of the State Treasury
Unclaimed Property Division
P.O. Box 11778
Columbia, SC 29211-1778
(803) 734-2101
www.state.sc.us/treas/

South Dakota
State Treasury Office
500 East Capitol Avenue
Pierre, SD 57501-5070
(605) 773-3378
www.sdtreasurer.com/unclaimed.asp

Tennessee
State Treasury Department
Unclaimed Property Division
Andrew Jackson Building,
10th Fl. 500 Deaderick St.
Nashville, TN 37243-0242
(615) 741-6499
www.treasury.state.tn.us

Texas

Chapter of Public Accounts
Unclaimed Property Division
P.O. Box 12019
Austin, TX 78711-2019
(800) 654-3463
www.window.state.tx.us/up

Utah
State Treasurer's Office
Unclaimed Property Division
341 South Main St., 5th Floor
Salt Lake City, UT 84119-2315
(801) 320-5360
www.treasurer.state.ut.us

Vermont
State Treasury Office
Unclaimed Property
Department
133 State Street
Montpelier, VT 05633-0001
(802) 828-2301
www.tre.state.vt.us

Virginia
Department of Treasury
Unclaimed Property Division
P.O. Box 2478
Richmond, VA 23218-2478
(804) 225-2142
www.trs.state.va.us/

Washington
Department of Revenue
Unclaimed Property Division
P.O. Box 47489
Olympia, WA 98504-7489
(360) 586-2736
https://dor.wa.gov/

West Virginia
Office of State Treasury
One Players Club Drive
Charleston, WV 25311
(800) 642-8687
www.wvtreasury.com

Wisconsin
State Treasurer's Office
Unclaimed Property Division
P.O. Box 2114
Madison, WI 53701-2114
(608) 267-7977
www.ost.state.wi.us/

Wyoming
Office of the State Treasurer
Unclaimed Property Division
2515 Warren Ave., Suite 502
Cheyenne, WY 82002
(307) 777-5590
https://treasurer.state.wy.us

*"The chance that you or someone you know has
unclaimed property is greater than you think. Finding out is*

free and easy."

— Alexi Giannoulias,
IL State Treasurer

CHAPTER 12
Free Money For Non-Profits

A lot of prisoners have asked me about starting a non-profit organization so they can help out their community and provide a valuable service. In this book, *Think Outside the Cell*, Joseph Robinson has a great chapter on this called, "Social Entrepreneurship." In *Free Money in America*, Rhonda Turpin writes about how some of the most important non-profits throughout the country have been started by felons. Angel Tree was started by an ex-prisoner after serving a 15-year prison sentence. The Prison Fellowship Program was started by another ex-prisoner. These are just a couple of the many non-profits started by ex-prisoners. Why couldn't you start the next big non-profit?

Here are some things you should remember when starting your non-profit:

- Most non-profit organizations or charities provide some type of benefit or greater good.
- You can draw a salary for running the non-profit and you can/should bring in money.
- If you started a charity, you must give away 80% of your donations each year to keep your tax-exempt status.
- You can try to get tax-exempt status for your non-profit from the IRS. Notice I said try. The IRS doesn't grant

everyone that status. Prisoner Joe Woods, a minister in the Universal Life Church, tried to get tax-exempt status from the IRS for his church while he was incarcerated, but was denied.

- Set up a website for your organization. Nowadays most non-profits use .org as the designation on their URL. For instance, *www.prisonlegalnews.org.*
- List your non-profit with these search engines: Guidestar.org; NetworkForGood.org; GreaterGood.com; Foundations.org; and CharityNavigator.com; Candid.org.
- Set up different ways for people to donate to your cause. Some examples are by gift donations, fundraising, monthly donation options, sponsorship of one of your programs, and online auctions.

You can sell products through your non-profit. Just because it's a non-profit doesn't mean it's not a business. It has to make money. Set up an email marketing plan and add some affiliate promotions with other online websites. Get the word out and build up your organization's coffers.

Think a non-profit or charity can't grow big? Think about United Way, the Boys and Girls Club, and the Red Cross. They are all non-profits. For an updated and expanded look at the ins and outs of running a non-profit, I suggest getting copies of the below listed books:

The Everything Non-profit Toolkit by Jim Goettler
Managing a Non-profit Organization: Updated Twenty-First Century Edition by Thomas Wolf
How to Form a Non-profit Corporation, 15th Edition by Anthony Mancuso
Free Money in America by Rhonda Turpin

For those of you who just can't wait till you read the above books, here's a brief overview of how you would start a non-profit organization.

How to Start a Non-profit Corporation

1. Choose a name and create a statement of purpose. For instance, if I wanted to start a non-profit, mine would be "Millionaire Prisoner, Inc." And my statement of purpose would be: "Changing lives one prisoner at a time."

2. After you come up with your name and statement of purpose, you'll have to create your Articles of Incorporation and Bylaws.

3. Form a board of directors. You can be Chairman of the Board.

4. Incorporate with your state government. You should contact your Secretary of State to get all the proper forms and requirements.

5. Keep detailed financial reports and start reporting your transactions to your state government.

6. Once you are incorporated, you should apply to the IRS for federal tax-exempt status. You'll want to get a copy of their publication, How to Apply For and Retain Exempt Status for Your Organization.

If you can get tax-exempt status, or 501(c)(3) status, then you can start getting grants from government and other tax-exempt organizations and foundations. But remember, this won't be easy while sitting in a prison cell. Just because something is hard doesn't mean it's impossible. If you're serious about forming a non-profit you should get a copy of How to Form A Non-profit Corporation, 15th Edition by Anthony Mancuso.

Are you thinking about starting a non-profit for the elderly? Or one in the educational field? How about in the public health arena? If so, you may qualify for $20,000 worth of government cars, beds, furniture, computers or land all for FREE for your non-profit. You can get this stuff through your State Agency for Surplus property (SASP). SASPs are state-run organizations that coordinate the federal program for the donation of federal surplus property to public, tax-supported entities and eligible, private, non-profit, tax-exempt organizations. To find your local SASP you can call "211" or a U.S. Government Information Specialist at 1-844-872-4681

Prison-to-Professionals (2P)

Remember the story I shared about Stanley Andrisse in the "Free Money for College" chapter? Well, in his book From Prison Cells to PhD, he said it was hard to get funding for his P2P program at first. But here is the proof of what is possible if you put your mind behind your actions:

Year one = P2P had revenue of $8,000 with seven scholars;
Year two = P2P had revenue of $40,000 with thirty scholars;
Year three = P2P had revenue of $150,000 with 120-plus scholars;
Year four = P2P had revenue of $500,000 with 200-plus scholars;
And in 2019, P2P and partners received a $7.2 million, five-year government grant from the National Science Foundation.

Proof that the money is out there, you just have to go get it. As I hope you now know, you can accomplish anything you want.

"Dreams don't belong in boxes. Dreams live in the clouds."
— Stanley Andrisse, MBA, PhD

Further Reading

One of the keys to my success has been to read how-to guides that were composed before the internet existed. Why? Because unless we prisoners have access to a contraband smartphone, we can't research on the web. So, to help speed up the process I try to do everything I can from my prison cell and only involve my outside personal assistant if I run into a dead end.

Two of the best books that show you how to get funding for your non-profit are as follows:

Development Today: A Fund-Raising Guide for Non-profit Organizations by Dr. Jeffrey Lant.

The Complete Guide to Planned Giving: Everything You Need to Know to Compete Successfully for Major Gifts by Debra Ashton

A couple more that you may want to get and study, are:

The Complete Guide to Getting a Grant by Laurie Blum

Raise More Money for Your Non-profit Organization by Anne L. New

If you study the above books and then use what you've learned with what's available online to assist you, the sky is the limit.

Additional Resources

Here are some of the more famous foundations and non-profits that could possibly help you or you could learn from:

The Ford Family Foundation
100 Wall St., 11th Floor
New York, NY 10005
(888) 313-0102
www.ford.com

The Rockefeller Foundation
420 5th Avenue
New York, NY 10018-2702
(212) 869-8500
www.rockfound.org

Girl Boss Foundation
2046 Hillhurst Avenue #112
Los Angeles, CA 90027
*https://www.girlboss.com/foundati
on*

Wal-Mart Foundation
702 Southwest 8th Street
Bentonville, AR 72716
*https://giving.walmart.com/apply-
for-grants*

Score Association
1175 Herndon Parkway,
Suite 900
Herndon, VA 20170
https://www.score.org/

Wheless Foundation
P.O. Box 1119
Shreveport, LA 71152

Simon & Schwab Foundation
P.O. Box 1014
Columbus, GA 31902

Coulter Foundation
P.O. Box 5247
Denver, CO 80217

Thatcher Foundation
P.O. Box 1401
Pueblo, CO 810002

Biddle Foundation, Inc.
61 Broadway, Room 2912
New York, NY 10006

Unocal Foundation
P.O. Box 7600
Los Angeles, CA 90051

The Piton Foundation
511 16th Street, Suite 700
Denver, CO 80202

Frank R. Seaver Trust
714 W. Olympic Boulevard
Los Angeles, CA 90015

Earl B. Gilmore Foundation
160 S. Fairfax Avenue
Los Angeles, CA 90036

The Commonwealth Fund
One East 75th Street
New York, NY 10021-2692

The Cullen Foundation
P.O. Box 1600
Houston, TX 77251

The James Irvine Foundation
One Market Plaza

San Francisco, CA 94105

William Penn Foundation
1630 Locust Street
Philadelphia, PA 19103

Blanchard Foundation
c/o Boston Sake
One Boston Place
Boston, MA 02106

Xerox Foundation
P.O. Box 1600
Stamford, CT 06904

Fairchild Industries
2031 Century Boulevard
Germantown, MD 20874

Charles and Els Bendheim
Foundation
One Parker Plaza
Fort Lee, NJ 07024

Broadcasters Foundation, Inc.
320 West 57th Street
New York, NY 10019

Copley Fund
P.O. Box 696
Morrisville, VT 05661

Cambridge Foundation
99 Bishop Allan Drive
Cambridge, MA 02139

Barker Foundation

P.O. Box 328
Nashua, NH 03301

The Hawaii Foundation
111 South King Street
P.O. Box 3170
Honolulu, HI 96802

Inland Steel-Ryerson
Foundation
30 West Monroe Street
Chicago, IL 60603

Northern Indiana Giving
Program
5265 Hohman Avenue
Hammond, IN 46320

Morris Joseloff Foundation, Inc.
125 La Salee Rd., W
Hartford, CT 06107

Deposit Guaranty Foundation
P.O. Box 1200
Jackson, MS 39201

Haskin Foundation
200 E. Broadway
Louisville, KY 40202

The Dayton Foundation
1395 Winters Bank Tower
Dayton, OH 45423

Bohen Foundation
1716 Locust Street
Des Moines, IA 50303

Yonkers Charitable Trust
701 Walnut Street
Des Moines, IA 50306

Miles Foundation
P.O. Box 40
Elkhart, IN 46515

Ametek Foundation
410 Park Avenue
New York, NY 10022

Horace B. Packer Foundation
61 Main Street
Wellsboro, PA 16901

The Clark Foundation
30 Wall Street
New York, NY 10005

Richard & Helen DeVos
Foundation
7154 Windy Hill, SE
Grand Rapids, MI 49506

The H & R Block Foundation
4410 Main Street
Kansas City, MO 64111

New Hampshire Fund
One South Street
P.O. Box 1335
Concord, NH 03302-1335

The Shearwater Foundation,
Inc.

c/o Alexander Nixon
423 West 43rd Street
New York, NY 10036

Muskegon County Foundation
Fraunthal Center, Suite 304
407 W. Western Avenue
Muskegon, MI 49440

There are plenty of other foundations and programs that provide money for non-profits. You can check with the following for more help:

The Foundation Center
79 Fifth Avenue, 2nd Floor
New York, NY 10003
(212) 620-4230
https://fdncenter.org

Candid
32 Old Slip, 24th Floor
New York, NY 10005-3500
https://candid.org

The Aspen Institute
One Dupont Circle, NW
Suite 700
Washington, D.C. 20036
(202) 736-1071
https://fields.org

The Grantsmanship Center
350 South Bixel Street, Suite 100
Los Angeles, CA 90017
https://www.tgci.com/funding-sources

CHAPTER 13
Free Money for Cellpreneurs

Some of you read my book, *Cellpreneur*. Or my first book, *The Millionaire Prisoner*. If you have, then you know I started two businesses from my prison cell. Because I didn't get permission from the prisoncrats beforehand, they seized all of my property and threw me in segregation for 30 days while they investigated me. I wish I would have known what I know now before I started those businesses. I bootstrapped $300 and a typewriter into thousands of dollars a year in passive income. But I could have sped it all up by using free help and grant money. In this chapter I'll show you what is available for any person starting a business. There's no way I could show you every single source of FREE money out there for cellpreneurs. What I hope to do is get you started. That way your whole financial future will change, and once you're out of prison you'll stay out. Let's get to it.

In the previous chapter I listed some organizations that can help you start a business, or more specifically, a non-profit. In this chapter I'll zero in on some FREE money sources that may interest some of you.

Federal Money for Business

The federal government gives away millions of dollars every year to businesses. You can find these programs in the *Catalog of Federal Domestic Assistance*. You can search the contents for free at *www.cfda.gov*. I will include some of the ones I know about in this chapter.

The U.S. government wants you to get ahead. They want you to get a job and establish a career. So much so that you can possibly get up to $10,000 to take entrepreneur training courses. Each state has local job training centers that provide money to people so they can upgrade their skills and get better jobs. To find out the closest one to your hometown you should contact your state's One-Stop Labor Information Center. Have them tell you where the local office is. I'll include the One-Stop Center's State Headquarters at the end of this chapter. Or you can find the local office online at: *www.doleta.gov/usworkforce/onestop/one-stopmap.cfm*.

Are you a freelancer? Do you have a product or service you could sell to the federal government? The government buys all kinds of services: legal, web design, landscaping, cleaning, massage therapists, and caterers. Matthew Lesko says his wife got over $100,000 to do consulting work. And his sister got over $350,000 from the government to frame pictures. To learn more about how to get these contracts you should contact your state's Office of Economic Development or your local Procurement Assistance Office. They will help match your product or service with the right agency. I'll include your state's Economic Development Office at the end of this chapter. If you want to find the local assistance office, you can at:

Small and Disadvantaged Business Utilization Office
Cameron Station, Room 48110
Defense Logistics Agency
Alexandria, VA 22304
(703) 76701661

www.dla.mil

My best friend started a landscaping business with one truck, one trailer, and some lawn care equipment. A few years later he signed a $100,000 contract to keep the grounds of the city cemetery. Not bad. He once told me something that I've never forgotten. He said that if his landscaping was ever damaged in a storm or from a tornado, he'd go to the government and get it all replaced for free. I believed him. Here it is 20+ years later and I read that he could get up to $75,000 in trees and bushes to replaced what was damaged. So, if you ever have landscaping, trees, or bushes damaged in a natural disaster, make sure you go get FREE replacements. You would do so by contacting:

Department of Agriculture
Farm Service Agency
1400 Independence Ave., S.W.
Washington, D.C. 20250-0506
(202) 720-7809
www.fsa.usda.gov/pas/publications/facts/html/tap04.htm

Are you from a small low-income town? You could get up to $300,000 to build a business or provide management and technical assistance to such smaller businesses. For more info contact:

New Markets Venture Capital Program
409 3rd Street, NW, Suite 6300
Washington, D.C. 20416
(202) 205-6510
www.sba.gov/Inv/

Are you a Minority/Native American trying to start a business? The federal government has all kinds of grants available for you, depending on your situation and status. For more information you should contact:

Business Development Specialist, Room 5071
Minority Business Development Agency
U.S. Department of Commerce
14th and Constitution Ave., NW
Washington, D.C. 20230
(202) 482-1940
www.mbda.gov

Office of Economic Development
Bureau of Indian Affairs
1849 C Street, NW
Mail Stop 4640
Washington, D.C. 20240
(202) 208-4796
www.doi.gov/bureau-indian-affairs.html

Associate Administrator for 8(a) Business Development
Small Business Administration
409 Third Street, SW
Washington, D.C. 20416
(202) 205-6421
(800) UASK-SBA
www.sba.gov/8abd

Charles H. Green is the former president/CEO of Sunrise Bank in Atlanta. He's now the executive director of the Small Business Finance Institute with over 40 years' experience in consulting with small business owners. Two of his books that you might want to read are: *Get Financing Now* and *The SBA*

Loan Book: The Complete Guide to Getting Financial Help Through the Small Business Administration.

SBA Lender Match

The Small Business Association has launched "Lender Match" to connect entrepreneurs and small business owners with lenders. It's FREE and easy to use. You can call 1-800-827-5722 or go to *sba.gov/funding-programs/loans/lender-match*.

You are not guaranteed to get a loan, but it would be easy to reach out to approximately 800 lenders. Here's what the SBA says about those who use Lender Match: "You'll receive an email with contact information of interested lenders two business days after you submit the form. From there, you'll start talking to lenders and completing applications. Some will reach out to you, and you're welcome to contact them as well."

Lender Match may be an option for you. Since it's FREE to use why not try it out? You never know what might happen.

For more about getting the money you need you may want to get a copy of *Startup Money made Easy* by Maria Aspan.

Women Cellpreneurs

If you're a female small business owner or freelancer, you can get income from a government contract. If you have assets less than $740,000 the federal government will put you at the top of this list. You can get free consulting on how to get this money by calling the SBA hotline at 800-827-5722 and ask for your local office for Women-owned Small Business (WOSB) Federal Contracting Program. Share that with your mother, sister, auntie, girlfriend, wife, and/or daughter. Matter of fact, share any of the tips in this book with them and watch how much they love you for it.

$10,000 to Creative Entrepreneurial Women who want to implement a new and creative business idea. For more information, contact:

Balance Bar Company Contributions Program
800 Westchester Avenue
Rye Brook, NY 10573
https://www.balance.com/grants/default.asp

Want to own a transportation related company or train women to run transportation companies? You can get a grant from the federal government to do just that. Contact them at:

Director Office of Civil Rights
Federal Transit Administration
U.S. Department of Transportation
400 Seventh Street, SW, Room 9102
Washington, D.C. 20590
(202) 366-4018
www.fta.dot.gov

You can also get contracts with the Department of Transportation. Contact the:

Office of Small and Disadvantaged Business Utilization
Office of the Secretary
400 Seventh Street, SW
Washington, D.C. 20590
1-800-532-1169
www.dot.gov

If you have a business or non-profit that helps women start businesses, you can get grant money from:

Office of Women's Business Ownership
Small Business Administration
409 Third Street, SW
Washington, D.C. 20416
(202) 205-6673
www.sba.gov/womeninbusiness

For welfare moms who want to start their own businesses they can get grant money from the Job Opportunities for Low Income Individuals (JOLI) Program by contacting:

Department of Health and Human Services
Office of Community Services
370 L'Enfant promenade, SW, Fifth Floor
Washington, D.C. 20447
(202) 401-9346
www.acf.hhs.gov/programs/joli/welcome.htm

If you feel like you have been discriminated against because of your sex or marital status you should contact the Federal Trade Commission (FTC). They enforce the laws that prohibit creditors and credit bureaus from doing such. They can send you the *Equal Credit Opportunity* pamphlet, which will give you tips on what to do. Contact them at:

Federal Trade Commission
600 Pennsylvania Ave., NW
Washington, D.C. 20580
1-877-FTC-HELP
www.ftc.gov/bcp/conline/pubs/credit/ecoa.htm

Here are some other organizations that women cellpreneurs may want to link up with:

National Association of Women Business owners (NAWBO)
601 Pennsylvania Ave., NW
South Building, Suite 900
Washington, D.C. 20004
https://www.nawbo.org/

National Women's Political Caucus (NWPC)
P.O. Box 65010
Washington, D.C. 20035
https://www.nwpc.org/

She Should Run
80 M St. SE, Floor 1
Washington, D.C. 20003
https://www.sheshouldrun.org/

Money For Disabled Cellpreneurs

I have a daughter who is in a wheelchair so I'm partial to Americans with disabilities. So is the Abilities Fund. They are a nationwide developer targeting Americans with disabilities and the organizations that support them. They deliver training, technical assistance services, and advisory support to individuals. For more information contact:

The Abilities Fund
332 S. Linn St., Suite 15
Iowa City, IA 52240
(866) 720-3863
(319) 338-2521
www.abilitiesfund.org

For more information about how to get a grant for a handicapped van see: *www.mobilityworks.com.*

Banks Friendly to Those in Need

There are several opportunities to use banks that are friendly to low-income people. The government supports these banks and credit unions because, like I wrote earlier, they want you to make your dreams come true. The U.S. Department of Treasury has a Community Development Financial Institution (CDFI) Fund. It awards money to banks that benefit needy communities across the country. When I read that I knew those are the banks we cellpreneurs need to send our loved ones to when we need a loan or investment. To learn where the nearest CDFI bank is to you contact:

CDFI Fund
601 13th St., NW, Suite 200
Washington, D.C. 20005
(202) 622-8662
www.cdfifund.gov

There are also banks that give you $5 for every $1 you put into a savings account! They're called Individual Development Accounts or IDA Saving Programs. They are for people who have little money to save, but who want to start a business, get training for a job, or fix a home, etc. To find these financial institutions that offer IDA accounts in your state, contact one of the following:

Prosperity Now
1200 G St.
NW #400

Washington, D.C. 20005
(202) 408-9788
www.prosperitynow.org/map

IDA Network
Corporation for Enterprise Development
777 N. Capitol St., NE, Suite 800
Washington, D.C. 20002
www.idanetwork.org

Want to start a home-based business? Would $700 be enough to get you started? There's an organization that works with over 250 different coordinating agencies to provide business training to get this grant. To see if there is a program near you contact:

Trickle Up
104 W. 27th St., 12th Floor
New York, NY 10001
(212) 255-9980
www.trickleup.org

Additional Network Opportunities

Those above are just a few of the opportunities and available help for cellpreneurs and their families and friends to get help. Here are some more:

Entrepreneurs' Organization (EO)
500 Montgomery Street, Suite 700
Alexandria, VA 22314
https://www.eonetwork.org

National Business Incubation Association

20 E. Circle Dr. #37198
Athens, OH 45701
(740) 593-4331
www.nbia.org

Your hometown and the county you live in all have grants that they make available to businesses in their areas. The same as the federal government. They want you to do business in your hometown and county. To find the right office, just do a search for "economic development office + your hometown" and you should get it. I'm from Danville, Illinois in Vermilion County, so I would run two searches as follows:

"Economic Development Office in Danville, Illinois"

"Economic Development Office in Vermilion County, Illinois"

Then I would contact them with my familiar line: "Hi, my name is Joshua Kruger, and I'm looking to start a business here. I'm trying to get a description of the grants you have available to assist me." If they don't know the answer, I'll ask them to point me in the direction of the person who does. Simple as that. It's funny what you can find out just by asking a question. Don't forget your state's One-Stop labor Centers and Economic Development Offices. You can find your state below. Contact them and ask for the local office nearest to your hometown (or town where you're going to start your business.)

Alabama

Alabama Development Office
401 Adams Ave., Suite 670
Montgomery, AL 36130-4106
1-800-248-0033
www.ado.state.al.us

One-Stop Career Center
Department of Industrial
Relations
649 Monroe Street
Montgomery, AL 36131
(334) 242-8990
https://dir.alabama.gov

Alaska

Alaska Department of
Commerce.
Community and Economic
Development
P.O. Box 110800
Juneau, AK 98111
(907) 465-5478
www.dced.state.ak.us/cbd/

One-Stop Career Center
Alaska Job Center Network
Department of Labor
P.O. Box 21149
Juneau, AK 99802-1149
(907) 456-2700
www.jobs.state.ak.us

Alaska Small Business
Development Center
University of Alaska-Anchorage
510 L Street, Suite 310

Anchorage, AK 99501-3550
(907) 271-4022
www.sba.gov/ak/

Arizona

Economic Development Office
Department of Commerce
1700 W. Washington
Suite 600
Phoenix, AZ 85007
(602) 771-1100
800-528-8421
www.commerce.state.az.us/

One-Stop Career Center
Arizona Department of
Economic Security
P.O. Box 6123
Phoenix, AZ 85005
(602) 542-3957
www.de.state.az.us/oscc/index.html

Arizona Small Business
Development Center
2411 West 14th Street
Tempe, AZ 85281
(480) 731-8720
www.dist.maricopa.edu/sbdc

Arkansas

Arkansas Economic
Development Commission
1 Capitol Mall
Little Rock, AR 72201
800-ARKANSAS
(501) 682-1121
www.1800arkansas.com

Arkansas Career Development
Network
Arkansas Employment Security
Dept.
#1 Pershing Circle
Little Rock, AR 72114
(501) 682-2003
www.state.ar.us/esd/

Arkansas Small Business
Development Center
University of Arkansas-Little
Rock
2801 S. University
Little Rock, AR 72201
(501) 324-9043
www.asbdc.uak.edu

California
Economic Development Office
Business, Transportation and
Housing Agency
980 9th Street, Suite 2450
Sacramento, CA 95814-2719
(916) 323-5400
https://commerce.ca.gov

One-Stop Office
800 Capitol Mall, MIC 83
Sacramento, CA 95314
800-758-0398
*www.sjtcc.cahwnet.gov/sjtccweb/on
e-stop/*

California Small Business
Development Center

California Trade and Commerce
Agency
980 9th Street, Suite 2450
Sacramento, CA 95814-2719
(916) 323-5400
www.commerce.ca.gov

Colorado
Office of Economic Development
1625 Broadway, Suite 1700
Denver, CO 80202
(303) 892-3840
www.state.co.us/gov-dir/oed.html

Job Service Centers
Colorado Dept. of Labor and
Employment
Office of Employment and
Training
1515 Arapahoe Street
Tower 2, Suite 400
Denver, CO 80202-2117
(303) 318-8000
https://navigator.cdle.state.co.us

Colorado Small Business
Development Center
Office of Business Development
1625 Broadway, Suite 1700
Denver, CO 80202
(303) 892-3794
www.state.co.us/oed/sbdc

Connecticut
Department of Economic and
Community Development
505 Hudson Street

Hartford, CT 06106
(860) 270-8000
www.ct.gov/ecd

One-Stop Career Center
Connecticut Department of
Labor
200 Folly Brook Boulevard
Wethersfield, CT 06109
(860) 263-6000
*www.ctdol.state.ct.us/ctworks/ctwor
ks.html*

Connecticut Small Business
Development Center
University of Connecticut School
of Business Administration
2100 Hillside Road, Unit 1094
Storrs, CT 06269-1094
(860) 486-4135
www.sbdc.uconn.edu

Delaware
Delaware Economic
Development Office
99 Kings Highway
P.O. Box 1401
Dover, DE 19901
(302) 739-4271
www.state.de.us/dedo/index.htm

Delaware Career Network
Department of Labor,
Employment and Training
4425 North Market Street
Wilmington, DE 19809-0828
(302) 761-8102

www.vcnet.net

Delaware Small Business
Development Center
University of Delaware
1318 N. Market St.
Wilmington, DE 19801
(302) 571-1555
www.delawaresbdc.org

District of Columbia
Office of Economic Development
1350 Pennsylvania Ave., NW
Suite 317
Washington, D.C. 20004
(202) 727-6365
www.dcbiz.dc.gov

DOES One-Stop Career Center
Department of Employment
Services
609 H Street, NE
Washington, D.C. 20002
(202) 724-7000
www.does.dc.gov

Small Business Development
Center
1110 Vermont Ave., NW, 9th
Floor
Washington, D.C. 20005
(202) 606-4000
www.sba.gov/dc

Florida
Florida Economic Development
Council

P.O. Box 3186
Tallahassee, FL 32315-3186
(850) 201-FEDC
www.fedc.net

Enterprise Florida
390 N. Orange Ave.
Suite 1300
Orlando, FL 32801
(407) 316-4600
www.floridabusiness.com

Agency for Workforce
Innovation
107 East Madison Street
Tallahassee, FL 32399-4120
(850) 245-7105
www.floridajobs.com

Florida Small Business
Development Center
University of West Florida
401 E. Chase Street, Suite 100
Pensacola, FL 32502
(850) 473-7830
www.sbdc.uwf.edu

Georgia
Office of Economic Development
60 Executive Park South, NE
Suite 250
Atlanta, GA 30329-2231
(404) 679-4940
www.dca.state.ga.us

One-Stop Career Center
Department of Labor

Employment Services
148 International Boulevard, NE
Atlanta, GA 30303-1751
(404) 232-3540
www.state.ga.us/index/gaemp.html

Georgia Small Business
Development Center
University of Georgia-Chicopee
Complex
1180 East Broad Street
Athens, GA 30602-5412
(706) 542-6762
www.sbdc.uga.edu

Hawaii
Department of Business and
Economic Development
P.O. Box 2359
Honolulu, HI 96804
(808) 586-2423
www1.hawaii.gov/DEBOT

One-Stop Career Center
Department of Labor
Workforce Development
Division
830 Punchbowl Street #112
Honolulu, HI 96813
(808) 586-8842
https://dlir.state.hi.us/

Small Business Development
Center Network
University of Hawaii-Hilo
308 Kamehameha Ave., Suite 201
Hilo, HI 96720

144

(808) 974-7515
www.hawaii-sbdc.org

Idaho
Economic Development Office
Idaho Commerce and Labor
700 West State Street
P.O. Box 83720
Boise, ID 83720-0093
(208) 334-2470
https://cl.idaho.gov

One-Steop Carper Center
Idaho Commerce and Labor
317 Main Street
Boise, ID 83735
(208) 332-3570
www.idahoworks.state.id.us

Idaho Small Business
Development Center
Boise State University
College of Business
1910 University Drive
Boise, ID 83725-1655
(208) 426-1640
www.idahosbdc.org

Illinois
Department of Commerce and
Economic Opportunity
620 E. Adams, 3rd Floor
Springfield, IL 62701
(217) 782-7500
www.commerce.state.il.us

Illinois Employment and
Training Center (IETC) Network
Department of Employment
Security
850 East Madison Street
Springfield, IL 62702-5603
(217) 785-5069
www.ides.state.il.us/

Indiana
Economic Development Office
Indiana Department of
Commerce
One North Capitol, Suite 700
Indianapolis, IN 46204
(317) 232-8800
www.state.in.us/doc/index.html

One-Stop Career Center
Indiana Dept. of Workforce
Development
Indiana Government Center
10 North Senate Avenue
Indianapolis, IN 46204
(317) 232-4259
www.dwd.state.in.us

Small Business Development
Center
One North Capitol, Suite 900
Indianapolis, IN 46204
(317) 234-2082
www.isbdc.org

Iowa
Department of Economic
Development

200 East Grand Ave.
Des Moines, IA 50309-1827
(515) 242-4700
www.state.ia.us/ided

One-Stop Career Center
Department of Workforce
Development
1000 East Grand Avenue
Des Moines, IA 50319-0209
(515) 281-5387
www.iowaworkforce.org

Small Business Development
Center
Iowa State University
College of Business
Administration
2501 N. Loop Drive
Building 1, Suite 615
Ames, IA 50010-8283
(515) 296-6714
www.iabusnet.org/sbdc/index.html

Kansas
Business Development Division
Dept. of Commerce and Housing
1000 SW Jackson St., Suite 100
Topeka, KS 66612-1357
(785) 296-3481
https://kdoch.state.ks.us/public

Kansas Job Service Career
Centers
Department of Human Resources
Division of Employment and
Training

401 SW Topeka Boulevard
Topeka, KS 66603-3182
(785) 296-5000
https://entkdhr.state.ks.us

Kansas Small Business
Development Center
Fort Hays State University
214 SW 6th Street, Suite 301
Topeka, KS 66603-3179
(785) 296-6514
www.fhsu.edu/ksbdc

Kentucky
Kentucky Cabinet for Economic
Development
2300 Capital Plaza Tower
500 Mero Street
Frankfort, KY 40601
(502) 564-7670
www.thinkkentucky.com

One-Stop Career Centers System
2300 Capital Plaza Tower
500 Mero Street
Frankfort, KY 40601
(502) 564-6606
www.kycwd.org

Kentucky Small Business
Development Center
University of Kentucky
Center for Entrepreneurship
225 College of Business and
Economics
Lexington, KY 40056-0034
(859) 257-7744

www.ksbdc.org

Louisiana
Department of Economic
Development
P.O. Box 94185
Baton Rouge, LA 70804-9185
(225) 342-3000
www.lded.state.la.us

One-Stop Career Center
Louisiana Occupational
Information System
P.O. Box 94125
Baton Rouge, LA 70804-9125
(225) 922-2675
www.ldol.state.la.us

Small Business Development
Center
Louisiana State University
One University Place
Shreveport, LA 71115
(318) 797-6144
www.lsus.edu/sbdc

Maine
Office of Business Development
Dept. of Economic and
Community Development
59 State House Station
Augusta, ME 04333
(207) 624-9804
www.econdevmaine.com

Maine Career Centers
Department of Labor

55 State House Station
Augusta, ME 04333-0055
(207) 624-6390
www.maincareercenter.com

Small Business Development
Center
University of Southern Maine
96 Falmouth Street
P.O. Box 3000
Portland, ME 04104-9300
(207) 780-4420

Maryland
Department of Business and
Economic Development
217 East Redwood St.
Baltimore, MD 21202
800-CHOOSEMD
www.dbed.state.md.us/

Career Net
Dept. of Labor, Licensing and
Regulation
Employment Services
500 North Calvert Street
Baltimore, MD 31302-2272
(410) 230-6220
www.careernet.state.md.us/

Maryland Small Business
Development Center
7100 Baltimore Ave., Suite 402
College Park, MD 20740
(301) 403-0501
www.mdsbdc.umd.edu

Massachusetts
MA Office of Business
Development
10 Park Plaza, Suite 4510
Boston, MA 02116
(617) 973-8600
www.state.ma.us.mobd

One-Stop Career Center Network
Division of Career Services
19 Staniford Street
Boston, MA 02114
(617) 626-5300
www.detma.org/jobseeker/centers

Small Business Development
Center
University of Massachusetts-
Amherst
227 Isenberg School of
Management
Amherst, MA 01003-9310
(413) 545-6301
https://msbdc.som.umass.edu

Michigan
Michigan Economic
Development
300 North Washington Square
Lansing, MI 48913
(517) 373-9808
https://medc.michigan.org

One-Stop Career Center
Michigan Works!
2500 Kerry Street, Suite 210
Lansing, MI 48912

(517) 371-1100
www.michiganworks.org

Michigan Small Business
Development Center
Grand Valley State University
510 W. Fulton St.
Grand Rapids, MI 49504
(616) 336-7480
www.mi-sbdc.org

Minnesota
Dept. of Employment and
Economic Development
500 Metro Square Bldg.
121 7th Place East
St. Paul, MN 55101-2146
1-800-657-3858
www.deed.state.mn.us

One-Stop Career Center
Employment Security
Commission
1520 W. Capitol St.
P.O. Box 1699
Jackson, MS 39215-1699
(601) 354-8711
https://mdes.ms.gov

Mississippi Small Business
Development Center
University of Mississippi
B19 Jeanette Philips Dr.
P.O. Box 1848
University, MS 38677-1848
(662) 915-5001
www.olemiss.edu/depts/mssbdc

Missouri
Department of Economic
Development
P.O. Box 1157
Jefferson City, MO 65102
(573) 751-4962
www.ded.mo.gov

Missouri Small Business
Development Center
University of Missouri
1205 University Avenue
Suite 300
Columbia, MO 65211
(573) 882-0344
www.missouribusiness.net/sbdc

Montana
Department of Commerce
Economic Development Division
301 South Park Avenue
P.O. Box 200501
Helena, MT 59620-0501
(406) 841-2700
https://commerce.state.mt.us/

Job Service Workforce Centers
Department of Labor and
Industry
P.O. Box 1728
Helena, MT 59624
(406) 444-4571
https://jsd.dli.state.mt.us

Montana Small Business
Development Center
Montana Dept. of Commerce
301 South Park Avenue
P.O. Box 200505
Helena, MT 59620-0505
(406) 841-2707
*https://commerce.state.mt.us/brd/br
d_sbdc.html*

Nebraska
Dept. of Economic Development
P.O. Box 94666
301 Centennial Mall South
Lincoln, NE 68509-4666
(402) 471-3111
www.neded.org

Nebraska Office of Workforce
Services
Department of Labor
550 South 16th Street
Lincoln, NE 68509
(402) 471-2600
www.dol.state.ne.us

Nebraska Business Development
Center
College of Business
Administration
Roskens Hall, Room 415
University of Nebraska-Omaha
Omaha, NE 68182-0248
(402) 554-2521
https://nbdc.unomaha.edu

Nevada

Nevada Commission of
Economic Development
108 E. Proctor St.
Carson City, NV 89701
1-800-336-1600
www.expand2nevada.com/

One-Stop Career Center
Nevada Dept. of Employment,
Training and Rehabilitation
Job Connect
500 East Third Street
Carson City, NV 89713-0021
(775) 684-0400
www.nevadajobconnect.com

Nevada Small Business
Development Center
UNR-College of Business
Administration
Business Building, Room 411
Reno, NV 89557-0100
(775) 784-1717
www.nsbdc.org

New Hampshire
Dept. of Resources and Economic
Development
172 Pembroke Road
Concord, NH 03302-1856
(603) 271-2591
www.nheconomy.com

One-Stop Career Center
Dept. of Employment Security
32 South Main Street
Concord, NH 03301

(603) 224-3311
www.nhes.state.nh.us

NH Small Business Development
Center
University of New Hampshire
The Whitemore School of
Business
108 McConnell Hall
Durham, NH 03824
(603) 862-2200
https://nhsbdc.org

New Jersey
NJ Economic Development
Authority
P.O. Box 990
Trenton, NJ 08625-0990
(609) 292-1800
www.njeda.com

One-Stop Career Center
Workforce New Jersey
Division of Employment and
Training
P.O. Box 940
Trenton, NJ 08625
(609) 292-5834
www.wnjpin.state.nj.us

NJ Small Business Development
Center
Rutgers Graduate School of
Management
49 Bleeker Street
Newark, NJ 07102-1913
)973) 353-1927

www.njsbdc.com

New Mexico
Economic Development
Department
Joseph M. Montoya Bldg.
1100 S. St. Francis Drive
Santa Fe, NM 97503
(505) 827-0300
www.edd.state.nm.us

One-Stop Career Center
New Mexico Works
Department of Labor
401 Broadway NE
Albuquerque, NM 87102
(505) 841-8409
www.dol.state.nm.us/

NM Small Business
Development Center
Santa Fe Community College
6401 Richards Avenue
Santa Fe, NM 97508
(505) 428-1362
www.nmsbdc.org

New York
Empire State Development
633 Third Ave.
New York, NY 10017-6706
1-800-782-8369
www.empire.state.ny.us

One-Stop Career Center
Department of Labor
Workforce Development

Building 12, State Campus
Albany, NY 12240
(518) 457-0380
www.wdsny.org

NY Small Business Development
Centers
SUNY
41 State St.
Albany, NY 12246
(518) 443-5398
www.smallbiz.suny.edu/

North Carolina
Economic Development Office
Commerce Finance Center
4301 Mail Service Center
Raleigh, NC 27699-4301
(919) 733-4151
www.commerce.state.nc.us/

Joblink Career Centers
NC Department of Commerce
4301 Mail Service Center
Raleigh, NC 27699-4301
(919) 715-3300
www.joblink.state.nc.us/

North Carolina Small Business
and Technology
Development Center
University of North Carolina
5 West Hargett St., Suite 600
Raleigh, NC 27601-1348
(919) 715-7272
www.sbtdc.org

North Dakota

Dept. of Economic Development and Finance
1600 E. Century Ave., Suite 2
P.O. Box 2057
Bismarck, ND 58502-2057
(701) 328-5300
www.growingnd.com

Job Service North Dakota
P.O. Box 5507
Bismarck, ND 58506-5507
(800) 732-9787
www.jobsnd.com

ND Small Business Development Center
University of North Dakota
118 Bamble Hall, Tox 7308
Grand Fords, ND 58202-7308
1-800-445-7232
www.ndsbdc.org

Ohio

Ohio Department of Development
77 S. High St., 28th Floor
P.O. Box 1001
Columbus, OH 43216-1001
1-800-848-1300
www.odod.state.oh.us

One-Stop Employment and Training
Bureau of Employment Services
145 Front Street, 6th Floor
Columbus, OH 43215

(614) 466-3817
www.ohioworkforce.org

Ohio Small Business Development Center
Department of Development
77 South High St., 28th Floor
Columbus, OH 43216-1001
(614) 466-2711
www.odod.state.oh.us/edd/osb/sbdc

Oklahoma

Economic Development Office
Department of Commerce
900 North Stiles
P.O. Box 26980
Oklahoma City, OK 73126-0980
(405) 815-6552
www.odoc.state.ok.us/index.html

One-Stop Career Center
Oklahoma Workforce Centers
Employment Security Commission
P.O. Box 52003
Oklahoma City, OK 73152-2003
(405) 557-5469
www.esc.state.ok.us

Oklahoma Small Business Development Center
Southeastern Oklahoma City University
Durant, OK 74701
(580) 924-0277
www.osbdc.org

Oregon
Economic and Community
Development Dept.
775 Summer St., Suite 200
Salem, OR 97301-1280
(503) 986-0123
www.econ.state.or.us/

Oregon Career Network
Oregon Employment
Department
875 Union Street, NE
Salem, OR 97311
(503) 947-1470
www.emp.state.or.us

Oregon Business Development
Center
Lane Community College
1445 Willamette St., Suite 1
Eugene, OR 97401-4087
(541) 687-0611
www.lanebdc.com

Pennsylvania
Dept. of Community and
Economic Development
Commonwealth Keystone
Bldg., 4th Floor
North Street
Harrisburg, PA 17120-0225
1-800-379-7448
www.inventpa.com

One-Stop Career Center
Team Pennsylvania Career Link

Department of Labor and
Industry
Seventh & Foster St., Room 1720
Harrisburg, PA 17120
(717) 787-5279
www.pacareerlink.state.pa.us

Pennsylvania Small Business
Development Center
Vance Hall, 4th Floor
3733 Spruce Street
Philadelphia, PA 19104-6374
(215) 898-1219
www.pasbdc.org

Rhode Island
Economic Development
Corporation
One West Exchange St.
Providence, RI 02903
(401) 222-2601
www.riedc.com

One-Stop Career Center
Department of Labor and
Training
1511 Pontiac Ave.
Cranston, RI 02920
(401) 462-8000
www.networkri.org

Bryant College
Small Business Development
Center
1150 Douglas Pike
Smithfield, RI 02197-1284
(401) 232-6111

www.risbcc.org

South Carolina
Economic Development Office
Department of Commerce
1201 Main Street, Suite 1600
Columbia, SC 29201-3200
(803) 737-0400
www.callsouthcarolina.com

1 Stop Partnership
Employment Security
Commission
P.O. Box 995
1550 Gadsden Street
Columbia, SC 29202
(803) 737-2258
www.sces.org/

SC Small Business Development
Center
University of South Carolina
Moore School of Business
Columbia, SC 29208
(803) 777-5118
www.uscbiz.net

South Dakota
Governor's Office of Economic
Development
711 East Wells Ave.
Pierre, SD 57501-3369
(605) 773-5032
www.sdgreatprofits.com

Job Service of South Dakota
SD Department of Labor

Kneip Building
700 Governors Drive
Pierre, SD 57501-2291
(605) 773-3101
www.state.sd.us/dol/sdjob/js-home.htm

SD Small Development Center
University of South Dakota
School of Business
414 East Clark Street
Vermillion, SD 57069-2390
(605) 677-5287
www.usd.edu/brbinfo/sbdc

Tennessee
Dept. of Economic and
Community Development
312 Eighth Avenue North
Eleventh Floor
Nashville, TN 37243-0405
(615) 741-1888
www.state.tn.us/ecd

Tennessee Career Center
Office of Workforce
Development
Andrew Johnson Bldg., 8th Floor
Nashville, TN 37243-0655
(615) 741-6652
www.state.tn.us/labor-wfd/

TN Small Business Development
Center
MTSU
P.O. Box 98
Murfreesboro, TN 37132

(615) 849-9999
www.tsbdc.org

Texas
Department of Economic
Development
P.O. Box 12728
Austin, TX 78711-2728
(512) 936-0100
www.tded.state.tx.us

One Stop Career Center
Texas Workforce Commission
101 East 15th Street
Austin, TX 78778
(512) 463-2654
www.twc.state.tx.us

North Texas Small Business
Development Center
Dallas County Community
College
1402 Corinth Street
Dallas, TX 75215
(214) 860-5831
www.ntsbdc.org

Utah
Business and Economic
Development Division
324 South State St., Suite 500
Salt Lake City, UT 84111
(601) 538-8700
www.utah.org/dbed/welcome.htm

Career Centers
Dept. of Workforce Services

P.O. Box 45249
Salt Lake City, UT 84145
(801) 526-9675
https://jobs.utah.gov

Small Business Development
Center
Salt Lake Community College
1623 South State Street
Salt Lake City, UT 84115
(801) 957-3480
www.slcc.edu/sbdc

Vermont
Dept. of Economic Development
National Life Building,
Drawer 20
Montpelier, VT 05620-0501
(802) 828-3080
www.thinkvermont.com

One Stop Career Resource
Dept. of Employment and
Training
5 Green Mountain Drive
P.O. Box 488
Montpelier, VT 05601-0488
(802) 828-4000
www.det.state.vt.us

Vermont Small Business
Development Center
P.O. Box 188
Randolph, VT 05061-0188
(802) 728-9101
www.vtsbdc.org

Virginia
Economic Development
Partnership
901 East Byrd Street
P.O. Box 798
Richmond, VA 23218-0798
(804) 371-8100
www.yesvirginia.org/

One-Stop Career Center
Employment Commission
P.O. Box 1358
Richmond, VA 23218-1358
(804) 786-1485
www.vec.state.va.us/

Virginia Small Business
Development Center
4031 University Drive, Suite 200
Fairfax, VA 22030
(703) 277-7700
www.virginiasbdc.org

Washington
Dept. of Community, Trade, and
Economic Development
128 10th Ave., SW
P.O. Box 42525
Olympia, WA 98504-2525
(360) 725-4000
www.cted.wa.gov

One-Stop Career Center
Employment Security
Department
212 Maple Park
P.O. Box 9046

Olympia, WA 98507
(360) 902-9302
www.wa.gov/esd/1stop

Washington State Small Business
Development Center
Washington State University
College of Business and
Economics
P.O. Box 644851
Pullman, WA 99164-4851
(509) 335-1576
www.wssbdc.org

West Virginia
WV Development Office
1900 Kanawa Blvd., East
Charleston, WV 25305-0311
(304) 558-2234
www.wvdo.org

One-Stop Career Center
Bureau of Employment
Programs
112 California Avenue
Charleston, WV 25305-0112
(304) 558-1138
www.state.wv.us/bep/jobs/

WV Small Business Development
Center
1900 Kanawa Blvd. East
Charleston, WV 25305-0311
(304) 558-2960
www.sbdcwv.org

Wisconsin

Economic Development Office
Department of Commerce
201 W. Washington Avenue
Madison, WI 53703
(608) 266-1018
www.commerce.state.wi.us

Partnership for Full Employment
(PFE)
Dept. of Workforce Development
102 East Washington Ave.
P.O. Box 7946
Madison, WI 53707-7946
(608) 266-3131
www.dwd.state.wi.us/dwd

Wisconsin Small Business
Development Center
University of Wisconsin-Stout
Center of Innovation
278 Jarvis Hall
Menomonie, WI 54715-0790
(715) 232-1457
www.wisconsinsbdc.org

Wyoming
Economic Development Office
Wyoming Business Council
214 W. 15th St.
Cheyenne, WY 82002-0204
(307) 777-2800
www.wyomingbusiness.org

Employment Resource Centers
Department of Employment
100 West Midwest
Casper, WY 82602
(307) 235-3254
https://wydoe.state.wy.us/erd

WY Small Business Development
Center
University of Wyoming
P.O. Box 3922
Laramie, WY 82071-3922
(307) 766-3505
www.uwyo.edu/sbdc

CHAPTER 14
Free Healthcare Services

A lot of you will get out of prison soon. What will you do for healthcare after prison? In this chapter we'll give you a lot of options for free medical help. In England, they have free healthcare. Not over here. Yet, there are some ways to get free medical help. Getting free medical will allow you to save money. It will also help you assist your family and friends. So, let's get to it.

One thing that I suggest you do before taking any serious medical leap is to get multiple opinions. I once read a book about a billionaire who got diagnosed with cancer. He didn't believe it, so he went to another doctor who told him the same thing. Finally, he went to the famous Mayo Clinic. They re-diagnosed him with a mild tumor and cut it out that day. No cancer at all. He was smart enough to get a third opinion. Now you can be smart also. Here are some places you can go to get free help and multiple opinions.

National Health Information Center
P.O. Box 1133
Washington, D.C. 20013
800-336-4797
www.health.gov/nhic

www.findahealthcenter.hrsa.gov
(Free health clinics closest to where you live!)

National Institutes of Health
Office of Communications
Building 1, Room 344
1 Center Drive, MCS 0188
Bethesda, MD 20892
(301) 496-4000
www.nih.gov

National Women's Health Information Center
U.S. Public Health Service
Office of Women's Health
1600 Clifton Rd., NE
Atlanta, GA 30333
800-944-WOMEN
www.4women.gov

https://healthhotlines.nlm.nih.gov/

Even if you have no health insurance you can still get free help from health clinics. When I was younger, I hurt my ankle pretty bad playing streetball. Of course, I was fresh out the joint, so I didn't have any health insurance. Lucky for me, my grandma knew where a free health clinic was, and I got my ankle fixed for free. Do you know where the closest free health clinic is to your hometown? If not, you can find out by contacting the below:

Health Resources and Services Administration
U.S. Department of Health and Human Services
888-275-4772

www.ask.hrsa.gov/primary.cfm

The Free Clinic Foundation of America
1240 Third Street S.W.
Roanoke, VA 24016
(540) 344-8242
www.freeclinic.net

A lot of us prisoners have been diagnosed with some form of mental illness. And lots of us are on some form of prescription medication. You can use one of the 24,000 free clinics in America to get continued mental health treatment once you're out of prison. To find the nearest one, go to *www.freementalhealth.com* and search.

You can also get free prescription drugs. Your doctor would need to write a note to the drug companies and fill out a form. Then the drug company would ship the drugs to your doctor's office. For more information you can contact the following:

Pharmaceutical Research and Manufacturers of America
1100 15th St., NW
Washington, D.C. 20005
800-PMA-INFO
www.pharma.org

Health Well Foundation
P.O. Box 4133
Gaithersburg, MD 20878
800-675-8416
www.healthwellfoundation.org
Email: *info@healthwellfoundation.org*
(Offers help with prescription medication.)

Needy Meds, Inc.
P.O. Box 219
Gloucester, MA 01931
(978) 865-4115
www.needymeds.com
Email: *info@needymeds.com*
(Offers help with prescription medication.)

The Partnership for Prescription Assistance
www.pparx.org
(888) 477-2669
OR
https://medicineassistancetool.org/
(800) 532-4274
(Offers help with prescription medication.)

Patient Access Network Foundation
P.O. Box 221858
Charlotte, NC 28222-1858
(866) 316-PANF
https://www.patientaccessnetwork.org
Email: *contact@patientaccessnetwork.org*
(Offers help with prescription medication.)

A lot of us wear glasses and have bad eyes. We get some pretty crappy eyecare in here. That doesn't have to keep up after we get out. You can get free eye care from several places.

Prism Optical, Inc.
10954 N.W. 7th Ave.
North Miami, FL 33186
(800) 637-4103
www.prismoptical.com
(Free catalog of eyeglasses.)

New Eyes for the Needy
P.O. Box 332
Short Hills, NJ 07078
www.neweyesfortheneedy.org
(New eyeglasses for low-income people.)

You can get FREE cataract eye surgery if you have no insurance or ability to pay. See *www.missioncataractusa.org,* or call (559) 797-1629.

If you have a local university near you that has an optometry school, you could get FREE or reduced-priced eye care. You will get treatment from student, but they will be supervised by some of the best optometrists. To see if you have a school near you, contact the:

American Optometric Association
243 N. Lindbergh Blvd.
St. Louis, MO 63141
(314) 991-4100
www.aoa.org

The Pearle Vision Foundation offers grants to non-profit organizations for vision-care assistance. For more info contact them at:

Pearle Vision Foundation
2465 Joe Field Road
Dallas, TX 75229
(972) 277-6191
www.pearlevision.com

Do you know someone in the free world who is a senior (age 65 or older)? You may be able to help them get FREE eye care. Have them check out the following:

Seniors Eye Care Program
Eye Care America
655 Beach Street
San Francisco, CA 94142
(415) 561-8500
(800) 222-3937
www.eyecareamerica.org/eyecare

Eye Care America-Glaucoma Program
Eye Care America
655 Beach Street
San Francisco, CA 94142
(415) 561-8500
800-391-EYES
www.eyecareamerica.org/eyecare

Your local Lions Club may also offer help with free eyeglasses. To find your local chapter contact:

Lions Clubs International
300 West 22nd St.
Oak Brook, IL 60523-8842
(630) 571-5466
www.lionsclubs.org

Another area where the prison has failed us medically is in the dentist's chair. The law books are filled with case law where prisoners have got subpar care from the prison dentist. But that doesn't have to continue once you get out. Here are some places you and your family can get FREE and low-cost dental work from.

American Dental Education Association
1400 K Street, NW, Suite 1100
Washington, D.C. 20005
(202) 289-7201
www.adea.org
(Find the local dentistry school to get free/discounted care.)

See also: *www.datreview.com/dentalschools.htm?source=overture*

National Foundation of Dentistry for the Handicapped
1800 15th St., Suite 100
Denver, CO 80202
(303) 534-5360
www.nfdh.org
($2,000 worth of free dental care for seniors and disabled!)

Don't forget to contact your local Community Action Agency to find out about any local programs for dental care. I read about Colorado giving free or discounted care to kids in their Kids In Need of Dentistry (KIND) program. See *www.kindsmiles.org*. Quantum Foundation in Florida developed a program for low-income residents to cut the prices of braces in half. See *www.quantumfind.org*. You can also contact your local dental society to find programs like this in your area.

A lot of you know that your county has a program that offers FREE condoms, HIV, Hepatitis, and STD testing. Before I got locked up, I would go get my condoms for free from the health clinic in my county. I would just walk in, ask for some condoms, sign a paper, and get a sack full of lifestyles condoms. My baby mama used the same health clinic for the pregnancy tests and prenatal care of her body before my twin daughters were born. There's nothing wrong with using these FREE services. To find your local county health clinic, call 211, your Health Department or public library. You could also check the following:

https://www.cdc.gov/publichealthgateway/healthdirectories/healthdepar tments.html

Do you want to quit smoking? You can get FREE help and assistance with nicotine patches. Call the National Quit Smoking Hotline at 1-800-784-8669. They'll help you develop a personal plan. They can also provide you with sources of FREE or discounted medications. See *https://www.cdc.gov/tobaco/*. For more you can watch Matthew Lesko's video at: *https://vimeo.com/257692375*.

A lot of you have hearing problems and/or need hearing aids. You can get FREE hearing aids or money for assistance in getting hearing exams and care. To find the local hearing professional nearest you who participates in this program, contact:

The Better Hearing Institute
515 King St., Suite 420
Alexandria, VA 22314

P.O. Box 1840
Washington, D.C. 20013
800-EAR-WELL
(703) 684-3391
www.betterheairng.org

The one area where you can help your family out is with the care of the kids in your family. Most states now have a Children's Health Insurance Program (CHIPS) that offers medical coverage to children who may not be covered. You can find out more at 1-877-543-7669; *www.insurekidsnow.gov*.

I'm sure you have seen the commercials for Shriners Hospitals. They provide FREE expert care for kids who have orthopedic injuries, diseases of the bones, joints and muscles, or burns. All children under age of 18 can be evaluated for free. To find a hospital close to you, contact them at:

Shriners Hospitals
2900 Rocky Point Dr.
Tampa, FL 33607-1460
1-800-237-5055
www.shrinershq.org

There are FREE camps for kids with asthma. One is called Camp Wheeze Away. TO find out more about these camps, contact:

The American Lung Association
61 Broadway, 6th Floor
New York, NY 10006
800-LUNG-USA
(212) 315-8700
www.lungusa.org

Federal law requires that pregnant women and kids up to 6 years old who are low-income get Medicaid health insurance. Kids can also get free protection from chicken pox, polio, mumps, whooping cough, German measles, tetanus, spinal meningitis, and Hepatitis B. Contact your county, State Department's of Health. Or call the National Immunization Information Hotline at 1-800-232-4636; *www.cdc.gov/nip.*

If your child has a hearing problem and doesn't have public support, they can get FREE hearing aids and follow-up care from:

Miracle-Ear Children's Foundation
5000 Cheshire Lane N, Suite 1
Plymouth, MN 55446-3715
800-234-5422
www.miracle-ear.com/resources/children_request.asp

God forbid one of the children in your family gets cancer. But if they do, your family could receive direct financial assistance for medical and non-medical expenses. For more information, contact:

National Children's Cancer Society, Inc.
1015 Locust Bldg., Suite 600
St. Louis, MO 63101-1323
(314) 241-1600
1-800-5-FAMILY
www.children-cancer.com
www.beyondthecure.org

Here are some other organizations that deal with specific medical issues. You may qualify for their FREE assistance if you have one of the ailments they cover.

American Kidney Fund
6110 Executive Blvd., Suite 1010
Rockville, MD 20852
1-800-638-8299
www.kidneyfund.org
(Helps with dialysis patients and kidney donor expenses.)

Association of Community Cancer Centers
11600 Nebel Street, Suite 21
Rockville, MD 20852-2557

(301) 984-9496
www.accc-cancer.org
(Helps with prescription costs for cancer patients.)

Cancer Care
275 Seventh Ave., Floor 22
New York, NY 10001
1-800-813-4673
www.cancercare.org
(Same as above, plus other support.)

Caring Voice Coalition, Inc.
8249 Meadowbridge Road
Mechanicsville, VA 23116
1-888-267-1440
www.caringvoice.org
(Helps patient with serious, chronic illnesses.)

Chai Lifeline
151 West 30th Street
New York, NY 10001
(877) CHAI-LIFE
www.chailifeline.org
(Helps children suffering from serious illness.)

Geriatric Services of America, Inc.
5030 S. Mill Ave. D-23
Tempe, AZ 85282
1-800-307-8048
www.geriatricservices.com
(Helps chronic respiratory disease patients.)

International Oncology Network (ION)

An Amerisource Bergen Specialty Group Company
3101 Gaylord Parkway
Frisco, TX 75034
1-888-536-7697 Ext. 6847
https://www.iononline.com

Leukemia and Lymphoma Society
1-800-955-4572
www.leukemia.org

National Organization for Rare Disorders
55 Kenosia Avenue
P.O. Box 1968
Danbury, CT 06813-1968
(203) 744-0100
www.rarediseases.org

It's a fact of life that we are all going to die one day. A lot of you will sadly lose family members to crime. Your family can get burial expenses through your state's Crime Victims Assistance Fund. For more information you should contact the following:

Office for Victims of Crime Resource Center
National Criminal Justice Reference Service
P.O. Box 6000
Rockville, MD 20849
1-800-851-3420
www.ncjrs.org

Office for Victims of Crime
U.S. Department of Justice
950 Pennsylvania Avenue, NW
Washington, D.C. 20530

(202) 514-2601
www.usdoj.gov/crimevictims.htm

For a national state directory of burial assistance programs,
see:
https://www.funerals360.com/ or watch the video at:
https://vimeo.com/257692375.

CHAPTER 15

Free Money From the IRS

All of the free money we prisoners got in the stimulus checks felt good, didn't it? Well, there are other ways the IRS tries to give back money. You just have to ask them for it.

Before we get into the actual ways to get FREE money from the IRS, I want to share some thoughts from some of the greatest thinkers ever.

"The avoidance of taxes is the only intellectual pursuit that carries any reward."

— John Maynard Keynes

Since the colonial days, Americans have been rebelling against paying taxes. Just like the founding fathers who organized the Boston Tea Party, the rich believe in their right to avoid taxes. But they don't have to start a revolution to do so, because the law is on their side. You can make it be on your side also. And it is your legal right to do so.

"Anyone may arrange his affairs so that his taxes shall be as low as possible; he is not bound to choose that pattern which best pays the Treasury. There is not even a patriotic duty to increase one's taxes. Over and over again the courts

have said that there is nothing sinister in so arranging affairs as to keep taxes as low as possible. Everyone does it, rich and poor alike and all do right, for nobody owes any public duty to pay more than the law demands."
— Judge Billings Learned Hand

So why don't more people learn how to lower their tax bills? Or get FREE money from the IRS? I don't understand it. But that's okay. We don't have to understand their thinking. All we have to do is understand the legal ways to get FREE money from the IRS. The poor call them tax loopholes. The rich call them tax credits or advantages. No matter what you call them, they are legal. And they can put FREE money back into your pocket or lower your tax bill. Let's look at some of them.

The IRS gives out an "Earned Income Tax Credit." Last I checked, it's anywhere from $500-$4,800. It depends on your circumstances. If you have two or more qualifying children, your EITC would've been $5,00 in 2009. If you had one qualifying child, it would've been $3,000. If you had no children, it was $457. This is free money. Everyone who doesn't meet the qualifying income limit is entitled to this tax credit! For more about this tax credit you need to get the free IRS publication *596: Earned Income Tax Credit.*

There are tons of other tax credits available. Too many for me to list. You can get tax credit for going to college. For buying a home. For saving money in an IRA (Individual Retirement Account).

One of the ways you can help out your baby mamas is to make sure they take advantage of the tax credits available to them. For instance, they can get money for what they pay in daycare costs. For a child under the age of 13 you can get up to 20% to 35% of those expenses. If their income is less than $15,000 a year, then they can get 35% of the daycare costs back. So, if they pay $4,000 a year in daycare costs, they can get $1,400 back. I bet that would make her happy if you showed her how to do that. You would need them to get an IRS Form #2441.

You can get a federal Lifetime Learning Tax Credit for taking any course that will improve your job skills. This credit is available for anyone who makes less than $100,000 and is up to $2,000. The Hope Scholarship Tax Credit is for anyone going to college for the first time who doesn't make more than $100,000 a year. You would need IRS Publication #970 for more information and Form #8863 to claim these credits.

I don't condone snitching. I'm doing life in prison because I wouldn't take a 20-year deal to testify against my rappy. But I know some of my fellow prisoners don't have a problem in doing it. The IRS will pay you 15%-30% (up to $20,000) of what they collect if you give them a tip on a tax cheat. Imagine if you were the one who turned in a millionaire for cheating on their taxes? Or a billionaire like Donald Trump? For more information you need IRS Publication #5251 "Whistleblower Award Claim." And to file an actual claim you would use IRS Form #211 "Application for Award for Original Information."

Don't forget to check your own state for tax credits. You may be able to get up to 50% of what you get from the federal EITC credit through your state as well. There's all kinds of tax credits available, depending on the state you live in. Here's some I've read about before:

$1,000+ for renters or homeowners in Wisconsin.
$300 for buying new appliances in Oregon.
$1,750 for installing solar panels in Hawaii.
$2,000 for seniors who pay property taxes in North Dakota.
$30,000 for fixing up an old home in North Carolina.
$250 if you donate to an extracurricular activity at a school in Arizona.

On the last point above, donating to 501(c)(3) non-profits is tax-deductible. I donate to the Education Justice Project in Illinois every year and they send me a receipt reminding me to claim my deduction on taxes. So, if you have a favorite charity that you donate to regularly, make sure you claim that deduction.

For those of you who are cellpreneurs making thousands of dollars (or more) a year from your cell, pay attention. You can deduct all your costs to do what you do. For instance, I'm a writer. So, all of my fees for books I bought while doing research, magazine subscriptions, pens, paper, and any other costs in regard to my book projects, I can deduct off my tax bill. For more information about how to do this you can read the following books:

Doing Business Tax Free: Perfectly Legal Techniques for Reducing or *Eliminating Your Federal Business Taxes* by Robert Cooke.

Tax Deductions for Professionals, 4th Edition by Stephen Fishman.

You can also get the following IRS Publications for FREE:

#1: Your Rights as a Taxpayer

#4: Student's Guide to Federal Income Tax

#17: Your Federal Income Tax for Individuals

#334: Tax Guide for Small Business

#448: Federal Estate and Gift Taxes

#501: Exemptions, Standard Deduction, and Filing Information

#502: Medical and Dental Expenses

#503: Child and Dependent Care Expenses

#504: Tax Information for Divorced or Separated Individuals

#505: Tax Withholding and Estimated Tax

#508: Education Expenses

#520: Scholarships and Fellowships

#521: Moving Expenses

#523: Tax Information on Selling Your Home

#524: Credit for the Elderly or the Disabled

#525: Taxable and Nontaxable Income

#526: Charitable Contributions

#529: Miscellaneous Deductions

#531: Reporting Income From Tips

#533: Self-Employment Tax

#535: Business Expenses

#536: Net Operating Losses

#538: Accounting Periods and Methods

#541: Tax Information on Partnerships

#542: Tax Information on Corporations

#547: Nonbusiness Disasters, Casualties, and Thefts

#550: Investment Income and Expenses

#552: Recordkeeping for Individuals

#554: Tax Information for Older Americans

#557: Tax-Exempt Status for Your Organization

#560: Self-Employed Retirement Plans

#583: Taxpayers Starting a Business

#587: Business Use of Your Home

#589: Tax Information on S Corporations

#590: Individual Retirement Arrangements (IRAs)

#596: Earned Income Credit

#598: Tax on Unrelated Business Income of Exempt Organizations

#907: Tax Highlights for Persons with Disabilities

#908: Tax Information on Bankruptcy

#911: Tax Information for Direct Sellers

#917: Business Use of a Car

#929: Tax Rules for Children and Dependents

#937: Employment Taxes

#947: Practice Before the IRS and Power of Attorney

#952: Sick Pay Reporting

#1544: Reporting Cash Payments of Over $10,000

www.irs.gov/*forms* and get whatever you need. No matter what, don't take no for an answer.

Internal Revenue Service
1111 Constitution Avenue NW
Washington, D.C. 20224
(202) 622-5000

CHAPTER 16
Americans With Disabilities

On February 16, 2000, my baby mama gave birth to two beautiful twin girls. They were premature and had complications. One is perfectly healthy. The other has been disabled her whole life and needs a wheelchair to get around. So, I can honestly say that I have loads of empathy for people with disabilities. For those of you who are disabled, or who have family and friends who are disabled, this chapter can help you out.

First and foremost, the federal American with Disabilities Act, 42 U.S.C. § 12101 et seq., and Section 504 of the Rehabilitation Act, 29 U.S.C. § 794, apply to prisoners. What these laws state is that people with disabilities have the same right to access programs, services, and activities as other people. And they cannot be discriminated against because of their disabilities. See *Crawford v. Indiana Dep't of Corrections*, 115 F.3d 481, 486 (7th Cir. 1997). And the Individuals with Disabilities in Education Act (IDEA) protects young prisoners with learning disabilities to have access to educational programs. See *Handberry v. Thompson*, 446 F.3d 335, 347-51 (2d Cir. 2006).

To take advantage of the ADA, you must generally be a "qualified individual with a disability." 42 U.S.C. § 12132. "Disability" under the ADA means:

(A)   A physical or mental impairment that
        substantially limits one or more of the major life
        activities of [an] individual;

(B)   A record of such impairment; or

(C)   Being regarded as having such an impairment
        (as described in paragraph (3)) 42 U.S.C. §
        12102(l).

In 2008, Congress passed the ADA Amendment Act which stated: "The definition of disability in this chapter shall be construed in favor of broad coverage of individuals under this chapter, to the maximum extent permitted by the terms of this chapter." 42 U.S.C. § 12102 (4)(A)

In their great handbook, *Prisoners' Self-Help Litigation Manual, 4th Edition,* John Boston and Daniel E. Manville do a superb job of breaking down prisoner rights under the ADA and RA. Most of this legal jargon that I'm using is based on what I learned from them, or by reading *Prison Legal News*. One could write a whole book about this subject. But one point I'd like to make here is that you don't have to be in a wheelchair to be considered "disabled." Here are some different ailments that the court considers a disability:

Drug addition – P.G. v. Jefferson County, 2021 U.S. Dist. Lexis 170593;

Colon medical issue – Rinehart v. Weitzell, 964 F.3d (8th Cir. 2020);

Neuromuscular disease – Fauconier v. Clarke, 966 F.3d 265 (4th Cir. 2020);

Deaf prisoner – Updike v. Multnomah, County, 870 F.3d 939 (9th Cir. 2017);

Front-cuffing permit – Kiman v. New Hampshire Dep't of Corrections, 451 F.3d 274, 288-89 (1st Cir. 20006);

HIV prisoner – McNally v. Prison health Services, 46 F.Supp. 2d 49, 58-59 (D. Me. 1999);

Blind prisoner – Kruger v. Jenne, 164 F.Supp. 2d 1330 (S.D. Fla. 2000);

Diabetes – Rouse v. Plantier, 997 F.Supp. 575, 582 (D.N.J. 1998);

Stomach and digestive problems – Scott v. Garcia, 370 F.Supp. 2d 1056, 1074-75 (S.D.Cal. 2005).

The above list is by no means exhaustive. You should Keycite® or Shepardize® the above cases to see the law in your Circuit. The key to all of the ADA and RA cases is that prison officials used the disability to discriminate against the prisoner. One warning though: if you are in a private prison that does not accept federal funding, the ADA doesn't apply. (See *Edison v. Douberly*, 604 F.3d 1307 (11th Cir. 2010).

Now that I got the legal stuff out of the way, we can look at some of the FREE money available to Americans with disabilities.

You can find lots of information on *www.disability.gov* or *disabilityinfo.gov*. You can also find all federal government programs that offer money for disabilities by searching the Catalog of Federal Domestic Assistance at *www.cfda.gov*. Here are some people who can also help:

Office of Special Education and Rehabilitation Services
U.S. Department of Education
400 Maryland Ave., SW
Washington, D.C. 20202-7100
(202) 245-7468
www.ed.gov/about/offices/list/osers/index.html

Disability Rights Education and Defense Fund (DREDF)
2212 Sixth St.
Berkeley, CA 94710

(510) 644-2555
www.dredf.org

There are several non-profits that help provide Assistance dogs to the disabled. Here are a few of them:

International Association of Assistance Dog Partners (IAADP)
38691 Filly Drive
Sterling Heights, MI 48310
(586) 826-3938
www.iaadp.org

Pilot Dogs, Inc.
625 West Town St.
Columbus, OH 43215
(614) 221-6367
www.pilotdogs.org

Southeastern Guide Dogs, Inc.
4210 77th St. East
Palmetto, FL 34221
1-800-944-2647
www.guidedogs.org

Guide Dog Foundation for the Blind
371 East Jericho Turnpike
Smithtown, NY 11787
1-800-548-4337
www.guidedog.org

Support Dogs, Inc.
11645 Lilbum Park Road
St. Louis, MO 63146

(314) 997-2325
www.supportdogs.org

PAWS WITH A CAUSE
National Headquarters
4646 South Division
Wayland, MI 49348
1-800-253-PAWS
www.pawswithacause.org

Loving Paws Assistance Dogs
P.O. Box 12005
Santa Rosa, CA 95406
(707) 586-0798
www.lovingpaws.com

Disabled Americans can get $1,000+ extra in their Social Security check from the Qualified Medicare Beneficiaries Plan or Specified Low-Income Medicare Beneficiaries Plan. To learn more, call the Social Security office at 1-800-772-1213. You can also contact the Medicare Hotline at 1-800-MEDICARE; *www.medicare.gov*.

$$ to buy a van, talking computer, or other helpful technology is available for the disabled. For more information you should check out:

RESNA
1700 North Moore St. #1540
Arlington, VA 22209
(703) 424-6686
www.resna.org

AAIDD
501 3rd Street NW, Suite 200

Washington, D.C. 20001
http://wwwaamr.org/

The ARC
National Headquarters
1825 K Street NW, Suite 1200
Washington, D.C. 20006
https://www.thearc.org

American Association of People with Disabilities
2013 H Street NW, 5th Floor
Washington, D.C. 20006
https://www.aapd.com/

IAC
150 W. 30th Street, 15th Floor
New York, NY 10001
https://www.iacny.org/

Dreamscape Foundation
5629 Strand Boulevard #404
Naples, FL 34110
https://dreamscapefoundation.org

Sprout
270 West 96th Street
New York, NY 10025
https://gosprout.org

Council for Exceptional Children
2900 Crystal Drive, Suite 100
Arlington, VA 22202-3557
https://www.cec.sped.org/

Yesterday's Children
360 Main Street
Ellsworth, ME 04605
https://www.ycimaine.org

One area where there are lots of grants of FREE money available is for housing for the disabled. You should contact your local community development office to find out what all is available. If you can't find it, try to get it through these:

National Association of Housing and Redevelopment Officials
630 Eye St., NW
Washington, D.C. 20001
(202) 289-3500
www.nahro.org

Information Center
Office of Community Planning and Development
P.O. Box 7189
Gaithersburg, MD 20898
1-800-998-9999
www.comcon.org

The Section 911 program from HUD provides funding to non-profits to develop rental housing for adults with disabilities. It's called "Supportive Housing for Persons With Disabilities 911." Contact your local HUD office or check it out online: *www.hud.gov/offices.*

HUD also offers a Shelter Plus Care Program that provides rental assistance to people with disabilities or chronic illnesses. Your state housing authority, local government, or public housing agency can apply for the funds. You would have to get your money from them.

Rebuilding Together helps renovate homes for the disabled FREE of charge. They build ramps, grab bars, and other fixes. They are a national non-profit organization. Check them out at:

Rebuilding Together
1536 Sixteenth Street, NW
Washington, D.C. 20036-1042
(202) 483-9083
https://www.rebuildingtogether.org

So does the UCP's Architectural Barrier Removal Program. For more information you can contact:

United Cerebral Palsy (UCP) National
1660 L Street, NW, Suite 700
Washington, D.C. 20036
1-800-872-5827
https://www.ucp.org

No matter what, do not let any disability stop you or your loved one from your dream life. The law is on your side. So are the organizations in this chapter.

CHAPTER 17

Free Money For Prison Picassos

The book I wrote before this one is called *Prison Picasso*. It shows cellpreneurs how to get real money from arts and crafts. The main thing I learned in my research for that book is that "starving artist" is a choice. Artists have plenty of opportunities to get FREE money if you know where to look. In this chapter I'll give you some tips to get assistance if you're an artist.

The two most important government agencies that offer money for artists are as follows:

National Endowment of the Arts
400 7th Street SW
Washington, D.C. 20506-0001
(203) 682-5400
www.arts.gov

National Endowment for the Humanities (NEH)
400 7th Street SW
Washington, D.C. 20506
(202) NEH-1121
www.negh.gov

One of the biggest sources of information for finding grants from non-profit organizations is:

The Foundation Center
79 Fifth Avenue
New York, NY 10003
(212) 620-4230
www.fdncenter.org

In her book, *Guide To Getting Arts Grants*, Ellen Liberatori suggests you should focus on the Foundation Center because it is "the most comprehensive research entity" for philanthropy. You can go to their website and to the "Find Funders" section.

Some other places you could search online are the following:

Grants.gov – Search for "arts," "grants for artists")
The Catalog of Federal Domestic Assistance (www.cfda.gov) (This is a searchable database of information about federal assistance.)

Any time you find an e-mail sign-up page for a foundation or nonprofit, or government agency that gives out grants, sign up. That way you are notified anytime a new grant is offered. Here are some of the grants that have been awarded in the past to people in the arts. You can check to see if they are still available.

$10,000 To Teach Art To Kids

Contact the following if you think you can utilize this grant:

U.S. Department of Education
Improvement Programs
400 Maryland Ave., S.W.
Washington, D.C. 20202-6140
(202) 260-2487
www.ed.gov/programs/artsed/index.html

$23,000 For Photo Exhibit

Sixth Street Photography Workshop was awarded $23,000 to produce a photography exhibit by the National Endowment for the Arts. Maybe you could be next.!

$200,000 To Make An Independent Film

Congress established the Independent Television Service to fund and present innovative public television programs. The ITVS has an "Open Call" where independent producers can propose single public television programs on any subject. For more information contact:

Independent Television Service
501 York Street
San Francisco, CA 94110
(415) 356-8303
www.itvs.org/producers

$20,000 To Produce A Film

The Miller Brewer Company (Yes, the beer company) has awarded business grants of $20,000 to make a film and $2,500 for other business ventures. They have a "Miller Urban Entrepreneurs Business Grant Competition" where people aged

21-30 can get grants for business ideas. For more information contact:

Miller Brewing Company
3939 W. Highland Blvd.
Milwaukee, WI 53208
(414) 931-2000
www.millerbrewing.com/inthecommunity/urbanbusinessgrant.asp

$5,000 To Make Comic Books

The Xeric Foundation wants to help comic book creators with some of the costs in self-publishing their work. I know some of my comrades have comic book/graphic novel dreams. Maybe this grant could be the catalyst that gets you started. Check them out at:

Xeric Foundation
351 Pleasant St.
PMB 214
Northampton, MA 01060-3900
(413) 585-0671
www.xericfoundation.com

$50,000 to $300,000 to Make a Film

The more I write this the more I realize that I should have never gone into crime. Instead, I should have got these grants and became the next Spike Lee or Michael Moore. Another foundation gives out grants to independent documentary films or series. For more about this grant, contact:

John D. and Catherine T. MacArthur Foundation

140 S. Dearborn St., Suite 1100
Chicago, IL 60603-5285
(312) 726-8000
www.macfound.org

$100,000+ for Songwriters

This grant is based on the legacy of Johnny Mercer. It aims to assist songwriters in developing their talents and help educate the public for music appreciation. Before you approach this foundation, you should search for "Johnny Mercer" on your tablet and listen to his music. I doubt any rappers or death metal would get this grant. For more information, check out:

The Johnny Mercer Foundation
c/o Prager and Fenton
675 3rd Avenue
New York, NY 10017
(212) 382-2790
www.johnnymercerfoundation.org/

$30,000 Grants for Visual Artists

This foundation below gives grants of up to $30,000 to individuals interested in media, communications, and the visual arts. They aim to promote artistic development. To learn more, you should contact the following:

The Penny McCall Foundation, Inc.
163 E. 81st St., Apt. 10A
New York, NY 10028
(212) 988-9714

$2,500 to Dance, Art or Take Photos

This foundation encourages emerging artists in these fields, especially music, theater, dance, and photography. They want to help artists whose works might have difficulty being aired because of the genre and/or social philosophy. Sounds to me like an avenue where a former prisoner could fit in at. Check them out at:

Puffin Foundation Ltd.
20 East Oakdene Avenue
Teaneck, NJ 07666-4111
www.puffinfoundation.org

$6,000 for Women Artists in Kentucky

This program provides grants to feminist artists to be used for artistic development and the exploration of new areas and/or techniques. They have the Artist Enrichment Program and the Art Meets Activism Program. Any female artists in Kentucky should contact this foundation to learn more:

Kentucky Foundation for Women
1215 Keyburn Building
332 West Broadway
Louisville, KY 40202-2184
(502) 562-0045
www.kfw.org

Attention: NYC and Los Angeles Filmmakers

Do you want to produce a film or video in New York City or Los Angeles? The below foundation offers the following grants:

The Roy W. Dean New York City Film Grant
The Roy W. Dean Los Angeles Video Grant
The Roy W. Dean Los Angeles Film Grant

For more information you should contact the following:

From the Heart Productions
Attn: Roy W. Dean Film and Video Grants
1455 Mandalay Beach Road
Oxnard, CA 93035-2845
(866) 689-5150
www.fromtheheartproductions.com/grant

$10,000 for Native American Artists

In the past, the Kookyangw Fund has provided grants to Native American graphic and visual artists. To see if they are still assisting Native American artists, you should contact the:

First Nations Development Institute
2300 Fall Hill Ave., Suite 412
Fredericksburg, VA 22401
(540) 371-5615
www.firstnations.org

$5,000 for Women Filmmakers

Are you a female who wants to complete a documentary, or animated film, or experimental video that promotes equal opportunities for women? Then the Film Finishing Fund offers cash awards to support independent and nonprofit women filmmakers. For more information, contact:

Women in Film Foundation
8857 W. Olympic Blvd., Ste. 201
Beverly Hills, CA 90211
(310) 657-5154
www.wif.org

Money for Artists Living with HIV/AIDS

The Visual AIDS Artist Material Grants are awarded to low-income artists living with AIDS/HIV who need money to obtain materials for their artwork. For more information, contact:

Visual AIDS
526 W. 26th St. #510
New York, NY 10001
(212) 627-9855
www.visualaids.org

$350 to $1,000 Grants for Sculptors

Are you an artist with a commitment to sculpture? Then you may qualify for this award. Check it out at:

National Sculpture Society, Inc.
237 Park Ave.
New York, NY 10017
(212) 764-5645
www.nationalsculpture.org/scholarships.asp

$5,000 to $10,000 to Individual Artists

Do you have exceptions talent, but no funding to pursue your art? Then you may qualify for a Tanne Award. To see if you do, you should contact the following:

Tanne Foundation
c/o Grants Management Associates
77 Summer Street
Boston, MA 02110
(617) 426-7172
www.tannefoundation.org

Grants for Emerging Artists and Craftspeople

If you're an artist or craftsperson whose work shows promise, but haven't got critical or commercial acclaim, you could get a grant. This foundation offers money every two years to artists, sculptors, photographers, crafters, and visual media. To learn more, contact the:

The Louis Comfort Tiffany Foundation
c/o Artists Space
38 Greene St., 3rd Floor
New York, NY 10013
https://louiscomforttiffanyfoundation.org/grants_program.htm

Here are some more foundations that give money to artists. You can check with them to see if they are a fit for what you're doing.

New Earth Foundation
2940 Southwest Drive, Suite 4A
Sedona, AZ 86336

(928) 204-1151
www.newearthfoundation.org

The Wallace Foundation
2 Park Ave., 23rd Floor
New York, NY 10016
(212) 251-9700
www.wallacefunds.org

The Lifebridge Foundation, Inc.
P.O. Box 793
Time Square Station
New York, NY 10108
(212) 757-9711
www.lifebridge.org/mission.htm

Film Arts Foundation
145 Ninth Street
San Francisco, CA 94103
(415) 552-8760
www.filmarts.org

The Jerome Foundation
125 Park Square Court
400 Sibley Street
St. Paul, MN 55101-1928
(651) 224-9431
www.jeromefdn.org

Creative Capital
15 Maiden Lane, 18th Floor
New York, NY 10038
https://creative-capital.org

Black Rock Arts Foundation
1900 Third Street, 2nd Floor
San Francisco, CA 94107
(415) 626-1248
www.blackrockarts.org

Elizabeth Greenshields Foundation
https://www.elizabethgreenshieldsfoundation.org/

Artwork Archive
P.O. Box 181185
Denver, CO 80218
https://www.artworkarchive.com
(Publishes a guide to grants and opportunities.)

I found an older version of the *Catalog of Federal Domestic Assistance* and here are some of the previous grants available to artists through the National Endowment for the Arts. (The number listed next to the title is the reference number in the *Catalog*. It still may be available.)

45.001 — $25,000 for Graphic Artists and Product Designers
45.007 — $37,500 To Exhibit a Local Art Show
45.009 — $20,000 For Painters, Sculptors, and Craft Artists
45.011 — Money For Regional Art Programs
45.022 — Money For Arts Groups To Have Better Management

The National Endowment for the Arts also gives millions of dollars to each state for their own grants to hand out. Most of these state art councils add their funding to it to make the pot even bigger. And some cities and towns have local art organizations that support artists. In my hometown, they had the Danville Art League. You need to find all of the places that you possibly could belong to. Most states' art councils require that you be a resident in that state to qualify. The same for local art leagues. Your local library could tell you where your local art council is. Or you can call "211" and ask them. Your state has an official website also. You can find your state's art council on it.

No matter what, do not give up. There is money out there for artists. You just have to find it. If you are serious about making money from arts and crafts while in prison, you need to get my book *Prison Picasso: The Millionaire Prisoners' Way To Sell Arts & Crafts* (Freebird Publishers). If you want to know more about getting an art grant, I highly recommend the following:

Guide To Getting Arts Grants by Ellen Liberator
Free Money for People in the Arts, Second Edition by Laurie Blum

The above books predate the internet advancements somewhat. But that is why they are perfect for a prisoner without access to the internet. You can learn how to do it by snail mail and by telephone. But no matter what, do not give up. Free money for artists is out there. You just have to find it. Then apply to get it.

CHAPTER 18

Free Crowdfunding Money

Need money for a lawyer? To publish your book? Buy art supplies or any other legit project you have going on? Crowdfunding presents opportunities for prisoners! In this chapter we shall explore these opportunities and give you some tips on how to take advantage of them.

Crowdfunding websites provide an interesting option for prisoners with imagination and originality to explore career-expanding opportunities, raise money and gain access to a commodity often in short supply behind bars—hope.

Basically, crowdfunding involves developing online campaigns for specific projects, charitable causes or services, or to develop certain products. People who want to support a campaign can donate funds from as little as $1 to as much as they want. Hundreds, thousands, or even tens of thousands of people may join together to support and fund a campaign, and once a project achieves its target funding amount, the money is paid to the campaign organizer so they can make the project a reality.

Before we get into the logistics of the "how-to" behind a successful crowdfunding campaign here are some examples of projects that benefitted prisoners:

$5,700 campaign to produce "Amazing Grace" by women in a New York prison.
$582 to finance a creative writing class at the Garner Correctional Institution in Connecticut.

$15,000 campaign through IndieGoGo by the Human Rights Defense Center to fund the Prison Ecology Project to fight toxic prisons.

$2,600 campaign by Claudia Whitman with the CURE's National Death Row Assistance Network to help fund a wrongful conviction investigation on behalf of Michigan prisoner Lacino Hamilton.

Since March 2014, the Cook County Jail has run a 10-week culinary program involving a small group of prisoners to help them learn marketable skills and obtain jobs in the food service industry upon their release. Chef Bruno Abate, an Italian native wo runs the program, called "Recipe for Change," became inspired after learning about an award-winning bakery at the Due Palazzi prison in Padua, Italy. In May of 2015, Abate wanted to take the culinary program to the next level. "When you know how to make pizza well, you can find a job anywhere," he said. Abate joined forces with prominent businessman Ronald Gidwitz to buy a pizza oven for the program. They raised almost $5,000 through an IndieGoGo campaign and another $11,000 through Gidwitz's personal network and were able to buy a top-of-the-line oven. They hope to eventually bake and sell pizzas to hungry customers outside the jail.

I'm sure you've seen more stores on TV or read about them in magazines. About how some people have used crowdfunding websites to raise money. Author Set Godin raised $287,342 for one of his book projects. Brainard Carey, and his wife Delina, raised $16,000 in 2011 for their non-visible art concept. Singer Amanda Palmer raised $1 million on crowdfunding. Tim Schafer's video game project received over $1 million in its first 24 hours, and ultimately got more than $3.3 million in pledges! The money is out there, you just have to know where to go to get it.

What Actually is Crowdfunding?

Crowdfunding is a way to raise money for a specific cause or project by asking a large number of people to donate small amounts of money in a relatively short period of time. Crowdfunding is done online where it's easy for supporters to share a cause or project with their social networks. Organizations, businesses, and individual people alike can all use crowdfunding for any type of project.

There are two main models of crowdfunding:

1. Donation-based funding, where donors contribute to a total amount for a cause or project. Normally in the model, the donors are promised a small gift in return for helping out.
2. Investment crowdfunding, where businesses seeking capital, sell ownership stakes online in the form of equity or debt. In this model, individuals who fund these businesses then become owners or shareholders and have a potential for financial return, unlike in the donation model. This became possible when Title II of the Jobs Act went into effect in 2013.

The JOBS Act

The JOBS Act was a new crowdfunding law that stands for "Jumpstart Our Business Startups (JOBS)." The JOBS Act lets businesses raise up to $1 million a year from crowdfunding without having to sell stock in an initial private offering (IPO). This law allows businesses to tell people about their funding needs without the complicated restrictions that used to be in place when a company offered its stock for sale. Besides the $1 million per year from crowdfunding, here are some other guidelines under the new law:

People who make up to $100,000 a year can contribute up to $2,000 or 5% of their yearly income to a company seeking funding.
People who make over $100,000 a year can contribute up to 10% of their yearly income to a company seeking funding, and
Businesses can only sell shares to the public through a middleman such as a broker or a website.

The ideas behind these changes in the law come from the still-new concepts of "microloans" and "person-to-person" or "peer-to-peer" (P2P) lending. These methods help you get large numbers of small amounts of money from many people. That, in itself, can be easier than getting one or two big loans from one lender or person.

Now that you know what crowdfunding actually is, we can look at where you should go to take part in it.

The Major Crowdfunding Platforms

There are thousands of crowdfunding platforms online. There are main crowdfunding websites, like Kickstarter and Indiegogo. There are also niche crowdfunding websites, like Pubslush and Smallknot. Let's look at some of them.

www.indiegogo.com

Indiegogo launched in 2007 and has raised millions of dollars since. It is open to any kind of project, anywhere in the world. Indiegogo offers plenty of tools and support to track your project. One of the things that I like best about Indiegogo is that you get to keep all the money you raised from your campaign (minus fees), even if you don't reach your fundraising goal. If you choose that plan, you'll pay 5% of whatever you get, plus 3% credit card processing fee.

www.kickstarter.com

Kickstarter launched in 2009 and is used to fund projects under such categories as art, design, film, games, music, food, photography, etc. It is not the platform for causes, charities, businesses and personal funding. I'm familiar with Kickstarter because a lot of authors have used it to fund their book projects. Kickstarter is the site Seth Godin used to raise $287,342 for one of his book projects. Kickstarter has 130+ people working for them and has helped fund 150,000+ projects. If you don't meet your goal, you don't get to keep any of the money. Kickstarter charges 5% commission plus 3-5% for credit card processing fees.

www.gofundme.com

GoFundMe is another famous crowdfunding site. It's different from Indiegogo or Kickstarter, in that you don't have to give perks (like a free copy of the book) to get financial help. GoFundMe has been used for more individual causes like school tuition, medical bills, travel expenses, or emergency housing. You can create a campaign for yourself or a family member or friend. GoFundMe does not charge a platform fee to run your campaign, but there is a standard payment processing fee deducted from the amount donated.

www.pubslush.com

Pubslush is a unique crowdfunding platform for only one category: books. One thing that I really like about Pubslush is that they advocate literacy by giving books to children in need.

www.publishizer.com

They call themselves "the first crowdfunding literacy agency." What you would do is put a book proposal online through Publishizer, with a short video to get pre-orders. Publishizer gets a 30% commission on pre-orders, but nothing once the book is published. If you get 500 pre-orders or more, you may attract one of the bigger publishers.

www.moola-hoop.com

This site is mainly used to help female entrepreneurs start and grow their small businesses. Moola-Hoop was founded by former IBM executives Brenda Bazan and Nancy Hayes. Unlike other platforms, Moola-Hoop doesn't have an all-or-nothing goal system. Instead, they allow women to reach milestones in the campaign. Once a milestone is reached, the campaign is funded up to that amount, where Moola-Hoop take a percentage.

www.patreon.com

Patreon is a little different than other crowdfunding platforms. On Patreon, funding is done on a continuum. You would create your project campaign and then offer different levels of investment. Depending on the level ($5 a month, $10 a month, etc.) you should have different levels of rewards for patrons, depending on how much they sign up for. Patreon takes a 5% fee on the revenue you generate.

www.smallknot.com

Smallknot was created by a securities lawyer on Wall Street who saw a way to keep crowdfunding in your neighborhood. Smallknot allows small businesses who are struggling. Instead of taking out a loan for 15,000, they can start a campaign on Smallknot. In return for donations, business owners promise to pay back the donations with products or services. Smallknot only charges a 3% fee.

www.appbackr.com

Everyone has heard the story. Someone got rich off developing the next great app. Are you a techie? Well, Appbackr is the crowdfunding site for app developers to find backers willing to help fund their project. Maybe this is the website for you.

www.fundable.com

Another crowdfunding site for small businesses. Fundable is an "all or nothing" platform, so if you don't reach your goal, you don't get nothing. Backers can either get rewards or equity in the business. You normally get 60-90 days to reach your goals.

www.hatchfund.org

Hatchfund is a charitable organization that helps fund projects towards art. Not just visual art like paintings, but also dance, theater, literature, music, and even architecture.

www.rockethub.com

RocketHub is another famous website because they've helped governments, educators, and communities in partnership to get the goals funded. RocketHub is open to any kind of project.

www.crowdfunder.com

Crowdfunder focuses on connecting entrepreneurs with investors through a global social network. Local business owners can use Crowdfunder to meet nearby angel investors in online and offline events.

These are just a few of the crowdfunding websites that I know about. But like I said earlier, there are thousands of them. Before you decide which crowdfunding website you will use, I highly recommend that you visit a great research website called *www.CrowdsUnite.com*. CrowdsUnite is the largest user review website in the world for crowdfunding platforms. No better place to get info on a site you want to use than from the actual users who have gone before you.

To help you reach your funding goals I will n ow share with you how a cellpreneur can set up a successful crowdfunding campaign.

The Successful Crowdfunding Plan

The first step is to understand that numerous people before you have been successful using these sites for their own projects. A prisoner I know used Kickstarter to raise a few hundred dollars so he could buy art supplies off the commissary. So, the first step is believing it's possible.

Here are the other steps to help make it more probable:

(1) *Pick the Right Platform*—As mentioned above, different crowdfunding sites have slight differences in how they fund, how you can promote, the fees they charge, and what types of projects they accept. For instance, on Kickstarter you have to wait till your goal is reached to get your money. But other sites, like IndieGoGo, allow you to choose to access the funds as they are raised. Some sites charge 3% in fees, others charge 5% plus credit card processing fees. The other issue is can you use YouTube and other social networks to promote your campaign. Or do you have to go through the crowdfunding site? All of these areas should be researched before you use a site.

(2) *Build A Network Ahead of Time*—It would be much easier to meet your funding goals if you have a built-in network of supporters. That's how singer Amanda Palmer raised $1 million. It's how Jerry McLaughlin and Rebecca Crowell raised $45,000 for their art book project. They used their Facebook community of artists and e-mail list of over 4,000 people. You should use the tips in *TMP4: Pen Pal Mastery* build this community.

(3) *Make Sure People Know What the Money is For*—This is key. Be specific. For instance, if you need money for art supplies, list them. Don't say, "I need $200 for art supplies." Say, "I need $200 total for the following art supplies." Then list each specific art supply and cost. If it's an art book project, like a comic book or even a how-to book, list each cost along with the total goal. You must do the research ahead of time and know exactly what you need the money for so you can tell your network.

(4) *Make Perks Easy and Simple*—It's normal practice for donors to get something in return for backing your project, or cause. You want these perks to be simple with different levels. Let's say you were requesting money for at supplies. You could give the following benefits:

$10 donation gets a public thank-you on Facebook.
$25 donation gets a hand-painted greeting card.
$50 donation gets a small painting.
$100 donation gets an 18 x 24 watercolor painting.

That's how you can do it. Make sure you are specific, so everyone knows ahead of time.

(5) *Post Updated to Donors*—Let people know and see your progress. For one, it's good karma. Two, you never know where a connection could go. Maybe you'll need more funds down the road. If a donor is happy with how you used the money the first time, they may back other projects in the future.

(6) *Use Video*—Most successful campaigns use a video to allow possible donors to see who and what they are giving money to. Pay attention to the next chapter, *How to Walk On Clouds by Using Videos.*

There you have it. A crash course on a successful crowdfunding campaign. Of course, you'll need someone on the outside to help you with this tactic. But don't let someone tell you it's impossible. Prisoners are using crowdfunding sites to get money for their causes and projects. Maybe you can do it also. Do your research first. Then go get the funding to achieve your dreams.

CAUTION-WARNING

Many prisons and jails have institutional rules that make crowdfunding projects difficult, if not impossible. Some have regulations that prevent prisoners from receiving funds from other prisoners, parolees or individuals not related to them. Others prohibit prisoners from having checking or savings accounts and deduct expenses for the cost of incarceration from money placed in their prison trust accounts. This is why most crowdfunding campaigns for prisoners and prison-related projects are usually organized and run by friends, family, and other contacts outside of prison.

Recommended Reading

For more information about how to use crowdfunding and other websites not mentioned in this chapter you can read the following:

The Crowdfunding Book by Patty Lennon
Step by Step Crowdfunding by Joseph Hogue
The Crowdfunding Bible by Scott Steinberg
A Crowdfunder's Strategy Guide by Jamey Stegmaier

No matter what, don't allow lack of funding to stop you.

CHAPTER 19

How to Walk On Clouds by Using Videos

In *The Crowdfunding Bible,* by Scott Steinberg, with Rusel DeMaria, they talk about the importance of "creating powerful online videos." Here's what they say: "Once upon a time, video production was the sole province of broadcast professionals. Nowadays, it's accessible to lone individuals working out of a spare bedroom or garage. Happily, for crowdfunding enthusiasts, assembling eye-catching clips doesn't have to cost a small fortune or even require hiring a dedicated cameraman." So true. And in this chapter, I'll give you all the tips you need to create an effective online video.

> *"When it comes to marketing online, the most powerful form of content is videos."*
> – Thomas Meloche

Most of what I wrote in *The Millionaire prisoner 3: Success University* (ps. 157-169) about using online videos to walk on clouds is still true to this day. I'll include most of that advice in this chapter also. But I'll also give you some additional tips that I've learned as well. Before I get into the actual "how-to" behind a successful video, let me share some information that will illustrate the power of videos.

In *The Copywriter's Handbook, 4th Edition*, my mentor Robert Bly wrote: "Video is taking over marketing and the world. According to a study by Cisco, in 2019 video will have accounted for up to 90% of all online traffic. And consumers are 85% more likely to buy your product after viewing your video."

Prison Lifestyle Video Succe$$

Some prisoners have had their 15 minutes of fame because of their videos going viral. Omar Broadway shot some raw prison footage on a contraband cellphone. HBO® picked up that video and turned it into a whole show. Of course, we can't talk about videos without talking about YouTube.

The publishing gods have a funny way of showing us writers stuff we should know. As I was putting the finishing touches on that online video chapter in *TMP3: Success University*, I got the July 2020 *Prison Legal News* in the mail. Anthony Accurso wrote an article titled, "The Popularity of YouTube Prison Lifestyle Videos." He detailed how Joe Guerrero has 1.2 million YouTube subscribers to his *After Prison Show*. After 700 videos, which started out as grainy amateurish vlogs (video + blog = vlog), he now earns six-figures as a social media influencer. His most popular video about how to make a tattoo gun got 2.3 million views. Christina Randall is a former prisoner that has 400,000 subscribers to her YouTube channel and most of them are women. Marcus "Big Herc" Timmons has become a social media star based off his videos and now makes a living speaking. People have always been, and always will be, fascinated by prisons, prison life and culture. Think of how well MSNBC's *Lock Up* WE channel's *Love After Lockup*, and C&I's *The Big House* do.

Speaking of *Love After Lockup*, I was recently watching their new show, *Love During Lockup*, and saw how one prisoner used a Jpay video on TikTok to meet the love of his life. Just more proof on the power of online videos.

At the end of King Guru's *Pretty Girls Love Bad Boys* he wrote: "If you can get someone to go on Facebook, Snapchat, or Instagram, look us up! Maybe once you see the blogs and pictures of how we're really living inside of these level 4 prisons then you'll know for yourself that everything that comes from The Cell Block is authentic. Maybe that's what it'll take for some of you to wholeheartedly follow our advice and finally start getting everything life has to offer." The key to what he said is "vlogs." Like other prisoners, you could start with YouTube or TikTok.

Steve Stockman is a writer and director of short films, commercials, music videos and TV shows. He wrote and directed the award-winning 2007 MGM feature film *Two Weeks*, starring Sally Field and Ben Chaplin. His website is *stevestockman.com*. Here's what he says about video in his great book, *How to Shoot Video That Doesn't Suck*, "Great video is a communication tool of unparalleled impact. It can change history, inspire movements, share and amplify emotions, and build community. Bad video is turned off. Nobody watches a bad video. Not your employee, even if you tell them to. Not your parents, even if you send them 'the cutest' video of your kids."

With all of this in mind, how can a prisoner use video to get FREE money? Here are some ideas:

Post a video of yourself online to get pen pals.
Sell more books or arts and crafts.
Use it as a supplement to an application or resumé.
Start a prison vlog to get more publicity.
Have other people give you testimonials and videos that support your expertise or product.

These are just some ideas. The sky is the limit. Just because you don't have lots of money doesn't mean you should skip this avenue of success. Not if you want to stand out. Even if you have to start out by having a family member or friend record your video visit and then post it online. Or having said family member, friend, or client/customer post a video to TikTok as a testimonial about you. Videos can change the game for you.

"You'll still be posting photos and writing posts, but nothing builds trust and value more than video."
— Keith Krance, founder of Dominate Web Media

How to Make Videos That Get Viewed

The best videos entertain the audience. They offer intrigue. Leaving the audience seeking more and wanting to know what happens next. So, the first key to video success is to know who our audience is. To make the best possible video ask yourself the following questions:

1. Who is your target audience?
2. What do you want the video to accomplish?
3. Who are you?
4. What is your product or project?
5. How is your background relevant to this project
6. Why should a viewer trust you?
7. What's so special about your project?
8. How will this product/project change the niche you're trying to reach?
9. What does your product/project look like?
10. How long will it take (if not done already)?
11. How will you use their money?
12. What rewards do people get for donating their money?

I got most of those questions from *The Crowdfunding Book,* by Patty Lennon. Answer these questions and put yourself in your viewer's place. Try to imagine what they'll feel when they watch your video. As Steve Stockman says, "The most memorable home videos and documentaries tell stories. Those stories don't just magically appear in the edit room. You have to imagine them before you start shooting." So, what's the story you're trying to tell?

Once you know who you're making your video for and what you want to accomplish, you must decide which kind of video you want to use. There are four main types of videos. They are:

1. A video testimonial
2. An interview video
3. The promotional video, and
4. The hot-to video

Each one has its own rules and best practices. Let's look at them.

The Video Interview

I've put this one first because it's something a prisoner could do easiest. Have your family member or friend record your interview through a video visit. Prepare ahead of time what you want them to ask you and what you'll say. Both of you should be relaxed and go with the flow. If both of you trust each other the interview will be better. here are some tips to remember:

Don't look at the screen or yourself in the corner of the screen. Look at the camera lens when answering questions. That way you'll be looking directly at the person watching your interview.

If you can, stand up during the interview. For one, it helps your voice. But two, it looks better on the Jpay and GTL video visit terminals. If you can't stand up, make sure you sit up straight. No slouching!

Try to use one of the prison clip-on desk lamps to help illuminate your face more. I clip mine on the back of the video terminal and point it at my face. My wife say it makes me look a whole lot healthier than just the regular bad cellhouse lighting.

If it's the other way around and you're conducting an interview, think about the following things:

Background. Because it matters. For instance, if they are an artist, have them sit in their studio. Are they an author? Have them sit in a library or with books behind them. Don't have them sit where people will be walking behind them. They are not newscaster.

Watch good documentaries on TV and see how the backgrounds are carefully chosen to fit the image of the person being interviewed. Remember, it's all about the story you're trying to tell, even in a video interview.

The Promotional Video

What are you trying to promote? Who is it for? Do they already know you? Or is it the first time they are meeting you? Try to think about your target audience (or your customer/client's) needs. Build a relationship with the viewer, not a sale. If you're selling a product or service, use a video sales letter (VSL). More on those in a minute.

If it's a video to promote you or your project in the hopes of getting donations on a crowdfunding site, remember these tips from Patty Lennon in *The Crowdfunding Book*:

Pick one tone, form, or topic for each video. Is it a behind-the-scenes documentary? A comedy skit? use that throughout the whole video.
Capture your audience's attention right away. Go big in the 5 to 15 seconds of the video.
Your crowdfunding video shouldn't be that long. 2-3 minutes in length maximum is best.
Keep it simple, stupid. 1-3 key bullet points. And don't repeat over and over.
Use the "TLC" tip for your video pitch. That stands for:
    T = Touch their heart and make them think.
    L = Make them laugh.
    C = Make them care (bonus points for making them cry.)
Add value to your viewer's life. If you're an author—give a tip from your book. If you're an artist/crafter—showcase an innovative technique. Got a prototype product? Do a demonstration video.
Make sure you have a call to action at the end of your video. A simple: "Donate by _____ to receive an exclusive reward of _____."
Try to have 10-15 seconds of testimonials. You can simply lead into them by saying: "But don't just take my word for it, take a look at what others are saying . . .

The Video Testimonial

I love watching late night/early morning infomercials. Not because I can buy from them. I can't, and never have. I watch them to learn tricks that I might be able to use in my own marketing. Especially now that I've studied video making. The best infomercials use testimonials. There's a long-form infomercial on right now where Larry King interviews a "credit secrets" book author. It uses a lot of testimonials. We know it works because they keep running it over and over again. I would love to be able to do that for my books and play them on the institution channels of many prisons across America. If you can utilize video testimonials, you'll get more FREE money donated to your cause.

The How-To Video

Use demonstration and explain only one thing per video. Think about Joe Guerrero's 2.3 million-viewed how-to-make-a-prison-tattoo-gun video. It's about one topic. Show your audience who you are and what you need money for. Think "show and tell" from grade school. Don't get distracted and off topic. If it doesn't pertain to the topic of the video, it shouldn't be in the video. When explaining things, try not to use jargon or long convoluted sentences. Do it like you were explaining it and showing it to a kid. Then at the end of your video you can include your "call-to-action."

The Video Sales Letter (VSL)

Video sales letters are used in several different ways. They can be used on the home page to see what you want visitors to your website to do. These are typically short 2-3 minutes or less in length. VSLs can also be used on second level pages on your website. These videos are longer, typically 5-7 minutes. Lastly, there are long form VSLs. These run anywhere from 14-45 minutes. When thinking about time and length of your videos, use your TV as a gauge of what's proper.

TV commercials are normally 30-second stories. A network hour is 44 minutes long. That leaves time for the network to put in commercial breaks. A movie trailer is normally 2-1/2 minutes long. Infomercials are either 30 minutes or 1 hours long. Here's how you compute those numbers into words when you write your video script.

Normally, it's 120 words per minute. So, a 30-second commercial will have 60 words. There can be more if the speaker talks rapidly. A 10-minute script would have 1,200 words. A 45-minute script would have 7,000 words. Once you write out your script you can use a voice-over estimate to see how long it will be. Upload your script at: *https://www.thevoicerealm.com/count-script.php*.

9 Rules For Creating an Effective VSL

When creating a pitch video, you are marketing. You're selling yourself and your project. Your video is your VSL. So, someone has to write the script. Here are master copywriter Robert Bly's nine rules for creating an effective VSL. You can find these in his book, *The Copywriter's Handbook, 4th Edition*:

1. Grab the audience's attention.
1. Tell an engaging story.
2. Keep it simple.
3. Use short sentences and words. No words with more than 9 letters.
4. Use short paragraphs of only 2 or 3 sentences.
5. If you have to prove a claim or fact, do it by inserting a chart or graph.
6. Explain the solution within the first minute or two.
7. Don't use more than two numbers in each sentence.
8. Use a positive and enthusiastic voice. But it should also sound authoritative.

Based off everything I have wrote so far, here's a fill-in-the-blank script you could use in an online video to seek donations.

"Hi, I'm _____, author (or creator) of _____. I've got a free _____ that's going to show you how to _____. If you've been struggling with _____, then you need this _____ because it will _____.

"Just donate $_____ and fill out the form on the side of this page. Let me know your shipping address, and I'll send it out right away.

"There's no catch. I'm doing this because I need the money so we can _____.

"I only have a very limited number of copies, so don't be left behind. This offer ends at midnight on _____, 2022. Don't wait.

"I know you'll be pleased. But don't just take my word for it, take a look at what others are saying about _____."

That's a possible script. Not that hard. The key to the one above would be giving them a reward for donating money. You should have different gifts for different levels of donation. Just remember, you're not directly selling them stuff. You're just giving them a FREE gift in return for their donation. A fair exchange isn't a robbery.

The Tech Side of Things

Most of us won't be able to hire a professional filmmaker right away. So, here's some technical stuff you can utilize when making videos.

Rick Gee of *www.marketingprofitstrategiesblog.com* says that all you need is a flip-video camera or a Kodak Zi8 pocket camcorder. That Kodak HD camcorder is less than $200 brand new. Patty Lennon in *The Crowdfunding Book* says that any of the newer iPhones are good for video. No matter what you use, make sure it has a minimum 720p high definition. But 1080p HD is perfect.

You can use YouTube to edit your videos for free by using their own free editing software. Great YouTube video experts to study are James Wedmore, Andy Jenkins, and Mike Stewart. Some other video editing software is:

Windows 10 Video Editor Program
Adobe Premiere Pro
Apple Final Cut Pro X
Adobe Premiere Elements (for beginners)

Whoever is shooting the video needs to do the following:

Turn off the "zoom" feature. Don't use it. Instead, set the lens all the way wide and move closer to what's being filmed. And don't ever use "digital zoom." Matter of fact, turn off all of your camera's digital features.

Keep the light at your back. Remember to think about your background.

Use the "rule of thirds" doctrine when shooting video of something standing (or sitting) still. This means the person should be off to the left or right of the center of the shot. In a third of the screen. If you've ever watched "American Greed" on CNBC, they do this perfectly.

Try to use external microphones like booms or clip-on mics. If you or your loved one are going to do periodic vlogs using a webcam, then you need a clip-on mic. Those cost less than $25 at electronic stores.

Remember to look at the camera and not the screen!

Edit your videos. Make them short and memorable. Edit what doesn't work. The mantra for editing videos is "When in doubt, cut it out." Make sure to turn off your computer's transition effects before you start editing.

When you first start out, your videos won't be the best. Joe Guerrero's videos started out as homemade, grainy mishaps. Now, after 700+ videos, he's an expert. Just remember that "no video is better than a bad video." You only get one chance to make a good first impression.

If you want more help, check out *www.thevideomarketing-guru.com*. You can also post your videos on *vimeo.com*. It's free. You can post your videos across many other platforms through Traffic Geyser (*http://trafficgeyser.com*). But you'll have to pay a fee there.

If you have a tablet (I have a GTL Inspire™) see if they got the following audiobooks:

How to Make Money With Online Videos
Optimizing You Videos for Free Traffic

Listen to those if you can to get some more ideas.

Recommended Reading

How to Shoot Videos that Don't Suck by Steve Stockman
Whoever Tells the Best Story Wins by Annette Simmons
No B.S. Guide to Powerful Presentations by Dan S. Kennedy and Dustin Matthews
Presenting Virtually by Patti Sanchez
Dot Com Secrets by Russell Brunson

Millionaire Prisoners do what unsuccessful prisoners won't do. To go to the next level and rise above the masses you can use videos. That's how you walk on clouds from a prison cell. That' how you can speak while you sleep.

My marketing mentor, Dan Kennedy taught me this wealth principle: "You get income from doing things. You get wealth, independence, and security from owning things." So true. And you can own the videos you create if done right. Make them so that you can use them over and over again in any automated process. Set it and forget it. Free money at its best! Learn to use videos.

If you want some more information on how to get FREE money to help shoot your videos, I suggest you read the following:

Shaking the Money Tree: The Art of Getting Grants and Donations for Film and Video by Morrie Warshawski

CHAPTER 20
FREE Credit Secret$

If you have read my first book, *The Millionaire Prisoner*, you know I'm against going into debt to buy things. When I was in the free-world if I didn't have cash to purchase something I just didn't get it. I was on the block and never had a credit card in my name. The only card I ever had was a Sears® charge card that my baby momma got in my name. And in prison I never use the "2-for-1" store. Because of my book royalties I can buy whatever I want in here. as it hard getting to this point? Not really. I just put my head down, worked on my books, and didn't pay attention to what everyone else around me was doing. But I do know that some of you are in debt or want to use credit cards. Okay, that's you decision. So, in this chapter I'll show you the FREE credit secrets you can learn. It will be up to you to implement them into your life.

Prisoner Credit Repair

In the last few years, I have seen several prisoners (and former prisoners) start businesses to help prisoners repair their bad credit. I smile because that's a play straight out of the *TMP* playbook. Get information that is FREE to all and write a book about it or sell the same information to others. Nothing wrong with that. Publishers have been doing it since they started printing books. If you like this idea, go back and read the FREE "Public Domain" money chapter. And get a copy of my next book, *TMP6: Publishing From Prison*. But, back to the topic at hand. Here are the prisoner credit repair programs that I've seen:

Pilgrim Cross Group B
P.O. Box 2315
Port Orchard, WA 98366
(Send SASE for more information.)

Ortiz Publishing Group
360 Bogert Rd.
River Edge, NJ 07661
(Send SASE for more information.)

Incarcerated Individuals Guide to Good Credit by Kimothy M. Wynn ($13.95 on Amazon.com)

I can't vouch for any of the above. I don't need good credit right now because I'm serving a life sentence. Besides, I wouldn't need to participate in any of these programs. Why? Because the federal government already puts out a ton of FREE information on credit. We call them "credit secrets," but there's nothing secret about how to get good credit. Here's how:

- Pay all of your bills on time. Never miss a payment for anything.
- Keep your oldest line of credit open and pay its payment every month on time. This could be a mortgage or credit card. Length of time matters.

If you have credit cards, pay their bills in full every month and stay away from your credit limit.

Simple, but effective advice. Let me share with you some of the other FREE credit secrets that are out there:

Your Credit Score

How do you know if you got good credit or bad credit? By checking your "credit score." Most of you have heard about them. Credit scores ranges from 300 to 840. The higher the better. Your goal should be to get yours above 760 and stay there. If you have a bank account, you can probably get a FREE monthly credit score from your bank. If not from them, you can get your credit score from *www.creditkarma.com* for FREE. Or you can get your full credit report by using *www.annualcreditreport.com*, or by calling 1-877-322-8228. You can also get another credit score from the Fair Issac and Company, called the "FICO" score at *www.myfico.com*. The Fico score is used more to assess credit risk.

Every 12 months you are entitled to a free credit report from each of the nationwide credit reporting companies. Here are the three credit reporting agencies:

Equifax
P.O. Box 740256
Atlanta, GA 30374
www.equifax.com

Experian
475 Anton Boulevard
Costa Mesa, CA 92626
www.experian.com

Trans Union
P.O. Box 2000
Chester, PA 19016

I like what Dr. Jan Yager suggests in *Help Yourself Now*:

"Since you get a free credit report from each of the bureaus only once a year, you might want to space out your requests. That will enable you to review your first report, report any errors, and see if those corrections have been made when you request the second report. It will also give you a chance to improve your score in between reports if you think that certain positive credit-related actions could help you to improve your score."

Great advice and you should follow it. Because your credit score is so much of a big deal there's a ton of information out there on it. Some of the best comes directly from the government itself. Why wouldn't it? They are the ones who wrote the laws on credit, debt, loans, and so on. So why not go directly to them to get your FREE info? You can and you should. Here's how.

Credit Protection Laws

Our government passes new laws every year. I personally think there are way too many laws. I believe we should be left alone mostly to self-govern. Of course, a convicted criminal like me would say that, huh? But there are laws that protect our rights when it comes to our money, banking, and credit. Here are some of them:

Fair Credit Reporting Act: It protects you because it requires credit bureaus to furnish correct and complete information.
Fair Debt Collection Act: If debt collectors contact you, this law says they are to treat you fairly.
Fair Credit Billing Act: This law is supposed to help you fix errors and mistakes on your bills.

Consumer Leasing Act: This requires lessors to give you specific information on lease costs and terms.

Electronic Fund Transfer Act: This law requires companies to disclose in writing all important terms and costs. Certainly relevant in this day and age with everything being done online.

Equal Credit Opportunity Act: This law prohibits anyone from denying credit because of sex, marital status, color, race, religion, national origin, age, or being on public assistance.

Truth in Lending Act: This requires creditors to disclose in writing certain cost information before consumers enter into any credit transactions. Also known as Consumer Credit Protection Act.

Credit Practices Rule: This prohibits certain security interests and collection remedies in consumer credit contracts.

Holder-in-Due Course Rule: This preserves consumers' claims and defenses involving performance of merchandise bought on credit against a non-seller owner of the credit contract.

Consumer Credit Protection Act: Landmark federal legislation establishing rules of disclosure that lenders must observe in dealings with borrowers. This act is enforced by the Federal Reserve Bank, and is also known as the Truth in Lending Act. (See above)

Credit Card Accountability, Responsibility, and Disclosure Act: This law went into effect fully in 2010 and was designed to curb fees and interest rate increases and other abusive practices by credit card companies.

The Federal Trade Commission (FTC) has lots of FREE publications that can help you on the road to great credit. You can reach them at:

Federal Trade Commission
Public Reference Room 130
6th and Pennsylvania Ave., NW

Washington, D.C. 20580
877-FTC–HELP
www.ftc.gov

Are you having a problem with a bank, lender, or another financial company? The Consumer Financial Protection Bureau (CFPB) can help you get a response from the company. The CFPB was established in 2010 to educate consumers about important financial decisions. It's a federal agency that implements and enforces Federal consumer financial law and ensures that markets for consumer financial products are fair, transparent, and competitive for everyone, including people who are incarcerated and their loved ones. If you are having a problem with almost anything financially related, you can submit a complaint to the CFPB. The CFPB will then work to get a response to your issue.

Examples of the issues you can submit complaints to the CFPB about include (but are not limited to):

Money transfers or virtual currency
Wrong information on a credit report
Identity theft
Mortgages
Credit repair
Debt settlement
Problems with bank accounts or prepaid cards
Debt collection issues
Many kinds of loans (student, vehicle or lease, payday, pawn, title, and other installment loans)

How do you submit a complaint to the CFPB? You do by one of three ways as listed below:

1. Phone: Call the CFPB toll-free at 855-411-2372, 8:00 a.m. to 8:00 p.m. EST, Monday through Friday, except federal holidays. They can help consumers in over 180 languages. [TTY/TDD at 855-729-2372].

2. Online: Visit *http://www.consumerfinance.gov/complaint.* You, or somebody else with you authorization can submit a complaint online. The online form provides information about the special requirements for somebody to submit a complaint on your behalf.

3. Mail: Your letter should have all of the following:

    (a) The date you're writing the letter, your name, current address, jail or prison ID number, and an e-mail address if you have one.

    (b) The name of the company and, if possible, the address of the company your complaint is against.

    (c) The product or service your complaint is about. Be specific as possible.

    (d) Tell the CFPB what happened in a few words. For example, you might say that your credit report includes a debt that you already paid or that is not yours. If possible, provide dates and other useful information.

    (e) Tell the CFPB what you think would be a fair resolution to your issue. Mail the complaint letter and any supporting documents to:

    Consumer Financial Protection Bureau
    P.O. Box 2900
    Clinton, IA 52733-2900

What happens after you file your complaint with the CFPB? They will do the following:

Confirm that they received your complaint and let you know if they need additional information.

They will forward the information you provided to the company for a response.

They will keep you updated about your complaint. If you cannot get online or don't provide an e-mail address with your complaint, you can call the CFPB toll free at 855-411-2372 for an update, or if you have questions. Have your complaint number ready when you call them. It will be on all of the letters or e-mails that you receive from the CFPB.

If you can get online, you can log in to see the status of your complaint and the company's response.

If you provided an e-mail address, the CFPB will e-mail you when the company has responded and you can review the response online. Some companies might mail a response directly to you.

There you have it. A federal governmental agency that will help you free of charge. Might as well get their help if you need to dispute something.

In research for this book, I requested a copy of my FREE credit report. Equifax showed me having nothing on my credit report. But Experian showed me having had two credit cards opened in 2010 with my addresses in California. Very odd and disturbing because in 2010 I was in Stateville prison in Joliet, Illinois. And I have never lived in California, and I have never had a credit card. One card had a credit limit of $14,000, the other $20,000! Lucky for me, whoever was using them was never late on a payment. I still went to the CFPB with my complaint.

> *"Your credit score is the only 'grade' that matters after you leave high school or college."*
>
> — Alex Von Tobel

If you are having problems with your bank or credit card company, you can get FREE legal help to fight them. Different banks are governed by different federal agencies, or your state's banking commissioner if it's a state-chartered bank. Here's what to know:

1. If it's a "FDIC insured" bank, you should contact:

    Federal Deposit Insurance Corporation
    Office of Consumer Affairs
    550 17th St., NW, Room F-130
    Washington, D.C. 20429
    (877) ASK-FDIC
    www.fdic.gov

2. If it's a "savings and loan" contact:

    Office of Thrift Supervision
    U.S. Department of Treasury
    1700 G. St., NW
    Washington, D.C. 20552
    (202) 906-6000
    1-800-842-6929
    www.ots.treas.gov

3. If it's a bank with the word "national" or "N.A." in its name, you should contact:

    Comptroller of the Currency
    Compliance Management
    U.S. Department of Treasury
    250 E St., SW
    Washington, D.C. 20219
    (202) 874-4800
    1-800-613-6743

www.ots.treas.gov

A Line of Credit

In the previous chapter I described a "letter of credit" or L/C. A "line of credit" or "LOC" is different from a letter of credit. A line of credit is a declaration by a bank or other entity that it will extend credit to a borrower up to a specific maximum amount. It's different than a loan. When you get a loan, the gull amount of the loan is given to you. And then you pay the loan off according to the terms of the loan. A line of credit is rarely used all at once. It will be easier to get a LOC when you are first starting out because most people don't even know about them. Here's how to get a line of credit:

1. Find a Line of Credit issuer. You can contact the commercial banks in the previous chapter, or the ones in this chapter.
2. Call them, or visit their websites, and ask for their Line of Credit application. It should be sent to you free of charge.
3. Make copies of the applications you receive. Save the original. You want to practice on the copy. You must fill out every question properly. And you want it to be letter perfect and done on a typewriter or computer.
4. After you have your application filled out properly, your next step should be a short, one-page business plan showing how you'll pay off your LOC.
5. Once you have taken these steps you want to submit your LOC applications to as many banks as you want.

A line of credit can be your avenue to success in building your financial empire. One place to get lines of credit from is credit card companies.

How to Play the Credit Card Game Successfully

In *FREE Money "They Don't Want You To Know About*, Kevin Trudeau talks about dealing with banks and credit card companies. He listed three important rules to practice:

Rule #1: Review your statements every month.
Rule #2: Call the company immediately to get rid of fees and high interest rates.
Rule #3: Negotiate the actual principal balance.

Great advice if you follow it. Always remember that there are lots of credit card companies out there. They are all in competition with each other. You should use them against each other to get the best deal possible. If you do it right you can build your credit and live well. Here's how:

Use websites like Credit Karma and Nerd Wallet to check out credit cards before you apply for them. On Credit Karma you can see how someone with your credit score and income will do when applying for any given credit card. Why does this matter? Because if you apply for a credit card and are denied, it will ding your credit score in the short term. By using Credit Karma ahead of time, you can put yourself in the best possible position.

The goal is to pay off your credit card in full every month. Besides your monthly APR interest rate, you need to look for any additional fees. For instance, annual card fees, inactivity fees, and balance transfer fees. Do your research before signing up for a card. Another thing to look at is how easily do you understand the cards' online system for checking your transactions, rewards, and dispute instances of fraud. It should all be safe, secure, and easy to understand.

Cash-back or travel rewards card? Or both? If you're in prison, then you do not need a travel rewards card. So, get a cash-back card and use it to order books, magazine subscriptions, and other online purchases. If you're free on parole, get a travel rewards card if you travel and eat out a lot. You can compare credit card rewards at www.bankrate.com.

Never cancel your oldest card unless you absolutely have to. Remember that length of your credit history matters! I wish I still had my SEARS® store card all this time (23 years) later. If you do need to cancel your credit cards, only cancel one per year so you don't lower your credit score too much.

Don't have lots of credit cards. I suggest only 3 at the most. A travel rewards card for when you travel and eat out. A cash-back rewards card for everything else. If you have a business, then I suggest a card just for business-related stuff. That's all you need. Anything else is just overkill.

Automate paying your monthly credit card bill. Set it up so you get a notice once a month reminding you to review your transactions, and schedule payment a day or two later.

Credit card statements are required by law to tell you how much APR (Annual Percentage Rate) interest you're paying. The average credit card debt accumulates at over 16 percent! But guess what? If you pay your monthly bill off, you won't pay that APR!

> *"Have enough credit where you're never using more than 20 percent of your credit limit at any point in time, and ideally pay it off each month. It's as simple as that."*
> — Ken Lin, CEO of Credit Karma

Every six to twelve months call the credit card company and ask for a credit increase. If you have been paying your monthly bill in full and have not been maxing out your credit limit, you should be able to get an increase. This will help your credit score also.

Once a year you should call up your credit card company and ask them what advantages you're eligible for. Do they have any promotions for customer retention? Ask them to send you a list of all their rewards. Then use them!

I used to be totally against credit cards. But that's because I grew up in the 1980s and early '90s. Businesses loved cash back then. Now some businesses don't even want cash. It's a new world out there. So, we might as well get paid to use a credit card. You can do that by using a cash-back rewards card and a travel rewards card. Just remember the golden rule of credit cards: *Never max out your credit limit and always pay off your monthly bill on time!* If you can do that, you'll build good credit over time. The key is to stay out of debt.

I want to tell you what you cannot do. You can't only pay the monthly minimum on your credit cards. No, that's what they want you to do. That's how you'll get in debt. Instead, pay off the whole monthly credit card bill every month. How do you do that? Don't max them out in the first place. It takes discipline, yes. But that's the key to getting wealthy.

Live Well Below Your Means

In *The Millionaire Prisoner, Part 1* I wrote about a simple practice to get wealthy: *live well below your means.* You do that so you can invest the rest. But some of you already have lots of debt from before you came to prison. Depending on how long you got, that debt could be wiped away. More on that later. But for now, I want to show you the best way to pay down your debt.

I know what it's like to come from a poor household. I was raised by a single mother on welfare. She had tons of credit card debt, student loans outstanding, and other debt. She ended up declaring bankruptcy on two separate occasions. Those experiences caused stress and pain in my childhood household. I vowed to never go into debt like that. But I also vowed to learn about money so I could help my family get out of the hood and live a better life. The first step is to help them get out of debt. You can do the same thing. Here's how:

1. Have them call the lender that you (or they) owe and ask them to refinance the debt. You have nothing to lose. You'll be surprised at the results.
2. Decide what debt you'll pay down first. Credit card debt? Student loans? Pay-day loans? The answer should be based on whichever debt you owe carries the highest interest rate. So, if one loan has a 16% APR versus another that has an 8% APR, you should pay down the 16% one first. All debt is not equal. Pay down your highest APR first.
3. There's another frame of thought popularized by financial experts like Dave Ramsey. It's called "the snowball effect." What they advocate doing is paying the minimum amount monthly on all of your debts. Then find the one that will be the easiest to pay off and pay it off. Then move on to the next easiest. And so forth until you have all of your debt paid off. I don't agree with that because all debt is not created equal. But some of you may like that method. No matter what, just start paying down your debt.
4. Once you have your debt down to a manageable level you should start investing the difference. What I mean is for you to find a better rate of return to offset the debt. For instance, say you owe on a loan at 6% APR, but you can get a return on your money at 8% APR in an investment. You should do it. That way you can use that 8% to pay off the 6% and still have 2% left over to reinvest or pay down

your debt. That way you can go from a consumer to a producer. It's all about changing your mindset.

That's how you pay down your debt and rebuild your credit. I know I make it sound easy and for some it will be. Others it will be harder. But it will be worth it. Besides getting out of prison, getting out of debt is another type of freedom!

"The difference between rich people and poor people is where they sign their checks. Poor people sign the front. Rich people sign the back."

— Ric Edelman

How To Stop Harassing Debt Collectors

Because of poor financial decisions before you came to prison, some of you have outstanding debts from unpaid bills and you're being harassed by debt collectors. Not only do they bother you, but now they are harassing your family members as well. This is illegal. The Fair Debt Collection Practices Act, known as the FDCPA (is U.S.C. Sec. 1692), was enacted to eliminate illegal and abusive debt collection practices. The FDCPA provides up to $1,000 per case for a violation of the Act, plus requires that the party violating the Act to pay all of your attorney's fees and costs. Here are some of the most common ways a debt collector can violate the Act:

1. You, your family, and your acquaintances are flooded with letters and phone calls from debt collectors or law firms.
2. The debt collector agency calls and leaves a message which fails to give the name of the agency, fails to give the

name of the debt collector, and/or fails to state that they are a debt collector.

3. Pre-recorded or automated calls to phone numbers that are not listed in your, or your family and friends' name may be a violation of the Act.

Under the Act, intent doesn't always have to be shown. So, even if a debt collector isn't intentionally trying to harass you or your family, they are still violating the law and you're entitled to compensation. There is a 1-year statute of limitations on violations of the FDCPA, so you are limited to collecting on violations that occurred in the last year.

If you believe that you or your family are being harassed by illegal debt collectors and their bogus practices, contact Attorney Allison Polesky. She runs the website: *www.prisonersdebthelp.com* and her firm specializes in protecting consumer's right under the FOCPA. Stop being harassed by illegal debt collectors now.

Debt Statute of Limitations

A lot of you know about the statute of limitations from your post-conviction appeals and prison lawsuits. But did you know that debt has a statute of limitations? It does. So, if you have money that you owe it may be wiped away just as the years go by. That's why banks and credit card companies sell old debt to collection agencies. Last I checked, here was the statute of limitations for credit card debt in each state:

Alabama = 3 years
Arkansas = 3 years
Alaska = 3 years
Arizona = 3 years
California = 4 years
Colorado = 3 years
Connecticut = 6 years

Delaware = 4 years
District of Columbia = 3 years
Florida = 4 years
Georgia = 4 years
Hawaii = 6 years
Idaho = 5 years

Illinois = 5 years

Indiana = 6 years

Iowa = 5 years

Kansas = 5 years

Louisiana = 3 years

Maine = 6 years

Maryland = 3 years

Massachusetts = 6 years

Michigan = 6 years

Minnesota = 6 years

Mississippi = 3 years

Missouri = 5 years

Montana = 5 years

North Carolina = 4 years

North Dakota = 6 years

Nebraska = 4 years

New Hampshire = 3 years

New Jersey = 6 years

New Mexico = 4 years

Nevada = 4 years

New York = 6 years

Ohio = 6 years

Oklahoma = 3 years

Oregon = 6 years

Pennsylvania = 6 years

Rhode Island = 4 years

South Carolina = 3 years

South Dakota = 6 years

Tennessee = 6 years

Texas = 4 years

Utah = 4 years

Virginia = 3 years

Vermont = 4 years

Washington = 3 years

West Virginia = 3 years

Wisconsin = 6 years

Wyoming = 8 years

I learned about this the hard way. When I got locked up, I had an outstanding balance on a SEARS® store card. I had my mother pay it off. That was a mistake. I could have let it be outstanding for 5 years (Illinois) and then used the statute of limitations defense. My mother could have kept her money. If you want to learn more about the statute of limitations on debt in your state, go to the law library and look it up. You'll be surprised at what you learn. Wouldn't it be nice to tell Mr. Bill Collector, "I'm sorry but that debt has expired as the statute of limitations has run out! Goodbye."? Just something to keep in mind.

If you have problems with debt you can get FREE counseling from one of the below non-profits:

National Foundation for Credit Counseling
801 Roeder Rd., Suite 900
Silver Spring, MD 20910
800-388-2227
www.nfcc.org

Credit Counseling Center of America
P.O. Box 830489
Richardson, TX 75083
1-800=493-2222
www.cccamerica.org

Debtors Anonymous
General Service Office
P.O. Box 920888
Needham, MA 02492-0009
https://debtorsanonymous.org

And check out Kevin Trudeau's *Debt Cures "They" Don't Want You to Know About.* They have a copy in my prison library. Maybe they have one in yours.

Two other books that you may want to get, and study are:

I Will Teach You to Be Rich by Ramit Sethi
The Debt-Free Millionaire: Winning Strategies to Creating Great Credit and Retiring Rich by Anthony Manganiello

Now that you know some secrets about credit, I will show you how to leverage your new power into riches!

12 U.S. Banks That Provide Credit Cards/Line of Credit

Previously, I talked about how to use credit cards to your benefit and also lines of credit. Here are the top 12 banks in the United States for just those purposes:

American Express National
  Bank
4315 South 2700 West
Salt Lake City, UT 84184
800-446-6307
www.americanexpress.com

Barclays Bank
125 South West Street
Wilmington, DE 19801
(888) 710-8756
www.barclaysus.com

Capital One Bank USA
4851 Cox Road
Glen Allen, VA 23060
(877) 383-4802
www.capitalone.com

Chase Bank USA
201 North Walnut Street
Wilmington, DE 19801
(800) 935-9935
www.chase.com

Comenity Bank
One Righter Parkway,
Suite 100
Wilmington, DE 19803
(800) 675-5685
www.comenity.net

Discover Bank
502 E. Market Street
Greenwood, DE 19950
(302) 349-4512
www.discover.com

HSBC Bank USA
452 Fifth Avenue
New York, NY 10018
(585) 238-7055
www.hsbc.com

1st Financial Bank USA
331 North Dakota
Dunes Blvd.
Dakota Dunes, SD 57049
(800) 733-1732
www.1fbusa.com

Merrick Bank
10705 South Jordan Gateway,
  Suite 200
South Jordan, UT 84095
(800) 204-5936
www.merrickbank.com

Synchrony Bank
170 West Election Rd.,
Suite 125
Draper, UT 84020
(866) 419-4096
www.synchronyfinancial.com

TCM Bank
2701 North Rocky Pointe Drive,
 Suite 700
Tampa, FL 33607
(800) 242-4770
www.icbabancard.org

Wells Fargo Bank
400 Hamilton Ave.,
2nd Floor
Palo, Alto, CA 94301
(612) 316-2348
www.wellsfargo.com

CHAPTER 21

Free Export/Import Money

As I was doing research for this book I kept coming across how people are making lots of money in the Export-Import field. For those of you who do not know what that is, here's a simple definition:

Export = Sending goods and services out of the country.
Import = Bringing goods and services into the country.

There are tons of companies that need help in doing this. Also, the government offers FREE money to those trying to do this. Why? Because they understand helping people sell goods and services overseas assists the American economy in growing. In this chapter, we'll look at how to get FREE money in the Export/Import world.

How many of you reading this are thinking this chapter doesn't apply to you? You're not a farmer trying to ship crops overseas. You don't have a product you want to introduce overseas. You don't have a shop you need to import goods into. So, what. You could get paid big money helping other businesspeople do just that. You could be a "finder" and match international buyers and sellers together for a fee. Look at it this way. *Penacon.com* was the middleman between my wife (who lives in England) and I meeting. "Red" on *The Shawshank Redemption* was the finder who got things for the other prisoners. They both got a fee for their service. Maybe you could do the same, but on a bigger scale. If this sounds interesting to you, just read on.

The Export Express program provides up to $500,000 to help businesses export products worldwide if you qualify. What would be your cut if you helped a small business get that? To learn more about that program you can get the *Export Programs Guide* from the:

Small Business Administration (SBA)
409 3rd Street, SW
Washington, D.C. 20416
800-827-5722
www.foreign-trade.com/us-export

Another great place to start getting help from is the Trade Information Center (TIC). They are part of the Department of Commerce and offer *A Business Guide to Federal Export Assistance.* They are staffed by trade specialists who can provide expert advice on everything overseas exporting. They also have access to the National Trade Data Bank. For more information, you can contact them at:

Trade Information Center
Department of Commerce
Room 4001
14th and Constitution Avenue, N.W.
Washington, D.C. 20230
800-872-8723
www.export.gov/exportprogramsguide

Another good place to get information from about exporting is the U.S. Trade and Development Agency. They exist to promote trade throughout the world. You can contact them at:

United States Trade and Development Agency
1000 Wilson Blvd., Suite 1600
Arlington, VA 22209
(703) 875-4357
www.ustda.gov

If you're looking for specific information on a market, or any company overseas, one of the best places to start with is the International Trade Administration. They are part of the Department of Commerce as well and have country desk officers who most likely have the information you need at their fingertips. They also offer a $5,000 grant just to travel overseas looking for customers for your business. To learn more you should contact them at:

U.S. Commercial Service
International Trade Administration
U.S. Department of Commerce
1401 Constitution Ave.
Washington, D.C. 20230
(203) 482-2867
https://www.export.gov/locations

The Export-Import Bank assists in the financing of exports of the U.S. goods and services. It also has credit information on thousands of foreign companies. In the past they have put out the *Eximbank Export Credit Insurance booklet*, and the *Program Selection Guide*. For more information contact:

Eximbank
811 Vermont Ave. NW
Room 929
Washington, D.C. 20571
800-565-3946
www.exim.gov

The Overseas Private Investment Corporation OPIC) is an agency that provides help to American companies investing in 140 countries. They have info-kits on each country they cover. They also offer direct loans, loan guarantees, and political risk insurance. OPIC sponsors seminars for investors. You can learn more by contacting them at:

Overseas Private Investment Corporation
1100 New York Avenue, NW
Washington, D.C. 20527
(202) 336-8799
www.opic.gov.

If you want to import goods you will need to follow certain guidelines established by the U.S. Customs Service. I know in the past they had pamphlets like, *Importing a Car*, that would show you all you needed to know. For more information you should contact the:

Public Information Division
U.S. Customs Service
U.S. Department of the Treasury
P.O. Box 7407
Washington, D.C. 20044
(202) 927-6724
www.custom.treas.gov

The following are extracted from an older version of the *Catalog of Federal Domestic Assistance* in my prison's law library. The five-digit number (such as 10.187) comes out of that reference. You can search the catalog for free at *www.cfda.gov*.

10.600 Foreign Market Development Cooperation Program

This program is to develop and expand long-term export markets for food-related products overseas. Money from this program can be used for market research and technical assistance to actual or potential foreign purchases of U.S. commodities.

10.601 Market Access Program

This program is a little bit different than the one above. Money from this program can be used for consumer advertising, public relations, trade fairs and exhibits, and technical assistance. Both of these are grants for food-related products exported overseas. More information can be found at:

U.S. Department of Agriculture
Deputy Administrator
Commodity and Marketing Programs
1400 Independence Ave., SW
Washington, D.C. 20250
(202) 720-4761
www.fas.usda.gov/mos/programs/

70.002 Foreign Investment Financing

This program is for financing in developing projects in other countries that help the social and economic growth of that country. At the same time, it should have a positive impact on the U.S. economy as well.

70.003 Foreign Investment Insurance

This program provides insurance to contractors and exporters who may be working in countries where there could be expropriation and political violence. Both of these are available through the Overseas Private Investment Corporation (OPIC) mentioned before. See *www.opic.com*.

Two other companies help exporters who need money to do business overseas. They are:

Private Export Funding Company (PEFCO)
280 Park Avenue
New York, NY 10017
(212) 916-0300
www.pefco.com

International Finance Corporation (IFC)
2121 Pennsylvania Avenue, NW
Washington, D.C. 20433
(202) 336-8799
www.ifc.org

One book that I've seen some prisoners with is the *CIA World Factbook*. It's produced every year and provides country-by-country data on everything you need to know. That would be a good book to have around if you are considering going into the Export/Import field. You can get them from Edward R. Hamilton Bookseller Co. For a free book catalog write to them at:

Edward R. Hamilton Bookseller Company
P.O. Box 15
Falls Village, CT 06031-0015
www.hamiltonbook.com

I learned about this other program from my free money mentor Matthew Lesko. You can ship anything to anywhere in the world for FREE! Say you live in Los Angeles and found something that you want to ship to your favorite pen pal in the United Kingdom. You can use a traveler who is going that way already. We convicts understand this because we've been doing it for years. We'll catch a guy moving to another cellhouse and give him something to transport to a friend of ours who lives where he's going. Or vice versa. Someone will send us a gift the same way. They are now doing this in the free world and cutting out expensive mailing costs. For more information, check out: *www.piggybee.com*. Or email: *hello@piggybee.com*.

Export Wholesale Riche$

You can make big money by exporting products overseas. The key to this strategy is you could get paid a finder's fee. How? By bringing a supplier and a buyer together. There are plenty of companies and businesspeople overseas looking for products. All you have to do is know where they can get those products. Then you can get a 1%-10% commission off each sale.

Or you can wholesale products yourself to overseas firms. You can sell bulk goods before you even purchase them from a wholesaler. I once read how a guy would buy a ton of children's clothes for $2,000 and then sell it to an overseas firm for $3,000. He said it would take him about a day to broker the deal. So, he made $1,000 in a day using the telephone and email. I like the sound of that. How about you?

Just to show you what's available I'm going to list 15 firms that wholesale or distribute products in America. But this list is by no means exhaustive. You'll find lots more by doing an internet search for "product wholesalers" or "product distributors." Or you can get the following eBooks from IWS by calling David Hicks at 1-800-323-0548 or email *admin@iwsmoney.com*:

Wholesaler and Distributor Directory
Director of High-Discount Merchandise Sources

Once you know how to find wholesale products all you need is the buyers. You can sell them to overseas department stores, buyer clubs, dollar stores, military bases, bargain basements, and "big box" stores among others. You can look in the "Products Wanted" section of your state or government exporting information. You want to look for the product type you have chosen. Then you would just contact them to broker the deal and collect your money. Here are 22 wholesalers so you can see what I am talking about:

Atlantic Dominion
Distributors
5400 Virginia Beach Blvd.
Virginia Beach, VA 23462
(800) 468-6612
*www.atlanticdominiondistributor
s.com*
(Wholesale distributor of over
10,000 items.)

Adventure Lighting
90 Washington Avenue

Des Moines, IA 50314
(515) 288-0444
www.adventurelighting.com
(Lamps/fixtures for the
commercial/industrial
market.)

Justin Blair & Company
4500 W. 31st St.
Chicago, IL 60623
(800) 566-0664
www.justinblairco.com

(Leading distributor of shoe store supplies.)

City Auto Supply
449 Littlefield Ave.
South San Francisco, CA 94080
(650) 616-4968
www.cityautosupply.com
(Supplier for the auto repair industry and public.)

Baby King
182-20 Liberty Avenue
Jamaica, NY 11412
(800) 424-2229
www.babyking.com
(Wholesale baby and kids' products.)

Beauty Solutions
151 Harvey West Blvd., Suite F
Santa Cruz, CA 95060
(888) 973-7546
www.beautysolutions.com
(Beauty products for salons, spas, and medical professionals.)

ABC Supply Co.
1002 Ann St.
Madison, WI 53713-2406
(608) 258-8880
www.abcsupply.com
(Largest wholesale distributor of building materials.)

Fusion Worldwide
One Marina Park Drive, Suite 305
Boston, MA 02210
(617) 502-4100
www.fusionww.com
(Distributor of electronic components.)

Sportsman's Supply Inc.
2219 Hitzert Court
Fenton, MD 63026
(636) 600-9301
www.ssisports.net
(Wholesaler of hunting, camping, marine, fishing, and golf goods.)

McGuff Medical
3524 West Lake Center Drive
Santa Ana, CA 92704-6987
(800) 854-7220
www.mcguffmedical.com
(5,000+ products for hospitals and doctor's offices.)

Campbell Wholesale
6849 East 13th St.
Tulsa, OK 74112
(918) 836-8774
www.campbellwholesale.net
(Food and beverage wholesaler offering convenience store products.)

Office Furniture Distributors

2901 Trade Center Drive, Suite 100
Carrollton, TX 75007
(866) 648-3635
www.ofdist.com
(Name of company says it all!)

National Performance Warehouse
11150 NW 32nd Avenue
Miami, FL 33167
(800) 344-0368
www.nationalperformance.com
(Truck parts and accessories for all makes and models.)

Unique Electronics
7750 Densmore Ave.
Van Nuys, CA 91406
(818) 988-1100
www.uniquetronics.com
(Wholesaler of difficult-to-find electronics and older models.)

MAC Wholesale
140 Laurel St.
East Bridgewater, MA 02333
(508) 378-3500
www.macwholesale.net
(National closeout wholesaler of giftware and home products.)

Lemon Tree Trading Co.
1000 S. San Pedro St., Unit C
Los Angeles, CA 90015
(213) 747-3410

https://www.wholesalefashionplace.com
(Wholesale clothing, high quality women's apparel, fashion accessories, etc.)

Factory Motor Parts Co.
(651) 405-3600
www.factorymotorparts.com

Bluefin Distribution
3321 E. La Palma
Anaheim, CA 92806
www.bluefincorp.com
customerservice@bluefincorp.com
(Distributor of toys, collectibles, novelties, and hobby products.)

REGO Trading
200 Liberty St.
Metuchen, NJ 08840
(732) 603-7346
www.regotrading.com
contact@regotrading.com
(Wholesale distributor of baby care products.)

Jinny Beauty Supply
3587 Oakcliff Road
Doraville, GA 30340
(800) 936-8733
www.jinny.com
(World's largest multi-cultural and ethnic beauty supply distributor.)

Ferguson
12500 Jefferson Avenue
Newport News, VA 23602
(757) 874-7795
www.ferguson.com
(Distributor of plumbing
supplies, heating and cooling
equipment, tools, safety
equipment, and fire protection
products.)

888 Digital
1416 East Linden Ave.
Linden, NJ 07036
(908) 583-9300
www.888digital.com
(Wholesale distributor of
consumer electronics.)

If you want to look more into this, I suggest you check out *Start Your Own Wholesale Distribution Business, Fourth Edition* by the Staff of Entrepreneur Media, Inc. & C.M. Spencer.

Letter of Credit

A "letter of credit" should not be confused with a line of credit. We'll discuss "lines of credit" in the next chapter. But for now, we're talking about a letter of credit or an "L/C." Basically, a L/C is a guarantee. Like "vouching" for your homie. Banks issue letters of credit as a way to ensure sellers that they will get paid as long as they do what they've agreed to do. A letter of credit can be key to achieving export success.

When an overseas bank issues a letter of credit in "your favor" this means that you will be paid for the products you export to the overseas company that obtained the L/C. All you would need to do is ship what was ordered.

When a commercial bank issues a letter of credit to you, the L/C gives you collateral you can use to get a loan for business use. Or you can use the L/C to pay for goods you're importing to sell in your own country.

Getting a letter of credit for an ex-prisoner won't be easy. But it is certainly doable. Banks charge a small fee for issuing an

L/C to you. This fee is often about $2.50 per $1,000 of L/C you obtain. So, for a $100,000 L/C you might pay $250 when the L/C goes into force.

A letter of credit is an easy way to associate yourself with an international bank that can give you trade leads for items you want to export. It's also a smart way to get free help in handling the paperwork for exports and imports. Letters of credit make it possible to do business worldwide. At the end of this chapter, I'll give you some commercial banks to look up once you get out to possibly get a letter of credit from. They could help you achieve your financial dreams.

The World is Flat

Because of the internet the world is now flat. You can find products and services to sell all over the world. Mike got his website redesigned by a guy in Pakistan. My first mail-order partner was in Egypt. So don't just think physical products. Think about services also. You could export your expertise and talk to everyone with an internet connection. My wife is in England. We talk everyday through email and phone. And we mix in the weekly video visit. A few years ago, that would not have been possible. But technology has leveled the playing field. So, think outside the box you live in. I'll see you at the top.

"Fun things happen when you earn dollars, live on pesos, and compensate in rupees."

— Timothy Ferriss

20 Selected Commercial Banks
1st Funding Source
7200 Gulf Blvd.
St. Pete Beach, FL 33706
(727) 710-2025

https://www.1stfundingsource.com

Busey Financial Services
7980 Summerlin Lakes Drive

Fort Myers, FL 33907-1816
(239) 790-8000
https://www.busey.com

California Center Bank
3435 Wilshire Boulevard,
Suite 700
Los Angeles, CA 90010
(213) 251-2222
https://www.calcenterbank.com

Encino State Bank
16000 Ventura Blvd., Suite 100
Encino, CA 91436
(818) 780-9055
https://www.encinostatebank.net

Heritage Bank N.A.
310 South First Street
P.O. Box 1124
Willmar, MN 56201-1124
(800) 344-7048
https://www.heritagebankna.com

American Chartered Bank
932 W. Randolph Street
Chicago, IL 60607
(312) 492-1124
www.americanchartered.com

Chase Bank
10 S. Dearborn, 2nd Floor
Chicago, IL 60603
(312) 732-8555
www.chase.com

New York Community Bank

1400 Old Northern Blvd.
Roslyn, NY 11576
(516) 683-4408
https://www.roslynsavings.com

Amsouth Bancorp
1900 Fifth Ave. N.
Birmingham, AL 35203
(205) 320-7151
https://www.amsouth.com

Bank of New York Co.
1 Wall St.
New York, NY 10286
(212) 495-1784
https://www.bankofny.com

Compass Bancshares
15 S. 20th St.
Birmingham, AL 35233
(205) 287-3000
https://www.compassweb.com

Regions Financial
417 N. 20th St.
Birmingham, AL 35203
(205) 944-1300
https://www.regions.com

Southwest Corporation
420 N. 20th St.
Birmingham, AL 35203
(205) 254-5000
https://www.southtrust.com

Pacific Century Financial
130 Merchant St.

Honolulu, HI 96813
(808) 643-3888
https://www.boh.com

Northern Trust Corp.
50 S. LaSalle St.
Chicago, IL 60675
(312) 630-6000
https://www.northerntrust.com

First Bank of Arizona NA
41 Wildlife Trail
Edgewood, NM 87015
(505) 362-2323
www.fnbaonline.com

JP Morgan International Bank
P.O. Box 36520
Louisville, KY 40233-6520
(800) 242-7338
www.jpmorgan.com

Fifth Third Bank
1701 Golf Road, Suite 900
Rolling Meadows, IL 60008
(847) 354-7372
www.53.com

First Midwest Bank
555 W. Dandee Road
Buffalo Grove, IL 60089
(847) 670-3120
www.firstmidwest.com

CHAPTER 22

Free Real Estate Money

This chapter may be the most important in this book for all of you trying to become multi-millionaires. If you have read my book *TMP3: Success University*, then you know about former prisoner Michael Santos. He got 45 years in federal prison under the 1980's draconian cocaine kingpin laws. He wrote several books while locked up, including *Success After Prison: How I Built Assets Worth $1,000,000 Within Two Years of Release*. For any prisoner about to go home, I highly recommend that book. He became a millionaire in real estate in California. Just another example of how a prisoner/parolee can do it. In this chapter we'll discuss tons of opportunities in the real estate market.

Lots of you watch all the real estate shows on HGTV. I like them also. You can see how much money they are getting by flipping houses. That's one option. You could also find cheap houses that buy, fix up, and then rent out. It's up to you. What you need to understand is that it's easy to find houses cheap in America. You can use Realtor.com (*https://www.realtor.com*) to find homes in your area for under a certain amount. Or you can use Zillow (*https://www.zillow.com/*). Say I got a $3,000 royalty check from my books and I wanted to buy a house. I could go to Realtor.com and put in $3,000 as my limit, then the town I was looking at, and it would show me all the properties that fit that stipulation. You can do it for any area code or city. You have no excuse to not find a property you could buy.

But you may be thinking you don't have $3,000 in book royalties coming in, so you can't buy houses or other properties. That's where you are lucky. There are plenty of FREE money opportunities in real estate out there. You just have to find them. I'll use this chapter to point you in the right direction to finding these sources of FREE money.

The first place you should start is with Uncle Sam! Yes, we all have a trillionaire rich uncle that we can go to for help. He wants to help us. All we have to do is ask. You should start with the following federal government office:

U.S. Department of Health and Urban Development (HUD)
451 7th Street SW
Washington, D.C. 20410
www.hud.gov

(For information specific to your state, go to *https://www.hud.gov/state* or you can find a local HUD counselor to help you at HUD Approved Counseling Agencies by calling 1-800-569-4287 or visiting: *https://www.hud.gov/offices/hsg/sfh/hcc/hcs.cfm*)

Always contact the above HUD Approved Counseling Agencies number or website to find a nonprofit organization that can help you. Why? Because they'll help you for FREE and they are approved by HUD to do this. You should never pay anyone to give you advice about HUD programs when there are thousands of counselors out there to help you for FREE!

Here are some of the FREE money programs I know HUD has released in the past and still might be available today. Remember that this information and # comes out of the *Catalog of Federal Domestic Assistance,* which can be searched for FREE at *www.cfda.gov.*

Money to Fix Up Houses That Are More Than One Year Old (#14.108 Rehabilitation Mortgage Insurance (203(k))

Loans To Buy Trailer Homes (#14.100 Manufactured Home Loan Insurance-Financing Purchase of Manufactured Homes as Principal Residences of Borrowers)

Loans to Co-op Investors (#14.112 Mortgage Insurance for Construction or Substantial Rehabilitation of Condominium Projects (234(d) Condominiums)

Loans To Homeowners Anywhere With 1 to 4 Family Units (#14.117 Mortgage Insurance-Homes (203(b))

Loans To Buy Single Family Homes For Disaster Victims (#14.119 Mortgage Insurance-Homes for Disaster Victims (203(h))

Money for Low to Moderate income Families Hurt by a Disaster or Urban Renewal (#14.120 Mortgage Insurance-Homes for Low- and Moderate-Income Families (221(d)(2)))

Money for Homes in Outlying Areas (#14.121 Mortgage Insurance-Homes in Outlying Areas (203 (i)))

Money for Homes in Urban Renewal Area (#14.122 Mortgage Insurance-Homes in Urban Renewal Areas)

Money for Homes in Older Areas of Town (#14.123 Mortgage Insurance-Housing in Older, Declining Areas (223 (e)))

Money to Buy a Co-op Apartment (#14.126 Mortgage Insurance-Cooperative Projects (213 Cooperatives))

Money to Buy a Trailer-Home Park (#14.127 Mortgage Insurance-Manufactured Home Parks (207 (m)))

Money to Buy a Hospital (#14.128)

Money to Buy a Nursing Home (#14.129)

Money to Buy Your House if it is in a Long-Term Ground Lease (#14.130)

Money to Buy Your Co-op (#14.132)

Money to Buy a Condominium (#14.133)

Money to Invest in Apartment Buildings for Middle Class Families (#14.135)

Money to Invest in Rental Housing for the Elderly (#14.138)

Money to Invest in Rental Housing in Urban Renewal Areas ($14.139)

Money to Fix Up Your Home (#14.142)

Money to Fix Up Multi-Family Projects (#14.151)

Money to Investors to Purchase or Refinance Multi-family Housing (#14.155)

Money to Build Housing for the Elderly That Also Provides Support Services (#14.157)

Money to Buy a House With Graduated Mortgage Payments (#14.159)

Money to Buy a Trailer and Trailer Lot (#14.162)

Money to Finance Co-op Buildings (#14.163)

Money to Developers in Financial Trouble (#14.164)

Money to Buy Houses in Areas Hurt by Defense Cuts (#14.165)

Money for Active-Duty Military to Buy Houses (#14.166)

Money to Buy a Home Using Increased Equity Payments (#14.172)

Money to Buy a Home Using an Adjustable-Rate Mortgage (#14.175)

Money for Non-Profits to Build Houses for Lower-Income Families (#14.179)

Money to Invest in Houses for Those With Disabilities (#14.181)

Rental Supplements for Investors Who Provide Houses to Low-Income Families (#14.182)

Money to Help Elderly Homeowners Convert Their Equity into a Monthly Income (#14.183)

Money for Low-Income Housing Tenants to Buy Their Building (#14.186)

Grants to Non-Profits Who Lend Money to Low-Income Families to Buy Houses (#14.240)

Money For Homes That Use New Building Ideas (#14.507)

Money For Apartment Buildings That Use New Ideas (#14.509)

Rent Supplements to Building Owners With Tenants That Have Low-Incomes (#14.856)

More Rent Supplements for Building Owners With Tenants That Have Low-Incomes (#14.857)

Grants to Organizations Who Help Low-Income Families Buy Houses (#14.858)

Loans for Families With Bad Credit Histories (#14.140)

Money to Provide Affordable Rental Housing for Low-Income Families (#14.239)

Money for Developers, Investors, and Builders of Low-Income Housing (#14.188)

Loans to Investors, Builders, Developers of Affordable Housing (#14.189)

Rental Voucher Program for Low-Income Indian Families (#14.855)

Money For Homes For Low-Income Indian Families (#14.850)

Those are just some of the many programs that were available from the federal government through HUD. But they are not the only department or organization that offers money for real estate. Here are some of the others:

Habitat for Humanity International
121 Habitat Street
Americas, GA 31709
1-800-422-4828
www.habitat.org
(Ask about their 0% interest mortgage rate program.)

You can get $12,000 worth of home repairs for FREE if you fit a certain income level. For an office near you, contact:

Rebuilding Together

1899 L Street NW #1000
Washington, D.C. 20036
(800) 473-4229
https://rebuildingtogether.org/

If you or someone you know has (or is having) problems with banks or lenders on their mortgages, you may be able to eliminate thousands of dollars in assessment fees. For more information, contact the U.S. Consumer Finance Protection Board (CFPB) at:

CFPB
1625 Eye St. NW
Washington, D.C. 20006
(885) 411-2372
www.consumerfinance.gov

The "Home Affordable Modification Program" gives people up to $65,000 in cash to reduce the size of their mortgage. For more information about this program contact 1-888-995-4673 or visit: *www.makinghomeaffordable.gov.*

After that housing meltdown crisis, the government came up with a program to offer a $100,000 grant so you can get a cheaper mortgage payment. Why would they do this? Because they want you to stay in your home! For more information, contact 1-888-995-HOPE or visit: *http://www.995hope.org.*

Volunteers of America is one of the largest non-profit housing organizations in the nation. They provide affordable housing options for the following people: seniors, low-income families, veterans, and persons with disabilities. You can check them out at:

Volunteers of America
1660 Duke Street

Alexandria, VA 22314
https://www.voa.org/housing

For seniors who need places to live in the following states: California, Texas, Pennsylvania, Colorado, Arizona, Georgia, Idaho and Maryland. You should contact the following:

Christian Church Homes
303 Hegenberger Road, Suite 201
Oakland, CA 94621-1419
(510) 632-6712
https://www.cchnc.org/housing-development

Besides HUD, there's another government entity that provides tons of FREE money for housing and real estate. That is the Rural Housing Service of the U.S. Department of Agriculture. They can be contacted by reaching out to the:

Rural Housing Service
U.S. Department of Agriculture
Room 5037, South Building
14th St., and Independence Ave., SW
Washington, D.C. 20250
(202) 720-4323
www.rurden.usda.gov/rhs/

Here are some of the money programs I have found out of the *Catalog of Federal Domestic Assistance (www.cfda.gov)* that the U.S. Dept. of Agriculture has given out in the past:

Money to Ensure Your Soil and Land Remains Intact (#10.063)
Money to Ensure that Your Water is Clean (#10.068)
Money to Improve Your Water and Soil (#10.069)

Money to Change Your County Property Into a Wetlands (#10.070)
Loans to Help Your County Property Recover From an Emergency (#10.404)
Money to Build Houses for Your Employees (#10.405)
Money to Buy, Fix Up or Build Houses in Small Towns ($10.410)
Money for Non-Profits to Build Houses in Small Towns (#10.415)
Money to Improve Your Water for a House in the Country (#10.416)
$5,000 Grants to Fix Up Your House in the Country (#10.417)
Money to Conserve Soil and Water in Small Towns (#10.900)
Money to Fix Up an Abandoned Coal Mine (#10.910)
Money to Fix Up Your Home in the Country (#10.433)

Those are some of the grants and loans available for rural homes and small-town housing that the government gives out. Veterans of the U.S. Military and Armed Forces can get grants to buy real estate through the VA:

U.S. Department of Veterans Affairs
Washington, D.C. 20420
(202) 273-7355
(800) 827-1000
www.va.gov

Here are some of those that are available for Veterans:

$150,000 to Help Veterans and Unmarried Spouses of Veterans to Buy or Fix Up A Home (#64.114)
$33,000 for Disabled Veterans to Fix Up A Home (#64.118)
$20,000 for a Veteran to Get a Manufactured Home (#64.119)
$12,610 to $541,000 to Help Homeless Veterans (#64.024)
$48,000 Grant for Veterans to Adapt Their Home For a Disability (#64.106)

There are numerous other programs and grants available to help people with their real estate needs. Each state has a Housing Authority that can help you. At the end of this chapter, I will list the last known contact information that I have for each one. You can always check with the National Council of State Housing Agencies (*www.ncsha.org*) for their most up-to-date contact information.

Your city and county government may also have a housing authority as well. For instance, in my hometown of Danville, Illinois, there is a Danville Housing Authority. Danville is in Vermilion County, Illinois, and there is also a Vermilion County Housing Authority as well. Maybe your city or county has the same. These entities may offer free money for rental assistance, home repairs, closing costs, and other grants for real estate purposes. Check with your local library or by calling "211" for more information about your local housing authority.

There are also thousands of local and national non-profit organizations that offer FREE money for all kinds of real estate costs. I will detail some on the next few pages to give you an idea of what's available.

National Association of Housing and Redevelopment Officials
630 Eye St., NW
Washington, D.C. 20001
(202) 289-3500
(877) 866-2476
www.nahro.org

Information Center
Office of Community Planning and Development
P.O. Box 7189
Gaithersburg, MD 20898
1-800-998-9999

www.comcon.org

Another office that offers low-interest loans and will know about any FREE money programs would be your local Community Action Agency. There are thousands of them around the country. To find the closest one to you, contact:
Community Action Partnership
1100 17th St., NW, Suite 500
Washington, D.C. 20036
(202) 265-7546
www.communityactionpartnership.org
(Some of the things that CAP offered in the past were $2,000 grants to fix up your home, help with weatherization and fuel bills, and even FREE furniture for those in need.)

The U.S. Department of Energy offers $2,500 to pay your insulation bills in their Weatherization Assistance Program. There are certain guidelines to qualify, and you must apply through your state weatherization agency. To find out where to apply and the eligibility requirements, contact:

EE44
U.S. Department of Energy
1000 Independence Ave., SW
Washington, D.C. 20585
1-800-DIAL-DOE
www.eren.doe.gov/buildings/home_weatherizing.html

Some people are not approved for the above program, but still can get $2,800 to help pay their heating bill through the Low-Income Home Energy Assistance Program (LIHEAP). That program is funded by the U.S. Department of Health and Human Services. To learn if you and your family are eligible for this program, you need to find your state LIHEAP coordinator. You can find that person by contacting:

Office of Community Services
Division of Energy Assistance
Administration for Children and Families
U.S. Department of Health and Human Services
370 L'Enfant Promenade, SW
5th Floor West
Washington, D.C. 20447
(202) 401-0351
1-888-294-8662
www.act.dhhs.gov/programs/liheap

Here are some other organizations that offer FREE money and down payment assistance on real estate. Contact them to see if you are eligible (or your family is):

American Family Funds, Inc.
3720 Airport Boulevard,
Suite C
Mobile, AL 36608
(251) 344-1084
www.americanfamilyfunds.com

Nehemiah Corporation of
America
1851 Heritage Lane, Suite 201
Sacramento, CA 95815
(877) 634-3642
www.getdownpayment.com

Neighborhood Gold, Inc.

3575 North 100 East,
Suite 275
Provo, UT 84604
1-888-627-3023
www.neighborhoodgold.com

The Home Down Payment
Gift Foundation, Inc.
1700 Rockville Pike,
Suite 400
Rockville, MD 20852
1-888-856-4600
www.homedownpayment.org

Ameri Dream Inc.

18310 Montgomery Village
Avenue, Third Floor
Gaithersburg, MD 20879
(866) 263-7437
www.ameridream.org

The Genesis Foundation
8834 N. Capital of Texas
Hwy. Suite 100
Austin, TX 78759
(512) 231-0270
www.thegenesisprogram.org

Homes For All, Inc.
13180 North Cleveland
Avenue, Suite 136
North Fort Myers, FL 33903
(941) 656-4633
www.ezdownpayment.com

Family Home Providers, Inc.
6030 Bethelview Road,
Suite #202
Cumming, GA 30040
(770) 887-4578
www.familyhomeproviders.org

The Horizon Community
Finance Fund
39178 10th Street West,
Suite F
Palmdale, CA 93551
1-800-348-8888
www.thehorizonfund.org

Gift America, Inc.
P.O. Box 676
Clarksburg, MD 20871-0676
(301) 231-0028
www.giftamerica.org

Newsong Buyer's Assistance
8022 South Memorial,
Suite 200
Tulsa, OK 74133
(918) 254-6999
www.buyers-assistance.com

Partners In Charity, Inc.
10 East Main St., Suite 114
East Dundee, IL 60118
1-800-705-8350
www.partnersincharity.org

Buyers Grant, Inc.
P.O. Box 271447
Flower Mound, TX 75027-
1447
www.buyersgrant.com

A New Horizon
500 Fairway Drive,
Suite 208
Deerfield Beach, FL 33441
1-800-556-1548, ext. 1227
www.anewhorizon.org

Global Gift

P.O. Box 6856
Albuquerque, NM
87197-6856
(505) 250-4706
www.globalgift.info/programs.htm

The Affordable Housing
Alliance
10318 4th Avenue West
Everett, WA 98204
(425) 353-7131
*www.housinggrants.org/
sellers.htm*

Agape Economic
Development, Inc.
17339 Barnhill Cerritos, CA
90703
(562) 924-9655
*www.homeloanassistance.com/
program.htm*

Alpha Assistance, Inc.
P.O. Box 2573
Desoto, TX 75123
(877) 684-7268
www.alphaassistance.com

American Assistance
Corporation
2800 E. Plano Pkwy.,
Suite 300
Plano, TX 75074

(972) 423-0394
www.american-assistance.com

Ameri Homes, Inc.
421 Coventry Drive
Nashville, TN 37211
(888) 446-6382
*www.free-down-payment-
program.com*

Amiya Institute
7100 Hayvenhurst Avenue,
Suite #320
Van Nuys, CA 91406
(888) 846-3750
www.homebuyaide.com

The Buyer's Dream Fund, Inc.
Waterstone Professional
Building
14077 Cedar Road, Suite 201
Cleveland, OH 44118
(216) 320-0870
www.libertygold.org

Consumer Debt Solutions, Inc.
158 Vineyard Avenue
Highland, NY 12528
(845) 691-9697
www.cdsgrants.com

Cornerstone Ministries
P.O. Box 836961

Richardson, TX 75083
(972) 497-9590
www.cornerstonegrant.org

Curtilage Fund
136 South Main Street, Suite
A-200
Salt Lake City, UT 84101
(801) 532-4669
www.curtilage.org/buyer.php

Deep South Community
Development Corporation
2964 Ember Drive, Suite 116
Decatur, GA 30034
(866) 262-1943
www.dsr.downpayment.com

Del Sol Foundation, Inc.
11428 Paramount Boulevard
Downey, CA 90241
(562) 858-3765
www.delsolfoundaiton.org

Down Payment Assistance
Foundation, Inc.
117 Oakwind Pointe
Acworth, GA 30101
(770) 966-1001
www.dpaf.com

The Down Payment Fund
315 West Mill Plain Boulevard,
Suite 210

Vancouver, WA 98660
1-800-620-2239
www.thedownpaymentfund.com

Dream Home Foundation
4880 S.W. Meadows Road,
Suite 300
Lake Oswego, OR 97035
(888) 801-6400
www.dreamhomefoundation.net

The Dreamhouse Fund
9450 SW Commerce
Circle #460
Wilsonville, OR 97070
(503) 582-0706
www.dreamhousecharity.com

Dream Maker Charity
424 N. 7th Street, Suite 200
Sacramento, CA 95814
1-800-894-1444
www.dreammakerprogram.com

The Esther Foundation
1716 North Meadowlark Road
Orem, UT 84097
(866) 937-8437
www.esther.ws

Foundation For Housing
Assistance
1387 Marlowe Avenue,
Suite 12

Cleveland, OH 44107
(216) 521-4663
www.ffha.net

Foundation for Life
Enhancement, Inc.
P.O. Box 670386
Dallas, TX 75367
1-800-493-5156
www.homegrants.net

The Franklin Foundation, Inc.
18401 Woodfield Road,
Suite G
Gaithersburg, MD 20879
1-800-506-3616
www.keygrant.org

Futures Home Assistance
Program
675 Southcrest Pkwy.,
Suite 100
Stockbridge, CA 30281
1-800-672-4055
www.onlinewithfutures.org

Giving in Kindness
Foundation, Inc.
(888) 645-4438
www.gikfoundation.com

Homestead Trust
3450 Ellicott Center Drive

Ellicott City, MD 21043
(410) 480-1967
www.homesteadtrust.org

Homebuyer Gift Charity
(724) 834-6065
www.homebuyergiftcharity.org

Keystone Grants, Inc.
11441 South State Street,
Suite A-374
Draper, UT 84020
(888) 785-7526
*www.keystoneplan.org/
homebuyers.php*

Main Street Foundation, Inc.
320 North Clayton Street
Lawrenceville, GA 30045
(866) 678-1977
www.getadownpayment.com

Mi Casa
8834 N. Capital of Texas
Hwy., Suite 110
Austin, TX 78759
(512) 795-8522
www.lulacmicasa.org

Mid-West Housing Authority
1442 East Primrose Street,
Suite 200
Springfield, MO 65804

(866) 239-1515
www.mid-westhousing.com

National Home Foundation, Inc.
15200 Shady Grove Road, Suite 350
Rockville, MO 20850
(301) 840-3844
www.nationalhomefoundation.org

The Noah Program
P.O. Box 14583
Spokane, WA 99214-0583
(509) 928-8310
www.noahprogram.org

Su Casita, Inc.

2928 Manor Road
Austin, TX 78722
(888) 562-8869
www.vlender.com/r/rort

Sustainable Living Foundation
618 Kenmore Avenue, Suite 2A
Fredericksburg, VA 22401
(540) 373-6277
www.sutainablelivingfoundation.org

The Zebra Project, Inc.
1950 North Park Place
Building 500
Atlanta, GA 30339
(770) 226-9300
www.zebraproject.org

Real Estate Investment Clubs

When you get out you may want to join a real estate investment club in your area. A real estate investment club can help you get to know local real estate investors and professionals, discover income opportunities, connect with lenders, and possibly pool money with others to buy properties you couldn't buy on your own. Real estate investment clubs are not the same as real estate investment trusts (REITs). REITs are formal organizations created to sell stock. Real estate investment clubs are general interest groups that anyone can join.

To find the closest Real Estate Investment Club nearest you, you should look on the following websites:

1. *www.nationalreia.org/find-a-reia*
2. *www.reiclub.com/real-estate-clubs-php*
3. *www.creonline.com/category/real-estate-clubs/*
4. *www.biggerpockets.com/rei/real-estate-clubs*
5. *www.meetup.com/topics/real-estate-investing*

State Housing and Financing Authorities

These offices of each state housing authority can provide help to first time home buyers, rehabbers, and other real estate needs. They can also point you in the right direction of other local housing agencies in your area that can help also.

Alabama Housing Finance Authority
P.O. Box 230909
Montgomery, AL 36123-0909
1-800-325-AHFA
www.ahfa.com

Alaska Housing Finance Corporation
P.O. Box 101020
Anchorage, AK 99510-1020
1-800-478-2432
www.ahfc.state.ak.us

Arizona Office of Housing Development
3800 N. Central, Suite 1500
Phoenix, AZ 85012
(602) 280-1365

www.housingaz.com

Arkansas Development Finance Authority
P.O. Box 8023
423 Main St., Suite 500
Little Rock, AR 72201
(501) 682-5900
www.state.ar.us/adfa

California Housing Finance Agency
1121 L St., 7th Floor
Sacramento, CA 95814
(916) 322-3991
www.calhfa.ca.gov

California Dept. of Housing and Community Development

P.O. Box 952050
Sacramento, CA 94252-2050
(916) 445-4782
http://housing.hcd.ca.gov

Colorado Housing and
Finance Authority
1981 Blake St.
Denver, CO 80202-1272
1-800-877-2432
www.colohfa.org

Connecticut Housing
Finance Authority
999 West St.
Rocky Hill, CT 06067-4005
(860) 721-9501
www.chfa.org

Delaware State Housing
Authority
18 the Green
Dover, DE 19901
(302) 739-4263
www.state.de.us/dsha

DC Housing Finance
Agency
815 Florida Ave., NW
Washington, D.C. 20001
(202) 777-1600
www.dchfa.org

DC Dept. of Housing and
Community Development
801 N. Capitol St., NE
Suite 8000
Washington, D.C. 20002
(202) 442-7200
http://dhcd.dc.gov

Florida Housing Finance
Corporation
227 N. Bronough St.,
Suite 5000
Tallahassee, FL 32301-1329
(850) 488-4197
www.floridahousing.org

Georgia Residential Finance
Authority
60 Executive Park South,
Suite 250
Atlanta, GA 30329
(404) 679-4940
www.dca.state.ga.us

Hawaii Housing and
Community Development
677 Queen Street, Suite 300
Honolulu, HI 96813
(808) 586-4882
www.hcdch.state.hi.us

Idaho Housing Agency
565 W. Myrtle
P.O. Box 7899

Boise, ID 83707-1899
(208) 331-4882
www.ihfa.org

Illinois Housing
Development Authority
401 N. Michigan Ave.,
 Suite 900
Chicago, IL 60611
(312) 836-5200
www.ihda.org

Indiana Housing Finance
Authority
115 W. Washington St.
Suite 1350, South Tower
Indianapolis, IN 46204
1-800-872-0371
www.in.gov/hfa

Iowa Finance Authority
100 E. Grand Ave.,
Suite 250
Des Moines, IA 50309
1-800-432-7230
www.ifahome.com

Kansas Housing Resources
Corp.
1000 SW Jackson St.,
Suite 100
Topeka, KS 66612-1354
(785) 296-5865

www.kshousingcorp.org

Kentucky Housing
Corporation
1231 Louisville Rd.
Frankfort, KY 40601-6191
1-800-633-8896
www.kyhousing.org

Louisiana Housing Finance
Agency
2415 Quail Dr.
Baton Rouge, LA 70808
1-888-454-20001
www.lhfa.state.la.us

Maine State Housing
Authority
353 Water St.
Augusta, ME 04330-4633
1-800-452-4603
www.mainehousing.org

Maryland Dept. of Housing
and Community
Development
100 Community Place
Crownsville, MD 21032-
2023
(410) 514-7000
www.dhcd.state.md.us

Massachusetts Housing
Finance Agency
1 Beacon St.
Boston, MA 02108-3110
(617) 854-1000
www.mhfa.com

Massachusetts Dept. of
Housing and Community
Development
100 Cambridge Street, Suite
300
Boston, MA 02114
(617) 573-1100
www.mass.gov/dhcd

Michigan State Housing
Development Authority
735 E. Michigan Ave.
P.O. Box 30044
Lansing, MI 48912
(517) 373-8370
www.mshda.org

Minnesota Housing
Finance Agency
400 Sibley St., Suite 300
St. Paul, MN 55101
1-800-657-3769
www.mhfa.state.mn.us

Mississippi Home
Corporation
P.O. Box 23369

Jackson, MS 39225-3369
(601) 718-4642
www.mshomecorp.com

Missouri Housing
Development Commission
3435 Broadway
Kansas City, MO 64111
(816) 759-6600
www.mhdc.com

Montana Dept. of
Commerce
Housing Division
P.O. Box 200501
Helena, MT 59620-0501
(406) 841-2700
*http://commerce,state.mt.us/ho
using*

Nebraska Investment
Finance Authority
200 Commerce Court
1230 O St.
Lincoln, NE 68508-1401
1-800-204-6432
www.nifa.org

Nevada Dept. of Business &
Industry
Housing Division
1802 N. Carson St., Suite
154
Carson City, NV 89701

1-800-227-4960
http://nvhousing.state.nv.us

New Hampshire Housing
Finance Authority
P.O. Box 5087
Manchester, NH 03108
1-800-640-7239
www.nhhfa.org

New Jersey Housing and
Mortgage Finance Agency
637 S. Clinton Ave.
P.O. Box 18550
Trenton, NJ 08650-2085
(609) 278-7400
www.state.nj.us/dc2/hmfa/ind
ex.html

New Mexico Mortgage
Finance Authority
344 4th Street, SW
Albuquerque, NM 87102
1-800-444-6880
www.nmmfa.org

New York Housing Finance
Agency
641 Lexington Avenue
New York, NY 10022
(212) 688-4000
www.nyhomes.org

N.Y. Division of Housing
and Community Renewal
25 Beaver St.
New York, NY 10004
(221) 480-6700
www.dhcr.state.ny.us

North Carolina Housing
Finance Agency
3508 Bush St.
Raleigh, NC 27609-7509
1-800-393-0988
www.nchfa.com

North Dakota Housing
Finance Agency
P.O. Box 1535
Bismarck, ND 58502-1535
1-800-292-8621
www.ndhfa.org

Ohio Housing Finance
Agency
57 E. Main St.
Columbus, OH 43215-5135
(614) 466-7970
www.odod.state.oh.us/ohfa

Oklahoma Housing Finance
Agency
100 NW 63rd Street,
Suite 200
P.O. Box 26720

Oklahoma City, OK 73126-0720
1-800-256-1489
www.ohfa.org

Oregon Housing and
Community Services
Department
P.O. Box 14508
Salem, OR 97309-0409
(503) 986-2000
www.hcs.state.or.us/

Pennsylvania Housing
Finance Agency
2101 North Front St.
P.O. Box 8029
Harrisburg, PA 17105-8029
(717) 780-3800
www.phfa.org

Rhode Island Housing and
Mortgage Finance
Corporation
44 Washington St.
Providence, RI 02903-1721
(401) 751-5566
www.rihousing.com

South Carolina State
Housing Financing and
Development Authority
919 Bluff Rd.
Columbia, SC 29201

(803) 734-2000
www.sha.state.sc.us

South Dakota Housing
Development Authority
221 S. Central Ave.
P.O. Box 1237
Pierre, SD 57501-1237
(605) 773-3181
www.sdhda.org

Tennessee Housing
Development Agency
404 James Robertson
Parkway, Suite 1114
Nashville, TN 37243-0900
(615) 741-2400
www.state.tn.us/thda

Texas Housing Agency
507 Sabine
Austin, TX 78701
(512) 475-3800
www.tdhca.state.tx.us

Utah Housing Corporation
554 South, 300 East
Salt Lake City, UT 84111
(801) 521-6950
www.utahhousingcorp.org

Vermont Housing Finance
Agency
One Burlington Square

164 St. Paul St.
Burlington, VT 05401-4364
(802) 864-5743
www.vhfa.org

Vermont State Housing
Authority
1 Prospect St.
Montpelier, VT 05602
(802) 828-3295
www.vsha.org

Virginia Housing
Development Authority
601 S. Belvedere St.
Richmond, VA 23220
(804) 782-1986
www.vdha.com

Washington State Housing
Finance Commission
1000 Second Ave.,
Suite 2700
Seattle, WA 98104-1046

(206) 464-7139
www.wshfc.org

West Virginia Housing
Development Fund
814 Virginia St., East
Charleston, WV 25301
(304) 345-6475
www.wvhdf.com

Wisconsin Housing and
Economic Development
Authority
P.O. Box 1728
Madison, WI 53701-1728
(608) 266-7884
www.wheda.com

Wyoming Community
Development Authority
155 North Beach
Casper, WY 86202
(307) 265-0603
www.wyomingcda.com

CHAPTER 23

How To Get FREE Money From Investors

Earlier in this book I wrote about how I got $3,000 from my mother to start my self-publishing empire. That was a gift I didn't have to pay back. (Though I have since given her that money back.) You can call that original 3K the "seed money" that got me started. Lucky for me, that was all I needed. But what do you do if you need additional money to help your business grow? You can look at all the FREE money opportunities mentioned in Chapter 13. Once you exhaust those, you may look at some of the following options.

Angel Investors
Venture Capital
Initial Public Offerings (IPOs)

I will write about angel investors and IPOs in this chapter, but not venture capital. That avenue is in a different league altogether. Most venture capital firms are looking for sizable returns on their investment. They usually invest millions of dollars in companies with proven sales and profitability. These firms don't take cold calls from people they don't know. But if you have a growing business they like, they'll probably contact you. Instead of them, you can reach out to Angel Investors yourself. And if they like your idea or company, they may contact the venture capital firms themselves. Because of this I'll focus on them instead.

Angel Investors

These types of investors have been around forever, but the actual term "angel investor" is relatively new. An angel investor typically provides money and guidance. Think Marcus Lemonis on CNBC's hit TV show *The Profit*. You can find angel investors easily by using the internet. Here are some of the places to go:

Angel.com – Join this network and post a description of your deal and your funding requirements for everyone to see.

Gust.com – Gust says it "connects startups with the largest collection of investors across the world." List your deal here also.

Go4funding.com – This site is more for existing business owners to post their capital needs and get closer with investors.

Startups.co/investor.com – You can connect with over 20,000+ investors on this website.

USangelinvestors.com – Here's what it says on their website: "US Angel Investors is an investment group of accredited private equity (angel) investors . . . who provide counsel and capital to startup companies in a wide variety of industries."

Gatheringofangels.com – They have helped over 400 young companies with early-stage capital from $20K to $12.5M.

Fundingpost.com – This website offers entrepreneurs the opportunity to access angel investors and venture capital firms.

If you're interested in approaching these people, make sure your "elevator pitch" is top notch. Watch ABC's *Shark Tank* on Friday nights. Or you can catch reruns on CNBC. Watch *The Profit*. Pay attention to the people who get deals. Then compare those with the ones who don't. What can you learn from their pitch? What can you use for yourself? What must you do? Or not do? Ask yourself these questions as you watch these TV shows to learn more.

One of the biggest mistakes I constantly see on *Shark Tank* is the over-evaluation of the idea (or company) by the entrepreneur. This causes the shark to be skeptical or ask for too much equity in return. Which causes the sides to fail in their negotiating and the entrepreneur to walk out of the Tank without a deal. Here's what MJ DeMarco says in *The Millionaire Fastlane*: "Any time you have an asset that has sustainable profits, an industry multiplier governed by prevailing market conditions determines the valuation of that asset. Other people or companies will buy that asset based on the asset's net profit multiplied by the assessed multiple."

In a 2009 *Inc.* magazine article, they listed some average multiples for each respective industry. Here they are from the highest to lowest:

Surgical and Medical Equipment	17.32
Patent owners and Lessors	14.56
Grocery Stores	11.34
Computer-Related Services	8.19
Engineering Services	6.32
Employment Agencies	5.40
Carpet Cleaning	5.22
Used Merchandise Stores	4.92
Plumbing/HVAC Services	4.52
Beauty Shops	4.10
Gas Stations	3.70
Physical Fitness Facilities	.56
Advertising	2.85
Bars/Drinking Places	2.70
Medical Labs	2.62

So, if you have a grocery store that has a net profit of $500,000 a year, you could sell it for $5,670,000! But you couldn't sell it for $50 million. That wouldn't be a realistic valuation. As you can see, you need to know the subjective price-to-earnings ratio for your company's respective industry. If you look at the above list from *Inc.* magazine, you'll see that two of the top industry multipliers are patent owners and lessors and also computer-related services. This is mainly about leverage. You can reach millions with a computer and an internet connection. Add in a proprietary web system and you have what angel investors dream of: a new tech product. No matter what your idea, product, or business is, make sure you know its true valuation before you go pitch possible investors.

If you want to learn more about how to pitch possible investors, you may want to get a copy of the following book:

Crack the Funding Code: How Investors Think and What They Need to Hear to Fund Your Startup by Judy Robinett.

Initial Public Offerings (IPOs)

You see it all the time. A young entrepreneur becomes a multi-millionaire after taking their company public with an IPO. What a lot of cellpreneurs don't know is that you can take a small company public just the same as you can with a large company. And you don't need a long record.

What business you'll be in?
When will the business start (or when it started)?
Why you are in that business?
How much you'll earn from the business?
Who will run the business?

What income any other officers can expect to earn from the business?
What yearly expenses will there be?
What's the market size for your business?
Who are your competitors (if any)?
Why your product or service is better?
How much money do you need to start (if you haven't started already)?
What are your expansion plans?

You can send your request to several different underwriters or firms and see which one will take your case. They can get paid from the proceeds of your IPO. If you sell stock in the IPO, you'll never have to repay the money you get. If you sell bonds in your company, you'll have to pay them off years later. But before you try to go public with an IPO you need to review the law on this matter. These laws are governed by the SEC.

The Securities and Exchange Commission (SEC) was formed to protect investors and to make sure the capital markets operate fairly and orderly. The SEC also has put forth rules and regulations to help small businesses raise capital and to ease the burden of undue regulations under federal securities laws. They even had a small booklet that was FREE to all who requested it called: *Q & A: Small Business and the SEC*. The SEC created an office to specifically help small businesses with these matters:

The Office of Small Policy
Division of Corporation Finance
U.S. Securities and Exchange Commission
450 5th Street, NW
Washington, DC 20549
(202) 942-4040
www.sec.gov

You want to get a copy of their Regulation "A" brochure. That's the regulation that governs taking a company public. You can also ask about "Rule 240." That rule allows you to sell up to $100,000 of stock in any one-year period of your company. But you must be careful with both of these types of deals. There are strict guidelines to follow. That's why you should hire a competent attorney who specializes in these matters. You could pay them out of the money you get once you go public with your IPO.

I remember reading about using penny stocks in an IPO as a way to generate FREE money. I happen to have a personal library of stock investing books. So, I picked up a copy of *Penny Stocks for Dummies* by Peter Leeds. Here's what he says about issuing shares in an IPO in that great book of his:

> *"The main benefit of being listed on a stock market is that it makes raising money easier. A company may start off with an initial public offer (IP), which sells a portion or all of the corporation to shareholders in exchange for the money they pay for the shares.*
>
> *"Issuing shares can be a great way for small companies to get up and running. Many of the greatest corporations in America started by issuing shares and did so again whenever they needed more cash."*

Maybe you could do the same with penny stocks. They do tend to get a lot of bad publicity sometimes, because it's easier for shady characters to sell them to the public. Think about the movie *The Wolf of Wall Street* starring Leonardo DiCaprio. That's a perfect example of how one can get rich hawking penny stocks. But that's not what I'm advocating here. What I'm suggesting is selling stock in your company for 1¢ a share. Then have your underwriter sell millions of shares. If you sell 46,000,000 shares at 1¢, it will give your company $460,000 (minus your underwriter's fee). Think about that. Where else could you legally get $460,000 that easily? This could be the way to go. But you'll never know until you do the research.

It's my job to give you all the available information that I have on the subject at hand. It's your decision to make a choice of what to do. With these thoughts in mind, I must share with you these words from *Get Financing Now* by Charles Green. I wrote about him in Chapter 13. His words are apt here for closing out this chapter.

"The average reader of this book will not be in a serious pursuit of an IPO, and when considering life in a publicly owned company — the costs, scrutiny, and pressure — probably wouldn't want to be. It's not a cakewalk, and there are plenty of pitfalls to getting there.

"If owners really want to go down that path, they must be sure to understand what they are getting into before planning their life in that direction. They should talk to other entrepreneurs who have been through the process and find out what life is like on a road show. What it's like to go through an SEC audit, and whether they would ever do it again."

CHAPTER 24

Free Money to Travel

One of my dreams s to get out of this cage and travel the world. My wife wants to take the Route 66 road trip. I also want to go to Australia and Thailand among other places. Because of these dreams why not get paid to do it? Or make it less expensive? In this chapter I'll give you some tips on how to do just that.

Before you decide to go anywhere you should check out the latest news on your proposed destination. Especially, if it's an overseas one. You can get Consular Information sheets for every country of the world. What do these "sheets" contain? Everything from the location of the U.S. Embassy or Consulate in the country, to health conditions, currency, and crime rates. You should also check to see if the State Department has issued any Travel Warnings for that particular country. You can get these Consular Information sheets from the following:

The Office of Citizens Services
U.S. Department of State
Room 4817 NS
2201 C St., NW
Washington, D.C. 20520
(202) 647-5225
http://travel.state.gov/travel_warnings.html

They also have put together a series of travel publications that can be retrieved for FREE online at: *http://travel.state.gov/travel_pubs.html*

Some of the FREE publications are:

U.S. Consuls Help Americans Abroad
Overseas Citizens Services
Travel Warnings on Drugs Abroad
Sending Money Overseas to a U.S. Citizen in an Emergency
A Safe Trip Abroad
Tips For Older Americans
Tips For Students
Tips For Residing Abroad
Tips For Travelers to the Caribbean
Tips For Travelers to Central and South America
Tips For Travelers to Mexico
Tips For Travelers to the Middle East

If you're going to travel overseas for business you may want to check out the Overseas Security Advisory Council (OSAC). The OSAC was established in 1985 by the U.S. Department of State to help protect private citizens working abroad, including those working for colleges and universities. OSAC publishes a series of publications that could help you:

Security Guidelines for American Families Living Abroad
Security Guidelines for American Enterprises Abroad
Emergency Planning Guidelines for American Businesses Abroad
Security Awareness Overseas
Guidelines for Protecting U.S. Business Information Overseas
Personal Security Guidelines for the American Business Traveler Overseas

Security Guidelines for Children Living Abroad

For more information about these publications and more, contact:

Overseas Security Advisory Council
Bureau of Diplomatic Security
U.S. Department of State
Washington, D.C. 20522
(202) 663-0533
www.ds-osac.org/default.cfm

Another great publication to check out is the latest version of the *CIA World Fact Book*. You can get them out of the latest Edward R. Hamilton Bookseller Catalog. Or you can contact the CIA itself and request its catalog. They make many publications, including maps, available to the public after they have been declassified. You can contact them at:

Public Affairs
Central Intelligence Agency (CIA)
Washington, D.C. 20505
(703) 351-2053
http://www.odci.gov/cia

Each state in the U.S. has an agency for tourism that can provide a wealth of FREE information. You can either reach them by phone or on the website. You can get a lot of FREE information from your State Travel and Tourism Hotlines or website. They will generally provide a travel guide, a calendar of upcoming events, and brochures from private, state, and regional tourist attractions. They can even give you specific advice about a particular place you want to visit in that state and any helpful information about that place. Here are the respective tourism hotlines for each state:

Alabama
(205) 242-4169
800-ALABAMA
www.state.al.us

Alaska
(907) 465-2012
www.state.ak.us

Arizona
(602) 542-4764
www.state.az.gov

Arkansas
(501) 682-1088
800-NATURAL
www.state.ar.us

California
(916)322-2881
800-TO-CALIF
www.ca.gov

Colorado
(303) 592-5510
800-COLORADO
www.colorado.gov

Connecticut
(203) 258-4286
800-CT-BOUND

www.ct.gov

Delaware
(302) 739-4271
800-441-8846
www.delaware.gov

District of Columbia
(202) 789-7000
800-422-8644
www.dc.gov

Florida
(904) 488-5607 Ext. 9187
www.myflorida.com

Georgia
(404) 656-3553
800-VISIT-GA
www.georgia.gov

Hawaii
(808) 586-2550
www.state.hi.us

Idaho
(208) 334-2470
800-635-7820
www.state.id.us

Illinois

(312) 814-4732
800-223-0120
www.illinois.gov

Indiana
(317) 232-8860
800-289-6646
www.state.in.us

Iowa
(515) 242-4705
800-345-IOWA
www.iowa.gov

Kansas
(913) 296-2009
900-2-KANSAS
www.state.ks.us

Kentucky
(502) 564-4930
800-225-TRIP
www.kentucky.gov

Louisiana
(504) 342-8125
800-33-GUMBO
www.louisiana.gov

Maine
(207) 287-5711
800-533-9595
www.state.me.us

Maryland
(410) 333-6611
800-543-1036
www.maryland.gov

Massachusetts
(617) 727-3201
800-447-MASS
www.mass.gov

Michigan
(517) 373-0670
800-543-2937
www.michigan.gov

Minnesota
(612) 296-2755
800-657-3700
www.state.mn.us

Mississippi
(601) 359-3297
800-WARMEST
www.state.ms.us

Missouri
(314) 751-3051
800-877-1234
www.state.mo.us

Montana
(406) 444-2654

800-VISIT-MT
www.state.mt.us

Nebraska
(402) 471-3794
800-228-4307
www.state.ne.us

Nevada
(702) 687-4322
800-NEVADA-8
www.nv.gov

New Hampshire
(603) 271-2665
www.state.nh.us

New Jersey
(609) 292-6963
800-JERSEY-7
www.state.nj.us

New Mexico
(505) 827-7400
800-545-2040
www.state.nm.us

New York
(518) 474-4116
800-CALL-NYS
www.state.ny.us

North Carolina
(919) 733-4171

800-VISIT-NC
www.ncgov.com

North Dakota
(701) 224-2525
800-435-5663
www.discovernd.com

Ohio
(614) 466-8844
800-BUCKEYE
www.ohio.gov

Oklahoma
(405) 521-3981
800-652-6552
www.state.ok.us

Oregon
(503) 986-0000
800-547-7842
www.oregon.gov

Pennsylvania
(717) 787-5453
800-VISIT-PA
www.state.pa.us

Rhode Island
(401) 277-2601
800-556-2484
www.state.ri.us

South Carolina

(803) 734-0136
www.myscgov.com

South Dakota
(605) 773-3301
800-S-DAKOTA
www.state.sd.us

Tennessee
(615) 741-2159
www.state.tn.us

Texas
(512) 462-9191
800-8888-TEX
www.state.tx.us

Utah
(801) 538-1030
www.utah.gov

Vermont
(802) 828-3237
800-338-0189
www.vermont.gov

Virginia
(804) 786-2051
800-VISIT-VA
www.virginia.gov

Washington
(206) 753-5600
800-544-1800
www.access.wa.gov

West Virginia
(304) 348-2200
800-225-5982
www.wv.gov

Wisconsin
(608) 266-2345
800-432-TRIP
www.wisconsin.gov

Wyoming
(307) 777-7777
800-225-5996
www.wyoming.gov

I'm a firm believer in the maxim: *proper preparation prevents poor performance*. Be sure to do your research first. There are plenty of FREE and low-cost options out there. Here are a few of them:

HI USA
8401 Colesville Road, Suite 600

Silver Spring, MD 20910
https://www.hiusa.org

(Used to be called American Youth Hostels. This is a nonprofit membership organization that allows travelers to stay in much lower-cost lodging throughout the US and internationally.)

Automobile Association of America (AAA)
1000 AAA Drive #28
Heathrow, FL 32746
https://www.aaa.com

(Yes, this is the roadside assistance organization. But they also offer travel information and discounts on all kinds of services.)

Road Scholar (*www.roadscholar.org)*
(Used to be called Elderhostel. They're a not-for-profit travel organization that promotes international opportunities for education, travel, and friendship.)

Now we can get into some more Free money travel ideas. Don't forgot you can find all the federal government money programs for travel in the *Catalog of Federal Domestic Assistance.* You can search that book for free at *www.cfda.gov.* Here are some interesting travel ideas I found that may interest you.

Do you have a teacher in your family? Or know one? They could climb aboard NOAA Research and survey ship and work with scientists. This is a way for them to get firsthand knowledge to take back to their classrooms. There were 15 different ships involved in a variety of scientific research they could choose from. This would be a free way for them to see the world. For more information, contact:

NOAA-Marine Operations Center

1801 Fairview Avenue E
Seattle, WA 98102-3767
(206) 553-8705
www.tas.noaa.gov

What about playing Indiana Jones and going on an archeological dig? Or studying marine biology in a coastal town somewhere? The U.S. Department of Agriculture has a program that allows you to do this. For more information contact:

Passport In Time Clearinghouse
P.O. Box 31315
Tucson, AZ 85751
800-281-9176
www.passportintime.com

Did you know you can get paid to take your work overseas? You could be one of the people who represent America at an overseas conference. Or maybe you're a musician and want to take a tour of Asia. The U.S. Department of State's Office or Citizen Exchanges manages these cultural program exchanges. For more information you should contact:

Office of Citizen Exchanges
Bureau of Educational and Cultural Affairs
U.S. Department of State, SA-44
301 Fourth Street, S.W.
Washington, D.C. 20547
(202) 619-5348
http://exchanges.state.gov

$7,000 to study overseas? The Benjamin Gilman International Scholarship Program offers money for needy college students to study abroad. The award provides for tuition, room and board, books, local transportation, insurance, and international airfare. For more information contact:

Gilman International Scholarship Program
Institute of International Education
520 Post Oak Blvd., Suite 740
Houston, TX 77027-9407
(713) 621-6300
www.iie.org/programs/gilman/index.html

Do you like flowers? No joking here. You can actually get money to go overseas and study flowers! The Harold F. Wilkins Scholarship provides grants to students to study the floral industry in a foreign country. Or to attend an International Floricultural Symposium or other related pursuits. For more information, contact:

American Floral Endowment
11 Glen-Ed Professional Park
Glen Carbon, IL 62034
(618) 692-0045
www.htctech.net

Want a grant of $16,000 to travel and live in Italy? Well, the Independent Research program awards these grants to live in Venice for historical research on the former Venetian empire, and modern-day society in Venice. Once the study is done you could get another $4,000 to help with publication of your research. Sounds like something I could do. Travel over there. Study society. Write a book about it all. Maybe you could do it? For more information, contact:

The Gladys Krieble Delmas Foundation

521 Fifth Avenue, Suite 1612
New York, NY 10175-1699
(212) 687-0011
www.delmas.org

Don't forget the Peace Corps. You would get two years to travel somewhere in the world to live among the native people. You would share your knowledge and help them out. For more information about how to join, contact:

Peace Corps
1111 20th Street, NW
Washington, D.C. 20526
800-424-8580
www.peacecorps.gov

Are you an artist who likes Japanese culture? You could possibly go to Japan in a Creative Artists' Program for six months to observe developments in their field. You would also get to meet your professional counterparts in Japan. For more information, contact:

Japan-U.S. Friendship Commission
1201 15th Street, NW
Suite 330
Washington, D.C. 20005
(202) 653-9800
www.jusfc.gov.

Do you like airplanes? You could get $5,000 for a research grant into airport design, safety, passenger comfort, and all aspects of air travel. For more information, contact:

Arnold W. Thompson Charitable Trust
8480 N. Lee Trevino Drive
Tucson, AZ 85742-9709
(520) 544-9307

Want to go to the Caribbean? You could get $3,000 for a research grant to study projects related to the Caribbean. For more information, contact:

Research Institute for the Study of Man
c/o Lambros Comitas
162 E. 78th Street
New York, NY 10021-0406
(212) 678-4040
www.rism.org

The American Council of Learned Societies (also known as ACLS) provides many different research grants. Here are some of them:

$40,000 to research Eastern Europe
$3,500 per month to research using foreign languages
$62,000 to travel and research social science projects
Money to study abroad in China

For more information about these grants, and others, contact:

American Council of Learned Societies (ACLS)
633 3rd Avenue, Suite 8C
New York, NY 10017-6795
(212) 697-1505
www.acls.org

You could get FREE rent and utilities if you're an artist who wants to go to New Mexico. Why would you go? To have a scenic, quiet haven where you can do your creative thing in peace. For more information contact:

The Helene Wurlitzer Foundation of New Mexico
P.O. Box 1891
Taos, NM 87571
(505) 758-2413
hwf@taosnet.com

$10,000 to travel to Europe or Russia for artists to work with other artists sounds good, right? Maybe it's for you. For more information, contact:

CEC Arts Link, Inc.
12 West 31st Street, 4th Floor
New York, NY 10001
(212) 643-1985
www.cecip.org

Do you want to go to India to do research? Then you should contact the below institute for more about their fellowship:

American Institute of Indian Studies
1130 E. 59th Street
Chicago, IL 60637-1539
(773) 702-8638
www.indiastudies.org

You probably already know that you could join the military and see the world all at the expense of the U.S. government. But did you know there are all kinds of government jobs in foreign countries available? For more information about these jobs you should contact the following:

Federal Job Information Center
Office of Personnel Management
1900 E St., NW
Washington, D.C. 20415
(202) 606-1800
https://www.usajobsopm.gov

Agency For International Development
Information Center
Ronald Reagan Building
Washington, D.C. 20523
(202) 712-4810
www.info.usaid.gov

U.S. Department of Commerce
Human Resources Management Office
U.S. and Foreign Commercial Service
1401 Constitution Ave., NW
Room 5001
Washington, D.C. 20230
(202) 482-4883
www.commerce.gov

Here's another great idea. My wife and I want to travel the Route 66 road trip from Chicago out west. I had the idea to rent an RV and we stop at campgrounds. I could write a book about the road trip with lots of photos. Then I researched this book and found out we could make $40,000 a year traveling around the U.S. in our RV. How? Plenty of companies need people and drivers to transport stuff across the country. Amazon certainly does with its distribution centers. There are others as well. For more info on how to do this you should contact:

Workamper News
110 Tulaka Blvd., Suite C
Heber Springs, AR 72543
800-446-5627
https://www.workamper.com
http://www.rv-dreams.com/workamping-wages.html

Or you could drive around the U.S. on vacation for FREE by helping move cars. Check out *www.movecars.com* for more information. Or how about flying around being a courier? Do a search on the web for "Air Courier Service" or contact AIR COURIER ASSOCIATION at 800-211-5119 or *www.aircourier.org*.

Lastly, if you're religious, don't forget missionary work. Your church, mosque, or other house of worship could finance your work in another country. Ask your religious leader about mission work under your faith. They should be able to point you in the right direction.

If you got kids you'll want to pay attention to the next chapter!

CHAPTER 25

Free Money For Kids

A lot of us have kids out there. We also have baby mamas out there. In this chapter I'll give you a bunch of money grants that kids can get or that you and your baby mama can get to help out. And yes, this applies to my female prisoners with baby daddy's out there. Plus, there's other free stuff in here as well.

My mother worked in daycare centers for years. When I was a kid and got suspended from school, I had to go to her work. I loved it. Helping her out with the little kids was a piece of cake compared to following all of the rules at school. Paying for childcare while you work can be costly. But did you know that you or your baby mama could get up to $1,200 a month for day care costs while you look for a job? The Child Care and Development Block Grant gives money to states to help families with their daycare needs. It could even give your baby mama (or wifey) money to start her own daycare. To find out if you're eligible for any of this money you should contact:

National Child Care Information Center
243 Church Street, NW
Vienna, VA 22180
800-616-2242
http://nccic.org

Last I checked, you can get free healthcare for your kids if you make less than $40,000 a year. Almost every state has a Children's Health Insurance Program (CHIPs). That program gives most kids who don't have health insurance the opportunity for coverage. You should contact your State Department of Health to see what kind of coverage your kids can get. Or you can call the federal government hotline to deal with it at 877-KIDS-NOW; 877-543-7669, or on the web at: *www.insurekidsnow.gov*.

$10,000 for kids aged 10 to 21 to start a business in small towns! That's the headline I read. And sure enough, the U.S. Department of Agriculture has a program for this. For more information on this you should contact:

Farm Service Agency
Loan Marketing Division
Ag Box 0522
Washington, D.C. 20250
(202) 720-1632
www.fsa.usda.gov

Does your kid seem to have a speech problem? Or do you want to get them tested for it? You may be eligible for $6,000 worth of FREE speech therapy. If your kid is 3 years old, it is part of the U.S. Individuals with Disabilities Education Act (IDEA) that they get this testing. Your local school district is supposed to do the testing. But if they are not doing it, you should contact the following:

Office of Special Education Programs
U.S. Department of Education
400 Maryland Avenue, SW

Washington, D.C. 20202
(202) 205-5507
www.ed.gov/about/offices/list/users/index.html

$500 to pay for childcare. $800 to spend on camping. $750 to buy health products for kids. What do all of these have in common? You can find them on a database online of more than 400 nonprofit and government organizations that help out kids who have health-related problems. You can find out more about all of these programs on *www.bravekids.org*.

Another foundation that helps out families with children who have health problems is the Firsthand Foundation. They provide grants to pay for expenses associated with clinical procedures and treatment, medical equipment and supplies, and expenses for relocation if needed. For more information you should contact:

Firsthand Foundation
c/o Cerner Corporation
2800 Rockcreek Parkway
Kansas City, MO 64117
(816) 201-1569
http://www.firsthandfoundation.org/grants.asp

Another great option is Youth Service America. They give out grants for all kinds of things. Kids aged 5-25 can get a $500 grant for community service work. Disabled youths can get $2,000 to volunteer. Young girls can get $500 to promote health and fitness. For more information about these and other grants, you should contact:

Youth Service America
1101 15th Street, NW, Suite 200
Washington, D.C. 20005

(202) 296-2992
http://www.ysa.org/awards/award-grant.cfm

$2,000 grants are available to women aged 19 and under if they will use the money to develop projects focused on activism and social change. For more information you should contact:
The Ellen Dougherty Activist Fund
Open Meadows Foundation
P.O. Box 150-607
Van Brunt Station
Brooklyn, NY 11215
(718) 768-2249
http://www.openmeadows.org

$10,000 to teenagers that don't smoke! Yes, that's right. Your kid could get a $10,000 scholarship just because they don't smoke. Ten kids get one every year. The Lorillard Tobacco Company does this in their Teen H.I.P. Awards. For more information about this and other grants you should contact:

Lorillard Tobacco Company Contributor Program
72 Green Valley Road
Greensboro, NC 27408
http://ww.lorillard.net

$5,000 for kids to write a book! Three different awards will be given annually to grade school kids (up to 10 years old), middle school aged (11-13) and teenagers (13-18). The book should portray living with a disability or that of a family member that is disabled. For more information you should contact:

The Schneider Family Book Awards

American Library Association
50 E. Huron Street
Chicago, IL 60611-2795
(800) 545-2433
http://www.ala.org

$1,000 for young entrepreneurs (ages 12 to 20) to start a business, club, or a civic-minded organization. This is open to those youth who want to improve their community. For more information contact:

Youth Venture
1700 North Moore Street, Suite 2000
Arlington, VA 22209
(703) 527-4126
http://www.youthventure.org

I love fried chicken! Do you? I know you're probably wondering why I just wrote that. Because KFC has its own grants and awards that it gives out to kids. They've given out $100 and a $50 KFC gift certificate. They've given out grand prizes of $5,000 and new computers. You should check them out to see what prizes your kid could possibly get. For more information contact:

KFC Corporation Contributions Program
c/o Corp. Contributions
P.O. Box 32070
Louisville, KY 40232
(502) 456-8300
http://www.yum.com/community/cdway.htm

The White House has special items for kids. All your kids have to do is write a letter to the President, Vice-President, or

First Lady. Make sure you kid puts their return address on the letter so they can get a response!

The White House
1600 Pennsylvania Avenue, NW
Washington, D.C. 20500
www.whitehouse.gov

Parents Anonymous

Parents Anonymous was founded in 1969 through the efforts of Jolly K., a caring mother who helped her family through the personal traumas and mental health issues of her kids. They have a helpline to provide free emotional support and resources to parents and caregivers. For more information contact:

Parents Anonymous
250 West First Street, Suite 250
Claremont, CA 91711
1-855-427-2736
www.parentsonymous.org

Temporary Assistance to Needy Families (TANF)

This is the program that replaced Aid to Families With Dependent Children (AFDC). It helps people who need funds to pay for basic necessities as they enter job training programs, finish their education, or care for small children. Each state has a specific office that deals with this program. To locate your state's office, you should contact:

Administration for Children & Families (ACF)

Office of Family Assistance
US Department of Health & Human Services
330 C Street, S.W.
Washington, D.C. 20201
https://www.acf.hhs.gov/ofa

Child Care Aware
1515 N. Courthouse Road, 2nd Floor
Arlington, VA 22201
800-424-2246
http://www.childcareaware.org/resources/map

(Find the best local childcare options in your area and other resources.)

Canines for Disabled Kids (CDK)
65 James Street, Suite 210
Worcester, MA 01603
https://caninesforkids.org

(Helps children with disabilities get independence by promoting service dog partnerships, understanding and awareness throughout the community.)

Children's Defense Fund (CDF)
25 E Street, NW
Washington, D.C. 20001
https://www.childrensdefense.org
cdinfo@childrensdefense.org

(Founded in 1973 by Marian Wright Edelman, the first black woman admitted to the Mississippi bar. They have offices in Washington, D.C., California, Minnesota, Mississippi, New York, Ohio, South Carolina and Texas. They offer after-school and summer programs for children. Their mission is to "Leave No Child Behind.")

KaBoom!
4301 Connecticut Avenue, NW, Suite ML-1
Washington, D.C. 20008
www.kaboom.org

(Offers grants and other help to build playgrounds for those who need a safe place to play, especially in underprivileged areas.)

Save the Children
501 Kings Highway East, Suite 400
Fairfield, CT 06825
www.savethechildren.org
(International nonprofit that offers food, healthcare, and education to children.)

Girlstart
1400 W. Anderson Lane
Austin, TX 78757
https://girlstart.org
(Encourage teen girls to go into the fields of Science, Technology, Engineering, and Math [STEM].)

The Masonic Angel Fund is a special charity designed for kids to help them. Some of the things they help out with are new winter coats, glasses or shoes, and even scholarships for music or art instruction. Referrals for all of these services are done through the school system, so you'll have to see if it's in your kids' school district. For more information contact:

The Masonic Angel Fund
P.O. Box 1389
Orleans, MA 02653
(508) 255-8812
www.masonicangelfoundation.org/goal.htm

Salvation Army
615 Slaters Lane
P.O. Box 269
Alexandria, VA 22313
(703) 684-5500
https://www.salvationarmyusa.org
(Has 250+ camps and 500+ clubs can attend for free!)

Most of us know about Angel Tree and the gifts they give to our kids during Christmas. But did you know that they also allow 10,000 kids to go to summer camp every year? For more information, contact:

Angel Tree
P.O. Box 1550
Merrifield, VA 22116
800-55-ANGEL
www.angeltree.org

Do you have kids, but don't know where they are at? Baby mama took them and no one in your family knows where they are at. You could possibly get FREE help locating them and other mediation services from:

Find-A-Child of America, Inc.
P.O. Box 277
New Paltz, NY 12561
800-I-AM-LOST
(914) 255-1848
www.childfindofamerica.org

When I was in school we would get free pizza from Pizza Hut for getting good grades. This may not sound like a big deal now that I'm 44 years old and doing life in prison but imagine a poor kid getting his own personal pan pizza that I didn't have to share with my twin brother. Now there are all kinds of benefits for kids who do good in school. Want to help your kids get good grades? Want to show them how to write good essays on all sort of topics easily? All you have got to do is show them how to use FREE government brochures and reports. Here are some ideas.

Say your kid has to write an essay on threatened or endangered plants or species. The U.S. Fish and Wildlife Service has lots of publications that deal with endangered species, including *Why Save Endangered Species?* As a matter of fact, they offer up-to-date information on all kinds of animals. They also offer FREE posters you could hang on your kids' wall. For more information contact:

Publications Unit
U.S. Fish and Wildlife Service
National Conservation Training Center
Conservation Library
Rt. 1, P.O. Box 166
Shepherdstown, WV 25443
(304) 876-7399
http://www.fw.gov/index.html

Free information and how to make a paper volcano is available at: *http://volcanoes.usgs.gov*.

Free information on earthquakes can be found at: *http://neic.cr.usgs.gov*.

Free information on how kids can copy leaves with crayons and how to make leaf prints with a stamp pad can be found at: *www.fs.fed.us*.

Do you have a young one who likes water and boats? You can get them some FREE coloring books that teach them water safety at: *www.uscboating.org*.

Want to teach your kid(s) about solar energy? You can find some publications just for kids from the Department of Energy here at: *www.eere.energy.gov/kids*.

If you have a young tyke that's ready to ride a bike and you want to teach them about safety and wearing a helmet, you can. The U.S. Consumer Product Safety Commission has a FREE coloring book for kids called *Sprocket Man*, that teaches kids about bicycle safety. They also have a brochure called *Kids Speak Out On Bike Helmets*. You can find them at: *www.cpsc.gov*.

If you want to teach your kids about the environment in a fun way, you can. The U.S. Environmental Protection Agency has coloring books, activity sheets, and even a Planet Protector Club for kids. You can learn more at: *www.epa.gov/kids*.

Want to teach your kid what to do during a disaster? The Federal Emergency Management Agency (FEMA) has Herman. He's a "spokes crab" and he will get your kid ready for a flood, wildfire, hurricane, tornado, earthquake, and even National Security emergencies. You can learn more at: *www.fema.gov/kids*.

What if your kid loves to take things apart or invent new things. Maybe they will be the next great inventor. The U.S. Patent and Trademark Office has created a great kids website to help encourage them to invent things. You can learn more at: *www.uspto.gov/go/kids/*.

Is your kid learning about space? NASA has a *Solar System Puzzle Kit* for kids and other great info in their Educators Resource Center at: *http://spacelink.nasa.gov.*

What if you need help teaching your kid how to learn? Well, then you need to check out the hundreds of FREE brochures the U.S. Department of Education has created just for you. Here are some titles:

Helping Your Child Learn To Read
Helping Your Child Learn History
Helping Your Child Learn Math
Helping Your Child Get Ready for School
Helping Your Child Improve in Test Taking
Helping Your Child Learn to Write Well
Helping Your Child Use the Library
Helping Your Child Learn Geography
Helping Your Child Learn Science
Helping Your Child With Homework
Helping Your Child Succeed in School

You can get these FREE by mail or online by contacting:

ED Pubs
P.O. Box 1398
Jessup, MD 20794-1398
877-4-ED-PUBS
www.edpubs.org

Our kids are the future, so we got to help them any way we can. Helping them learn is one of the greatest skills we can give them. I wouldn't be the author I am today if it wasn't for my mom teaching me how to read and write and how to use the library. Will you kid(s) be able to say the same about you?

CHAPTER 26

Free Money For Everything Else

We have come to the last chapter in our FREE money journey. In this chapter I will throw out all the cornucopia of free stuff I found along the way during my research. Some of it may not help you. But it could help someone you know. So, pay it forward. Let's get to it.

Do you have family members who are over 55 years old and just sitting at home? Would you like to show them how to get an extra $1,000 a month by volunteering? You can. The government has a program called "Senior Community Service Employment Program (SCEP)." This money is paid by the government for seniors to help local non-profit organizations do good in the community. For information on the programs in your area have them call 877-US2-JOBS, or go to: *https://www.servicelocator.org/program*. The can also watch Matthew Lesko's video on this at: *https://vimeo.com/257724828*.

The U.S. Department of Energy keeps a current database where you can quickly identify cash savings programs that encourage you to reduce your utility bills. You could save up to $5,000 on new appliances. Get cash rebates, tax credits and discounts with energy saving upgrades. This database shows you programs from federal, state, and local governments as well as utility companies. You can search for your state at *https://www.dsireusa.org.* Or you can call the main switchboard at 202-586-5000 and ask for help with the "Tax Credits, Rebates, and Savings" database.

Money saved is money earned! You can save up to 40% on your car repairs. All you have to do is stop going to the garage and let the mechanic come to you. Some of you know a hype who does great work and you laughed at 40% because you can get an 80% discount. Okay, I'll give you that. But for those of us who are going completely legit once we get out, here's where to do your research: 1-800-701-6230 or *www.yourmechanic.com.*

You can get FREE cellphones plus 500 free minutes a month. How? Once again, from the U.S. government who subsidizes cellphone carriers to provide free service to people who have trouble paying their bills. To see which services are available in your area contact:

assurancewireless.com (888) 898-4888
www.safelink.com (800) 378-1684
https://www.lifelinesupport.org (888) 641-8722 (Press 1)

You can do the same with internet for $9.95 and a computer for $150. Yes, the U.S. government subsidizes internet providers also. There is no credit check, no installation fee, no term contract, and in-home WIFI is included. For more information contact:

Internet Essentials
(888) 710-4156
https://internetessentials.com
Or watch the video at: *https://vimeo.com/257608996.*

How about a FREE car? New cars are expensive. But it's hard to take care of yourself and your family if you can't even afford a car. That's why there are non-profit organizations all over America that provide FREE and low-cost automobiles, if you can't afford to buy one. Here are some of them:

Cars 4 Christmas
(913) 643-3137
http://www.cars4christmas.org

Working Cars for Working Families
(617) 542-8010
http://workingcarsforworkingfamilies.org

800 Charity Cars
1-800-242-7489
https://800charitycars.org

Lutheran Services
1-800-664-3848
http://www.lutheranservices.org/aboutus

Ways to Work
866-252-7171
http://www.slideshare.net/benben9602/free-car

Did you know you can get your grandma as much as $500 just to buy fresh fruit and vegetables from those roadside stands? It's called the "Seniors Farmers Market Nutrition Program (SFMNP)." It's available nationwide through your local County Cooperative Extension Service for people ages 60+. Call 1-800-677-1116 to apply at a local office or visit: *https://www.fns.usda.gov/sfmnp/overview*.

What would you do if a tornado or earthquake demolished your house and car? And your insurance didn't cover fees for hotels, rental assistance, or other home repairs? You could be eligible for $25,000 of assistance from FEMA. You can contact FEMA at: 1-800-621-FEMA or *http://www.fema.gov/rrr/inassist.shtm*.

Is there a Jack in the Box restaurant in your hometown? Then you could be eligible for a $2,500 hardship grant. Employees and customers have been awarded grants for education expenses and human service projects. For more information, contact:

Jack in the Box Foundation
c/o Tax Department
9330 Balbao Avenue
San Diego, CA 92123-1516
http://www.jackinthebox.com/foundation

Here's another one for your mom or grandma. If they are over the age of 65 and low-income, they may qualify for a $6,000 grant. This grant is available no matter where you live. For more information about this program, you can contact:

Sarah A.W. Devans Trust
c/o Rice, Heard & Bigelow, Inc.
50 Congress St., Suite 1025
Boston, MA 02109
(617) 557-7509
axis@riceheard.com

$20 million in grant money is available for those who work or who have retired from Abbott Laboratories. Grants, loans, financial education and counseling services are provided due to financial hardships. If you know someone who works (or has worked) at Abbott, have them contact:

The Clara Abbott Foundation
200 Abbott Park Road
Abbott Park, IL 60064-3537
http://clara.abbott.com

$5,000 for heroic acts. If you have a family member or friend that has demonstrated voluntary heroism in saving or attempting to save the lives of others, you could help them get this award. It is also given to awardees and to the dependents of those who have lost their lives or who have been disabled in such heroic acts. For more information, contact:

Carnegie Hero Fund Commission
425 6th Ave., Suite 1640
Pittsburgh, PA 15219-1823
(412) 281-1302
1-800-447-8900
http://www.carnegiehero.org

Grants of $1,000 to $7,500 are available for support in higher education, music, social services, and medical needs. It doesn't matter where you live. For more information, contact:

The Chazen Foundation
P.O. Box 801
Nyack, NY 10960
http://www.chazenscholar.com/project.php3

$5,000 to $25,000 grants are available to support Christian churches, education, missionary, welfare programs, and needy individuals. For more information, contact:

Agape Fund
800 Middlebrook Road

Prescott, AZ 86303
http://www.communionchapel.org/agape_fund_guidelines.htm

There are grants available to Italian-Americans in financial need, including senior citizens. For more information, contact:

Italian-American Community Services Agency
678 Green St.
San Francisco, CA 94133-3896
(415) 362-6423
http://italiancommunityservices.org/index.htm

Your mom or grandparent could be a "Foster Grandparent" and get $3,000 worth of incentives for helping needy kids. If they meet certain income guidelines and are 60 or older, they could be eligible. They would receive a modest tax-free stipend to offset the cost of volunteering, and are reimbursed for transportation, some meals, and accident and liability insurance. For more information about this program, they should contact:

National Senior Service Corps
1201 New York Ave., NW
Washington, D.C. 20525
800-424-8867
www.seniorcorps.gov/about/programs/fg.asp

There are many more programs out there that supply FREE money. Once you start your search, you will see what I've seen. There's no excuse to not have what you need in life if you live in America. Someone, somewhere, is willing to help you. I hope this book helps you and your family get the help you need. If you know of a program that specifically helps prisoners or their families that I do not list here, please send it to me. Tell me what you know about it and how it helped you or your family. I'll be sure to include it in any updated versions we make of this book.

No matter what, keep your head up and your eyes on the prize. Prison doesn't have to be the end. It could be the start. See you at the top!

"I will have to remember 'I am here today to cross the swamp, not to fight all the alligators.'"
The Art of Possibility
by Rosamund & Benjamin Zander

ABOUT THE AUTHOR

Josh Kruger is *The Millionaire Prisoner*™. He's a Cellpreneur, author, and leading authority on how prisoners can live productive and happy lives by thinking outside the cell, networking, and breaking down carceral barriers.

He and his work has been seen in *The Commercial News*, *The New Gazette*, *Prison Legal News*, *Kite Magazine*, *Straight Stuntin*, *Inmate Shopper*, *The Best Resource Directory for Prisoners*, and *Conscious County Courier*, among others.

In 1999, Josh was arrested for felony murder, home invasion, and robbery. He refused to turn state's evidence against his co-defendant in return for a 20-year sentence. At the subsequent 2000 bench trial he received a directed verdict of acquittal when the state of Illinois prosecutor refused to participate over an evidence dispute. Josh was released, but eventually rearrested after the state successfully got the not guilty verdict vacated on appeal. See *People v. Kruger*, 327 Ill. App. 3d 839, 764 N.E.2d 138 (4th Dist. Ill. 2002). At the 2003 jury trial, Josh was convicted based on a theory of accountability, but found not guilty of intentional murder. He was still sentenced to life in prison without parole. *People v. Kruger*, 363 Ill. App. 3d 1113, 845 N.E. 2d 96(4th Dist. Ill. 2006).

After reading several of Zig Ziglar's books, Josh reached out to the late, great motivational speaker and began corresponding with Ziglar. He adopted Zig's philosophy that you can have everything you want in life if you just help enough people get what they want.

Tired of depending on friends and family for support, the graduate of Crown Financial Ministries decided to leverage his extensive juvenile and adult prison experiences into a freelance writing career. In 2011, Josh launched his micro-publishing empire from his maximum-security prison cell by self-publishing two booklets, *How to Get FREE Pen-Pals* and *How to Win Your Football Pool*. Prison authorities seized his property and threw him in segregation by alleging that he was violating prison rules. Not to be dismayed, Josh kept going and published his first book, *The Millionaire Prisoner*. His goal was to help prisoners turn their prison into a stepping-stone to success.

A fierce defender of prisoner rights, especially those under the First Amendment, Josh has filed numerous successful lawsuits challenging prison conditions and bogus censorship practices. See *Kruger v. Boland, et al*, 15-CV-1261 (C.D. Ill 2015); *Kruger v. Pfister, et al*, 15-CV-1325 (C.D. Ill.); *Kruger v. Lashbrook, et al*, 18-CV-512 (S.D. Ill); *Kruger v. Baldwin, et al*, 19-CV-268 (SD. ILL); *Kruger v. Lashbrook, et al*, 20-CV-24 (S.D. Ill). He believes that prisoners should have the same rights extended to them that free-world people have, and that the protection afforded by the Constitution does not stop at the prison gates. He will fiercely defend his name and *The Millionaire Prisoner* brand.

It took Josh only 30 days to write his second book, *Pen Pal Success* which is based on his personal experiences from behind the iron veil of prison. After the success of both of his books, a lot of prisoners started asking him how he did it. So, he wrote *Cellpreneur: The Millionaire Prisoner's Guidebook*, to show prisoners how to legally start a business from their prison cell. He also compiled *Celebrity Female Star Power: The Millionaire Prisoner's Address Book*, after his cellmate—JuBoy—showed him how much prisoners love celebrities. His latest two book projects continue on the *TMP* brand. *Prison Picasso*, shows prison artists and crafters how to make big money from their arts/crafts while inside. *TMP4 Pen Pal Mastery* shows prisoners how to master the pen pal game and what works now and what doesn't work now.

Josh has vowed to never stop writing or fighting for prisoner rights and prison reform. His mission is to change lives, one prisoner at a time. He can be reached directly on the GTL app at: *www.connectnetwork.com* or on Facebook (Meta) at JoshuaKruger. Or by snail mail at:

Josh Kruger
#K50216
P.O. Box 99
Pontiac, IL 61764

MIKE ENEMIGO PRESENTS

THE CELL BLOCK
BOOK SUMMARIES

MIKE ENEMIGO is the new prison/street art sensation who has written and published several books. He is inspired by emotion; hope; pain; dreams and nightmares. He physically lives somewhere in a California prison cell where he works relentlessly creating his next piece. His mind and soul are elsewhere; seeing, studying, learning, and drawing inspiration to tear down suppressive walls and inspire the culture by pushing artistic boundaries.

THE CELL BLOCK is an independent multimedia company with the objective of accurately conveying the prison/street experience with the credibility and honesty that only one who has lived it can deliver, through literature and other arts, and to entertain and enlighten while doing so. Everything published by The Cell Block has been created by a prisoner, while in a prison cell.

THE BEST RESOURCE DIRECTORY FOR PRISONERS, $19.99 & $7.00 S/H: This book has over 1,450 resources for prisoners! Includes: Pen-Pal Companies! Non-Nude Photo Sellers! Free Books and Other Publications! Legal Assistance! Prisoner Advocates! Prisoner Assistants! Correspondence Education! Money-Making Opportunities! Resources for Prison Writers, Poets, Artists! And much, much more! Anything you can think of doing from your prison cell, this book contains the resources to do it!

321

A GUIDE TO RELAPSE PREVENTION FOR PRISONERS, $15.00 & $5.00 S/H: This book provides the information and guidance that can make a real difference in the preparation of a comprehensive relapse prevention plan. Discover how to meet the parole board's expectation using these proven and practical principles. Included is a blank template and sample relapse prevention plan to assist in your preparation.

LOST ANGELS: $15.00 & $5.00: David Rodrigo was a child who belonged to no world; rejected for his mixed heritage by most of his family and raised by an outcast uncle in the mean streets of East L.A. Chance cast him into a far darker and more devious pit of intrigue that stretched from the barest gutters to the halls of power in the great city. Now, to survive the clash of lethal forces arrayed about him, and to protect those he loves, he has only two allies; his quick wits, and the flashing blade that earned young David the street name, Viper.

LOYALTY AND BETRAYAL DELUXE EDITION, $19.99 & $7.00 S/H: Chunky was an associate of and soldier for the notorious Mexican Mafia – La Eme. That is, of course, until he was betrayed by those, he was most loyal to. Then he vowed to become their worst enemy. And though they've attempted to kill him numerous times, he still to this day is running around making a mockery of their organization .... This is the story of how it all began.

MONEY IZ THE MOTIVE: SPECIAL 2-IN-1 EDITION, $19.99 & $7.00 S/H: Like most kids growing up in the hood, Kano has a dream of going from rags to riches. But when his plan to get fast money by robbing the local "mom and pop" shop goes wrong, he quickly finds himself sentenced to serious prison time. Follow Kano as he is schooled to the ways of the game by some of the most respected OGs whoever did it; then is set free and given the resources to put his schooling into action and build the ultimate hood empire...

DEVILS & DEMONS: PART 1, $15.00 & $5.00 S/H: When Talton leaves the West Coast to set up shop in Florida he meets the female version of himself: A drug dealing murderess with psychological issues. A whirlwind of sex, money and murder inevitably ensues and Talton finds himself on the run from the law with nowhere to turn to. When his team from home finds out he's in trouble, they get on a plane heading south...

DEVILS & DEMONS: PART 2, $15.00 & $5.00 S/H: The Game is bitter-sweet for Talton, aka Gangsta. The same West Coast Clique who came to his aid ended up putting bullets into the chest of the woman he had fallen in love with. After leaving his ride or die in a puddle of her own blood, Talton finds himself on a flight back to Oak Park, the neighborhood where it all started...

DEVILS & DEMONS: PART 3, $15.00 & $5.00 S/H: Talton is on the road to retribution for the murder of the love of his life. Dante and his crew of killers are on a path of no return. This urban classic is based on real-life West Coast underworld politics. See what happens when a group of YG's find themselves in the midst of real underworld demons...

DEVILS & DEMONS: PART 4, $15.00 & $5.00 S/H: After waking up from a coma, Alize has locked herself away from the rest of the world. When her sister Brittany and their friend finally take her on a girl's night out, she meets Luck – a drug dealing womanizer.

FREAKY TALES, $15.00 & $5.00 S/H: *Freaky Tales* is the first book in a brand-new erotic series. King Guru, author of the *Devils & Demons* books, has put together a collection of sexy short stories and memoirs. In true TCB fashion, all of the erotic tales included in this book have been loosely based on true accounts told to, or experienced by the author.

THE ART & POWER OF LETTER WRITING FOR PRISONERS: DELUXE EDITION $19.99 & $7.00 S/H: When locked inside a prison cell, being able to write well is the most powerful skill you can have! Learn how to increase your power by writing high-quality personal and formal letters! Includes letter templates, pen-pal website strategies, punctuation guide and more!

THE PRISON MANUAL: $19.99 & $7.00 S/H: *The Prison Manual* is your all-in-one book on how to not only survive the rough terrain of the American prison system, but use it to your advantage so you can THRIVE from it! How to Use Your Prison Time to YOUR Advantage; How to Write Letters that Will Give You Maximum Effectiveness; Workout and Physical Health Secrets that Will Keep You as FIT as Possible; The Psychological impact of incarceration and How to Maintain Your MAXIMUM Level of Mental Health; Prison Art Techniques; Fulfilling Food Recipes; Parole Preparation Strategies and much, MUCH more!

GET OUT, STAY OUT!, $16.95 & $5.00 S/H: This book should be in the hands of everyone in a prison cell. It reveals a challenging but clear course for overcoming the obstacles that stand between prisoners and their freedom. For those behind bars, one goal outshines all others: GETTING OUT! After being released, that goal then shifts to STAYING OUT! This book will help prisoners do both. It has been masterfully constructed into five parts that will help prisoners maximize focus while they strive to accomplish whichever goal is at hand.

MOB$TAR MONEY, $12.00 & $4.00 S/H: After Trey's mother is sent to prison for 75 years to life, he and his little brother are moved from their home in Sacramento, California, to his grandmother's house in Stockton, California where he is forced to find his way in life and become a man on his own in the city's grimy streets. One day, on his way home from the local corner store, Trey has a rough encounter with the neighborhood bully. Luckily, that's when Tyson, a member of the MOBTAR, a local "get money" gang comes to his aid. The two kids quickly become friends, and it doesn't take long before Trey is embraced into the notorious MOB$TAR money gang, which opens the door to an adventure full of sex, money, murder and mayhem that will change his life forever... You will never guess how this story ends!

BLOCK MONEY, $12.00 & $4.00 S/H: Beast, a young thug from the grimy streets of central Stockton, California lives The Block; breathes The Block; and has committed himself to bleed The Block for all it's worth until his very last breath. Then, one day, he meets Nadia; a stripper at the local club who piques his curiosity with her beauty, quick-witted intellect and rider qualities. The problem? She has a man – Esco – a local kingpin with money and power. It doesn't take long, however, before a devious plot is hatched to pull off a heist worth an indeterminable amount of money. Following the acts of treachery, deception and betrayal are twists and turns and a bloody war that will leave you speechless!

HOW TO HUSTLE AND WIN: SEX, MONEY, MURDER EDITION $15.00 & $5.00 S/H: *How To Hu$tle and Win: Sex, Money, Murder Edition* is the grittiest, underground self-help manual for the 21st century street entrepreneur in print. Never has there been such a book written for today's gangsters, goons and go-getters. This self-help handbook is an absolute must-have for anyone who is actively connected to the streets.

RAW LAW: YOUR RIGHTS, & HOW TO SUE WHEN THEY ARE VIOLATED! $15.00 & $5.00 S/H: *Raw Law For Prisoners* is a clear and concise guide for prisoners and their advocates to understanding civil rights laws guaranteed to prisoners under the US Constitution, and how to successfully file a lawsuit when those rights have been violated! From initial complaint to trial, this book will take you through the entire process, step by step, in simple, easy-to-understand terms. Also included are several examples where prisoners have sued prison officials successfully, resulting in changes of unjust rules and regulations and recourse for rights violations, oftentimes resulting in rewards of thousands, even millions of dollars in damages! If you feel your rights have been violated, don't lash out at guards, which is usually ineffective and only makes matters worse. Instead, defend yourself successfully by using the legal system, and getting the power of the courts on your side!

HOW TO WRITE URBAN BOOKS FOR MONEY & FAME: $16.95 & $5.00 S/H: Inside this book you will learn the true story of how Mike Enemigo and King Guru have received money and fame from inside their prison cells by writing urban books; the secrets to writing hood classics so you, too, can be caked up and famous; proper punctuation using hood examples; and resources you can use to achieve your money motivated ambitions! If you're a prisoner who want to write urban novels for money and fame, this must-have manual will give you all the game!

PRETTY GIRLS LOVE BAD BOYS: AN INMATE'S GUIDE TO GETTING GIRLS: $15.00 & $5.00 S/H: Tired of the same, boring, cliché pen pal books that don't tell you what you really need to know? If so, this book is for you! Anything you need to know on the art of long and short distance seduction is included within these pages! Not only does it give you the science of attracting pen pals from websites, it also includes psychological profiles and instructions on how to seduce any woman you set your sights on! Includes interviews of women who have fallen in love with prisoners, bios for pen pal ads, pre-written love letters, romantic poems, love-song lyrics, jokes and much, much more! This book is the ultimate guide – a must-have for any prisoner who refuses to let prison walls affect their MAC'n.

THE LADIES WHO LOVE PRISONERS, $15.00 & $5.00 S/H: New Special Report reveals the secrets of real women who have fallen in love with prisoners, regardless of crime, sentence, or location. This info will give you a HUGE advantage in getting girls from prison.

THE MILLIONAIRE PRISONER: PART 1, $16.95 & $5.00 S/H

THE MILLIONAIRE PRISONER: PART 2, $16.95 & $5.00 S/H

THE MILLIONAIRE PRISONER: SPECIAL 2-IN-1 EDITION, $24.99 & $7.00 S/H: Why wait until you get out of prison to achieve your dreams? Here's a blueprint that you can use to become successful! *The Millionaire Prisoner* is your complete reference to overcoming any obstacle in prison. You won't be able to put it down! With this book you will discover the secrets to: Making money from your cell! Obtain FREE money for correspondence courses! Become an expert on any topic! Develop the habits of the rich! Network with celebrities! Set up your own website! Market your products, ideas and services! Successfully use prison pen pal websites! All of this and much, much more! This book has enabled thousands of prisoners to succeed and it will show you the way also!

THE MILLIONAIRE PRISONER 3: SUCCESS UNIVERSITY, $16.95 & $5.00 S/H: Why wait until you get out of prison to achieve your dreams? Here's a new-look blueprint that you can use to be successful! *The Millionaire Prisoner 3* contains advanced strategies to overcoming any obstacle in prison. You won't be able to put it down!

THE MILLIONAIRE PRISONER 4: PEN PAL MASTERY, $16.95 & $5.00 S/H: Tired of subpar results? Here's a master blueprint that you can use to get tons of pen pals! *TMP 4: Pen Pal Mastery* is your complete roadmap to finding your one true love. You won't be able to put it down! With this book you'll DISCOVER the SECRETS to: Get FREE pen pals & which sites are best to use; successful tactics female prisoners can win with; use astrology to find love, friendship & more, build a winning social media presence. All of this and much more!

THE MILLIONAIRE PRISONER 5: FREE MONEY, $24.95 & $7.00 S/H: Wish you could find more FREE MONEY like your stimulus? Seeking an end to your money problems? Look no further! Here's a master blueprint that reveals all that's available! *Tmp 5: Free Money* is your complete roadmap to finding all the FREE MONEY options out there for convicts. You won't be able to put it down!

GET OUT, GET RICH: HOW TO GET PAID LEGALLY WHEN YOU GET OUT OF PRISON!, $16.95 & $5.00 S/H: Many of you are incarcerated for a money-motivated crime. But w/ today's tech & opportunities, not only is the crime-for-money risk/reward ratio not strategically wise, it's not even necessary. You can earn much more money by partaking in any one of the easy, legal hustles explained in this book, regardless of your record. Help yourself earn an honest income so you can not only make a lot of money, but say good-bye to penitentiary chances and prison forever! (Note: Many things in this book can even he done from inside prison.) (ALSO PUBLISHED AS *HOOD MILLIONAIRE: HOW TO HUSTLE AND WIN LEGALLY!*)

THE CEO MANUAL: HOW TO START A BUSINESS WHEN YOU GET OUT OF PRISON, $16.95 & $5.00 S/H: $16.95 & $5.00 S/H: This new book will teach you the simplest way to start your own business when you get out of prison. Includes: Start-up Steps! The Secrets to Pulling Money from Investors! How to Manage People Effectively! How To Legally Protect Your Assets from "them"! Hundreds of resources to get you started, including a list of "loan friendly" banks! (ALSO PUBLISHED AS *CEO MANUAL: START A BUSINESS, BE A BOSS!*)

THE MONEY MANUAL: UNDERGROUND CASH SECRETS EXPOSED! 16.95 & $5.00 S/H: Becoming a millionaire is equal parts what you make, and what you don't spend – AKA save. All Millionaires and Billionaires have mastered the art of not only making money, but keeping the money they make (remember Donald Trump's tax maneuvers?), as well as establishing credit so that they are loaned money by banks and trusted with money from investors: AKA OPM – other people's money. And did you know there are millionaires and billionaires just waiting to GIVE money away? It's true! These are all very-little known secrets "they" don't want YOU to know about, but that I'm exposing in my new book!

HOOD MILLIONAIRE; HOW TO HUSTLE & WIN LEGALLY, $16.95 & $5.00 S/H: Hustlin' is a way of life in the hood. We all have money motivated ambitions, not only because we gotta eat, but because status is oftentimes determined by one's own salary. To achieve what we consider financial success, we often invest our efforts into illicit activities – we take penitentiary chances. This leads to a life in and out of prison, sometimes death – both of which are counterproductive to gettin' money. But there's a solution to this, and I have it...

CEO MANUAL: START A BUSINESS BE A BOSS, $16.95 & $5.00 S/H: After the success of the urban-entrepreneur classic *Hood Millionaire: How To Hustle & Win Legally!*, self-made millionaires Mike Enemigo and Sav Hustle team back up to bring you the latest edition of the Hood Millionaire series – *CEO Manual: Start A Business, Be A Boss!* In this latest collection of game laying down the art of "hoodpreneurship", you will learn such things as: 5 Core Steps to Starting Your Own Business! 5 Common Launch Errors You Must Avoid! How To Write a Business Plan! How To Legally Protect Your Assets From "Them"! How To Make Your Business Fundable, Where to Get Money for Your Start-up Business, and even How to Start a Business With No Money! You will learn How to Drive Customers to Your Website, How to Maximize Marketing Dollars, Contract Secrets for the savvy boss, and much, much more! And as an added bonus, we have included over 200 Business Resources, from government agencies and small business development centers, to a secret list of small-business friendly banks that will help you get started!

PAID IN FULL: WELCOME TO DA GAME, $15.00 & $5.00 S/H. In 1983, the movie *Scarface* inspired many kids growing up in America's inner cities to turn their rags into riches by becoming cocaine kingpins. Harlem's Azie Faison was one of them. Faison would ultimately connect with Harlem's Rich Porter and Alpo Martinez, and the trio would go on to become certified street legends of the '80s and early '90s. Years later, Dame Dash and Roc-A-Fella Films would tell their story in the based-on-actual-events movie, *Paid in Full*.

But now, we are telling the story our way – The Cell Block way – where you will get a perspective of the story that the movie did not show, ultimately learning an outcome that you did not expect.

Book one of our series, *Paid in Full: Welcome to da Game*, will give you an inside look at a key player in this story, one that is not often talked about – Lulu, the Columbian cocaine kingpin with direct ties to Pablo Escobar, who plugged Azie in with an unlimited amount of top-tier cocaine at dirt-cheap prices that helped boost the trio to neighborhood superstars and certified kingpin status... until greed, betrayal, and murder destroyed everything....(ALSO PUBLISHED AS *CITY OF GODS*.)

OJ'S LIFE BEHIND BARS, $15.00 & $5 S/H: In 1994, Heisman Trophy winner and NFL superstar OJ Simpson was arrested for the brutal murder of his ex-wife Nicole Brown-Simpson and her friend Ron Goldman. In 1995, after the "trial of the century," he was acquitted of both murders, though most of the world believes he did it. In 2007 OJ was again arrested, but this time in Las Vegas, for armed robbery and kidnapping. On October 3, 2008 he was found guilty sentenced to 33 years and was sent to Lovelock Correctional Facility, in Lovelock,

Nevada. There he met inmate-author Vernon Nelson. Vernon was granted a true, insider's perspective into the mind and life of one of the country's most notorious men; one that has never been provided...until now.

THE MOB, $16.99 & $5.00 S/H: PaperBoy is a Bay Area boss who has invested blood, sweat, and years into building The Mob – a network of Bay Area street legends, block bleeders, and underground rappers who collaborate nationwide in the interest of pushing a multi-million-dollar criminal enterprise of sex, drugs, and murder.

Based on actual events, little has been known about PaperBoy, the mastermind behind The Mob, and intricate details of its operation, until now.

Follow this story to learn about some of the Bay Area underworld's most glamorous figures and famous events...

COCAINE QUEEN, $17.95 & $5.00 S/H. She was a loving mother.

She was also a ruthless and treacherous drug lord who's suspected of murdering more than one husband.

Who was she?

Griselda Blanco, the Queen of Cocaine, aka The Godmother.

of Columbia, to the mansions of Miami, *Cocaine Queen: The Reign of Griselda Blanco*, is a based-on-actual-events story that takes you on a dangerous ride along the bloody rise to power of the most notorious female drug lord in history, as she kills anyone who gets in her way of complete dominance of the American cocaine market....

COCAINE QUEEN 2, $17.95 & $5.00 S/H. She was a loving mother.

She was also a ruthless and treacherous drug lord who's suspected of murdering more than one husband.

Who was she?

Griselda Blanco, the Queen of Cocaine, aka The Godmother.

From the streets of New York, to the ghettoes of Columbia, to the mansions of Miami, *Cocaine Queen: The Reign of Griselda Blanco*, is a based-on-actual-events story that takes you on a dangerous ride along the bloody rise to power of the most notorious female drug lord in history, as she kills anyone who gets in her way of complete dominance of The American cocaine market....

SOSA: THE PRICE OF POWER (BOOK ONE), $19.95 & $5.00 S/H: The 1983 classic gangster film *Scarface wooed* over a billion fans worldwide, but it ended in the abrupt, violent massacre of Tony and his squad at the behest of ruthless Bolivian crime boss, Alejandro Sosa.

Since then, *Scarface* has birthed a nation of diehards who have been waiting decades for a Hollywood response. The wait is now over. Tony is dead, but his legacy lives inside of Elvira, who has resurfaced in the riveting masterpiece saga entitled: *Sosa; The Price of Power*. First, Sosa must scramble to pick up the pieces which were left shattered by the betrayal of Tony.

The true *Scarface* fan will be glued to the coldblooded cunning, the bigger-than-life characters who Sosa surrounds himself with, and the skilled moves he makes on an international scale. For the blonde bombshell, the game becomes life or death. Who can't remember Tony's enemies: Gaspar Gomez, the Diaz brothers and others? They are the Miami Cuban Mafia and are hunting Elvira down for the huge nine-figure fortune her husband left behind....

SOSA: THE REIGN (BOOK TWO), $19.95 & $5.00 S/H: In book one of this mega-hit series, *Sosa: The Price of Power*, Elvira appealed to Sosa to protect her from the Miami Cuban Mafia (MCM), who were trying to force her to hand over millions of dollars left by her dead husband. Surprised but eager, Sosa sent a couple of his best assassins to Miami to neutralize the MCM and muscle them into backing off the pregnant bombshell. Now Elvira (who may or may not know

Sosa had Tony Montana hit) has made a new ally and friend, but with her husband out of the picture, Sosa finds himself in need of a solid business contact inside of the USA.

With Dr. Orlando Gutierrez assassinated, Sosa and his powerful crime syndicate literally has brand-new life and partners: The CIA. Sosa was expressly requested by the Americans to assist them with helping the Nicaraguan Contra Army stay afloat in the fight against the Sandinista Government. In return, Sosa demands that U.S. Marine Colonel Oliver North allow his organization – La Corporacion Mafia Cruenza – be allowed to fly fifty jets several times per week into the United States.

While Sosa, his Mafia, the CIA and President Ronald Reagan's National Security Advisor were involved in one of the most blatant and unethical conspiracies in American history, Elvira focuses on her pregnancy... and learns what real power feels like. As she absorbs that feeling, she learns also that she can't outrun demons buried in her past. To deal with them, she writes a book entitled *Dark Flight.*

It was a can of worms best kept closed....

MOB TALES, $16.95 & $5.00 S/H. In 1992, Suge 'The Mobfather' Knight launched Death Row Records with a rumored 1.5-million-dollar investment from then-incarcerated drug kingpin Michael 'Harry O' Harris. Under Suge Knight's leadership, Death Row would go on to boast a roster consisting of some of the greatest names in hip-hop history, such as Dr. Dre, Snoop Dogg, and Tupac Shakur. Suge ultimately generated well over 200 million dollars selling records that detailed life in the streets.

Now, from his prison cell, Suge Knight has partnered up with incarcerated publishing boss Mike Enemigo, and longtime Mob affiliate O.G. Silk, to create Death Row Publishing, and drop a new series, *Mob Tales*, as a platform to shed light on some of the hottest incarcerated street-lit authors in the game today. Each book in this series will be a collection of stories written by those who have lived that of which they write, and who are surely to be among the next generation of street-lit legends.

AOB, $15.00 & $5.00 S/H. Growing up in the Bay Area, Manny Fresh the Best had a front-row seat to some of the coldest players to ever do it. And you already know, A.O.B. is the name of the Game! So, When Manny Fresh slides through Stockton one day and sees Rosa, a stupid-bad Mexican chick with a whole lotta 'talent' behind her walking down the street tryna get some money, he knew immediately what he had to do: Put it In My Pocket!

AOB 2, $15.00 & $5.00 S/H.

AOB 3, $15.00 & $5.00 S/H.

PIMPOLOGY: THE 7 ISMS OF THE GAME, $15.00 & $5.00 S/H: It's been said that if you knew better, you'd do better. So, in the spirit of dropping jewels upon the rare few who truly want to know how to win, this collection of exclusive Game has been compiled. And though a lot of so-called players claim to know how the Pimp Game is supposed to go, none have revealed the real. . . Until now!

JAILHOUSE PUBLISHING FOR MONEY, POWER & FAME: $19.99 & $7.00 S/H: In 2010, after flirting with the idea for two years, Mike Enemigo started writing his first book. In 2014, he officially launched his publishing company, The Cell Block, with the release of five books. Of course, with no mentor(s), how-to guides, or any real resources, he was met with failure after failure as he tried to navigate the treacherous goal of publishing books from his prison cell. However, he was determined to make it. He was determined to figure it out and he refused to quit. In Mike's new book, *Jailhouse Publishing for Money, Power, and Fame*, he breaks down all his jailhouse publishing secrets and strategies, so you can do all he's done, but without the trials and tribulations he's had to go through...

All books are available on thecellblock.net website.

You can also order by sending a money order or institutional check to:

The Cell Block
PO Box 1025
Rancho Cordova, CA 95741